FAIRY TALE
PHYSICS

BOOKS 1 - 4

Sarah Allen

Fairy Tale Physics Books 1–4

© 2024 Sarah McCarthy

Illustrated by Vladimir Djekic, Kimberly Delain, and Marie Delwart

Edited by Jennifer Murgia

Also by Sarah Allen

The Fairy Tale Physics Series
Newton's Laws: A Fairy Tale
Fluid Mechanics: A Fairy Tale
Light: A Fairy Tale

Physics Story Games
The Case of the Seven Reflections:
A Fairy Detective Optics Mystery
The Sorceress of Circuits:
A Steampunk Electricity Adventure

Stick Figure Physics
Electric Circuits
Momentum
Rates of Change
Work, Energy, and Power
Basic Fluid Dynamics
The Complete Stick Figure Physics Tutorials

Math Books
Practical Percentages
Algebra 1: Exponents and Operations
Algebra 1: Foiling and Factoring

Contents

About this Book

Hello! Welcome to the Fairy Tale Physics collection!

Each fairy tale includes some explanations of the science concepts behind the story, some activities, and even some math!

Feel free to read these stories in whatever way is most fun for you!

My intention in writing this was to create something that you could adapt to your own preferences. Reading the stories without pausing to read the explanations or problem-solving guides—especially the first time through—is totally great and probably the most fun. But I wanted there to be more in-depth explanations and hands-on things to try for those who want them.

Please read what you enjoy and skip the rest. The stories can be read in any order, and there are a wide range of activities and jumping-off points for exploration. Go wherever your curiosity takes you!

If you have any questions or would like to learn more about my project to teach physics through stories, you can email me at SarahAllenPhysics@gmail.com or reach out on my website www.MathwithSarah.com.

Newton's Laws: A Fairy Tale

ONCE upon a time, in a small village in the south-west corner of a tiny kingdom, there lived a farmer who had three sons. The eldest son was the strongest in the village. He regularly lifted whole oxen and set them back down again, just to show that he could. The middle son was the smartest in the village. He had fixed his father's irrigation system so that every plant got the optimal amount of water and, when he was only five, had redesigned the town's mill so that it ground twice as much wheat into flour every day.

The third and youngest son was called Kip and, as far as anyone could tell, he was not particularly special in any way. But he was happy. He loved his father and his brothers and the farm he grew up on, and he loved exploring. By the time he was twelve he knew every secret path and hideaway in the forest.

When it came time for the three sons to go out into the world, the father gave them each their inheritances. To the eldest he gave his farm, because he knew he would have the strength to work it. To the middle son, he gave his money, so that the boy could attend the university and become a wise scholar. And to Kip he gave all that he had left: an apple.

1

Kip, who was a small boy with mousy brown hair, looked at the apple. Then he looked at his eldest brother, who was already out plowing the fields. Then he looked at the middle brother, who was counting out gold coins and muttering calculations to himself.

Kip's father cleared his throat. "I know it's not much. It was all I had left. But I... I have a good feeling about this apple."

Kip would have liked to have been given the farm—everything from the way the trees moved in the wind to the secret glens of irises in the forest was familiar to him. But something in him yearned for the unknown. There might be more iris glens or snowy peaks or rushing rivers to discover. But if he had been given the farm, he might never have had the courage to leave it.

He would have liked to have been given the money, too. That way he could have bought a good travelling cloak and some food, and maybe a few nights at inns along the way. And... he couldn't really think of a consolation to that. Money would have been useful.

Kip didn't want his father to feel bad for only having an apple left to give him, so he smiled and hugged his father. "I have a good feeling about it, too," Kip said.

Kip packed his few possessions into a worn-out sack, waved goodbye to his father and brothers, and set off up the dusty road to seek his fortune.

The first night he slept in the woods on the side of the road. It was cold, and the ground was hard, but Kip lit a small fire and hummed a song to himself. He was hungry, but he didn't eat the apple. He was going to discover something great; he was sure of it.

The second night it rained, and Kip was unable to light a fire. He wrapped himself in his cloak and shivered, while the dark trees dripped water down on him.

The next day he had nothing at all to eat. He knew the apple would taste sweet and juicy, and he could have eaten every bit of it, even the core, but something told him to save it. The weather was cold enough that it wouldn't spoil quickly, and things would get better soon. He knew they would.

The next night it rained again and midway through the night the temperature dropped, and the water froze, and the rain changed to snow. Afraid he would freeze to death, Kip continued walking, barely able to keep to the road in the icy, moonless dark. He didn't even think about eating the apple. All he could think about was staying warm.

The next morning, when the sun came up and light filtered down in golden sunbeams, making the snow-covered branches sparkle, Kip came to a small village. He found a bakery and offered to sweep the floor in exchange for bread. Seeing how tired and cold Kip was, the baker agreed.

Kip swept and dusted, polished the windows until they were so clear they were almost invisible, cleaned the soot out of the chimney, and split wood. The baker was so impressed with his hard work that he gave Kip two whole loaves of bread and some cheese. Grateful, and warm now from the work, Kip went outside to wander the town and eat his food. He narrowly avoided being run over by a man galloping past on a black horse. Kip caught a glimpse of fine oiled leather and shining brass buckles as he stumbled back. When he had caught himself, he turned to watch the man ride away and realized it was a royal messenger.

A group of townspeople were clustered around something in the central square, talking excitedly.

4

"What is it?" Kip asked, approaching the group. A man turned and answered him gruffly.

"The king's dead." He touched his fist to his forehead and bowed his head in reverence. Kip did the same.

"How old is the new king?" a young boy asked.

"Didn't have any children," a woman answered, shaking her head.

"Who's going to be king, then?" Kip asked, feeling stupid. He took a bite of his bread.

The first man shrugged. "Doesn't say. The royal proclamation says that the council will decide."

Maybe it was because he'd just eaten the most delicious food he'd ever had, after being the closest to starving he'd ever been, but Kip felt a rush of excitement. It felt like a sign. Of what, he didn't know, but he knew what he needed to do next.

"Which road goes to the capital?" he asked the crowd, his mouth still full.

The man looked at him, and then chuckled. "This one here thinks he's going to be king."

"No, I don't," Kip mumbled, but the huddle of people laughed at him.

"You'd best be on your way, your majesty," the woman said, giving a mock bow. She pointed to the scroll tacked on the post. "It says they'll make their choice in nine days. The capital's at least a week's walk from here."

"Yes, hurry!" another man said, sniggering. "You've not much time, Your Highness!"

Blushing, Kip turned and walked away. The last bite of bread was heavy in his mouth, and he suddenly found he couldn't swallow.

"You're going the wrong way!" one of them called out.

Kip choked the last bite of bread down and kept walking. He listened for sounds of them following him, but their laughter faded away. When he could no longer hear them, he doubled back, turning down a side street and skirting the main square, finding his way to the other end of the village, where a sign pointed the way to the capital.

Kip walked alone for two more days, following the road as it wound into the mountains. He ate the last of his food on the second day. Again, he considered eating the apple—what good was it going to do him anyway? But something kept him back.

That afternoon another black horseman galloped past, a leather satchel at his side. More announcements from the capital, Kip thought, excitement swelling in his chest. He wondered what they were.

The next day Kip continued to walk, although now he was beginning to feel slightly faint from hunger. Which was why he thought he might be hallucinating when, late in the afternoon, he came across an old man lying face up in the middle of the road.

He was tall and skinny, with bony, hairy ankles that protruded from his midnight blue robes. His long white beard had blown back in the wind and covered his face. Several feet away, his pointed blue wizard's hat sat in a mud puddle.

"Are you all right, sir?" Kip asked.

The man grunted, sucked in some of his beard, and, coughing, spat it back out. His hands scrabbled at his face, brushing the white hairs away and smoothing them down his belly. His bright blue eyes snapped open, and he glared at Kip.

"Fine, lad. Perfectly fine." He closed his eyes again.

Kip considered this. He had been raised to respect his elders, and it seemed wrong to leave such an old man lying in the middle of the road. He went over, picked up the hat, and wiped as much mud as he could off it.

"You dropped this, sir," he said, holding the hat out to the man.

The man glared at his hat, then at Kip, but he took the hat and stuffed it back onto his head.

"Do you need anything?" Kip asked.

The man sighed. "Can't a person have a moment's peace? I was trying to work something out, and I almost had it, until you came along."

Kip thought that if one wanted a moment's peace, they would be more likely to get it not by lying down in the middle of the road. "Sorry to bother you," was all he said. He could have walked away at that point. But something told him not to go just quite yet.

"Are you hungry?" Kip asked.

"Starving, actually," the man said, perking up.

And Kip knew what he'd been saving the apple for. He pulled it excitedly from his bag, shined it on his shirt, and held it out over the man's face so he could see it clearly.

"Here, have my apple," Kip said.

The man shrieked in terror, causing Kip to drop the apple, which hit the man full in the face as he tried to leap out of the way.

"Aaargh!" the man yelled, holding his head and stumbling away.

Kip moved after the old man, trying to help. "I'm so sorry, are you all right?"

The man stopped groaning and, still rubbing his face, looked at Kip. "It's not your fault. Apples have it out for me."

"Oh, um…" Kip tried to think of something sympathetic to say. Maybe… Apples could be that way? He'd always had a hard time with cherries. He didn't think he could manage to say either of those with a straight face.

"As you can surely see, I am a wizard. I was cursed by my arch nemesis, Leibniz the Evil, two hundred years ago," the man explained. He eyed the apple where it lay on the ground a few feet away. Kip followed his gaze, and to his complete shock, saw the apple roll over once, then twice, inching its way toward the wizard. He took a step back.

"It's fine, don't worry. It's got nothing against you. Just put it away, will you?"

Kip wasn't sure he wanted the apple anymore.

"At least get it away from me," the wizard said.

Reluctantly, Kip approached the apple, reached down, and picked it up. He half expected it to shake, or shock him,

8

or burn like acid, but it did none of those things. It was still an ordinary, if very shiny and red, apple. Not at all comfortable with the idea, he put the apple back in his pack. Still, it hadn't given him any trouble so far on his journey, and it was still his inheritance.

"Good. There you go," the wizard said. "I don't suppose you've got anything else?"

"No," Kip said. "Sorry."

The man examined him. Then he stuck out a bony hand. "Wizard Newton, the Great."

Kip had heard of several wizards, but not this one. "Kip." He shook the wizard's hand.

"Just Kip? Not Kip the Wise or Kip the Slightly Misshapen?"

Kip wondered if he was just pulling random titles out of midair, or if he thought either of those might apply. He himself didn't think he was very wise, and he hoped he wasn't misshapen.

"Just Kip."

"Pleased to make your acquaintance, Just Kip." He removed his hat and swept into a low bow. He shivered and looked around.

"It appears to be getting dark. Would you like to join me for dinner this evening?"

Kip knew better than to refuse an invitation from a wizard. Maybe the wizard might be able to conjure food for them. "Yes, thank you, sir."

Wizard Newton rubbed his hands together. "Wonderful. You make us a fire, and I will find us something to eat."

9

Kip found a dry place under some thick pines and gathered some twigs and pine needles. Then he cleared a space, although there was little danger of starting a forest fire in this weather, and piled up some small dry twigs and fir cones. They were drier than most of the wood, but they were still damp, and he struggled for several minutes to get a good blaze going. He had just begun adding larger twigs to the fire when Newton returned.

"I think I found a squirrel's cubby hole," Newton said, dropping a handful of moldy nuts next to the fire. "Roast those up for us, will you?"

Kip picked through the pile. A few dirty roots, which might have been turnips, some wilted leaves, and a handful of nuts. Kip's hunger and his politeness warred with his fear of food poisoning, but it was two against one, and he brushed the roots off, tied them to a stick, and attempted to roast them.

"Can't you call animals to us, or make plants flower out of season, or anything?" Kip asked. He was sure he'd heard of wizards doing that.

"Silly magic tricks. I'm not that kind of wizard."

"What kind of wizard are you?"

"Careful not to burn it, lad," Newton said, gesturing to the root, which was starting to smoke. Kip adjusted the root over the fire. "So, what are you doing out here on the road?"

Kip explained about his brothers and his father, and about seeing the sign in the village.

"Ah, so you're on your way to the Capital! Excellent, lad. I'm headed there, too. I was a great friend of the king, many years ago. It's a terrible thing, his passing. And terrible that he hasn't left an heir. Those advisors of his are ridiculous. They'll tear up the kingdom with this fool plan of theirs."

"What plan?"

"Oh, you haven't heard?" Kip shook his head. "Well, they've decided how they'll pick the next king."

Kip perked up at this.

"Don't get too excited, lad. They said they thought about it and the thing a king needs to do is make laws. Laws that people will follow. So, they said that whoever wants to be king must make three laws and force the whole kingdom, everyone in it, to follow those three laws. Whoever is successful at the end of the week must present their three laws in the royal throne room for judgement."

Kip's enthusiasm diminished. How was anyone supposed to be able to do that? They'd need an army.

"Exactly," Newton said, causing Kip to jump. Had the wizard read his mind? "The worst part is, there is one person powerful enough to actually do that. Leibniz the Evil, my arch nemesis. He's a very powerful wizard, and completely unethical. If he takes over, he'll enslave everyone."

"But if he's the only one capable of succeeding at the challenge, how are we going to stop him?" Kip asked without thinking.

Newton looked at him. Then he patted him on the shoulder. "You're a good lad."

"Are you powerful enough to complete the challenge?"

Newton was examining the root. "What? No, I'm not that kind of wizard."

Kip wanted to ask, but he didn't think he'd get an answer.

Newton looked up and tapped the side of his nose. "But I've got an idea. That's why I was headed to the capital."

"Oh, what?"

"I'll just think of three things everybody already does and make those my laws."

Kip could see the logic of that, but he wondered if the advisors would allow it. It seemed rather against the spirit of the challenge. Also, what was something everyone already did? Breathing? He realized he was holding his breath. That wouldn't work. Unless they made a law about how often you had to breathe, or you would be put to death. But there were probably people who could hold their breath for a really long time. Also, maybe not everything needed to breathe.

"Yes, interesting thought, isn't it? I was just thinking things out when you came along, although I hadn't gotten very far. You seem like a likely lad. Will you help me? Assist me in this and I swear to you on my hat that I will make your fortune when I'm king."

Kip considered this, but only for a second. Something told him that this was exactly what he'd been waiting for. "Yes. I will help you."

"Wonderful!" The wizard reached out and clapped him on the back. Kip narrowly missed tumbling into the fire. "Let's eat!"

Newton's First Law

THE next morning, they continued down the road. The wizard was surprisingly quick, and Kip had to hurry to keep up. As they walked, the wizard kept up a constant stream of talk, rattling off idea after idea and shooting them back down again almost as quickly.

"Let's see . . . nothing can stay in the air . . . there's birds, though. But maybe nothing can stay in the air forever? Possibly true but difficult to prove, also Lieb'll just levitate something. That . . ." He glanced at Kip, cleared his throat, and went on. "Everything must rot. Nope, there's rocks."

"Rocks fall apart eventually," Kip volunteered.

"Not the same as rotting."

True. But there was something similar there. He thought about the baker's shop. "What about, like, everything gets more disorderly on its own?"

"Disorderly? What do you mean by that?"

"I mean, have you ever seen something clean itself?"

"Cats."

"But, would you say the cat is getting more orderly?"

"Hard to say, with cats."

"But, like, we're always having to clean, right? If something isn't cleaned, it gets dirtier, right? Always? Isn't that weird?"

"We're not looking for weird here, boy. We're looking for laws."

Kip sighed. He still thought it was a pretty good idea.

They continued walking, and he continued making suggestions, and the wizard continued shooting down both his own and Kip's ideas with equal rapidity.

Toward midmorning a group of soldiers came galloping up the road. Out in front was a tall woman with high leather boots and a red doublet. She swung out of the saddle as the horse pulled to a stop, whipping out a sword as she did so.

"Kneel in the name of Prince Eric!" she shouted.

Kip and the wizard stared at her.

"Kneel in the name of Prince Eric or I'll cut you down where you stand!" she cried.

Reluctantly, Kip and the wizard knelt.

"Good. Now, if anyone says, 'Prince Eric' in the future, you kneel."

"OK," Kip said, but he doubted he would. "Who is Prince Eric? I thought the king didn't have any children."

"Prince Eric was like a son to him. He was captain of the guards, and we guards think of him like a father. He's a good man, and the only choice for king."

"Why didn't the king appoint him his successor, then?" Kip asked.

"He died unexpectedly."

"Aren't you going to tell us to do something else?" Newton asked.

"What?"

"Well, it's three laws, not one. What are your other two?"

"Oh, no stealing. And no murdering."

Newton shrugged. "Those are pretty good."

"Prince Eric thinks so."

"Hard to get people to follow, though."

"Not for a true king."

Newton snorted, but Kip kind of admired the woman's devotion and Prince Eric's optimism.

"Now, let's practice," the woman said. "Get up."

She was still pointing the sword at them, so they got up.

"Prince Eric," she said, waving her sword in the air. Obediently, they got back down again.

"Very good." The woman smiled and hopped back on her horse. "Good day, then. Don't forget."

"Bye!" Kip called out, waving as they passed.

"Prince Eric, Prince Eric, Prince Eric," Newton muttered under his breath, stomping back down the road, and decidedly not kneeling.

The road wound higher into the mountains, cutting through dense forests and steep cliffs. They were walking along a narrow patch of road on the side of a fairly steep, rocky incline, and Newton was still muttering to himself, picking up rocks and tossing them, when he tripped and tumbled over the edge.

Kip lunged for him, trying to grab him before he went over, but he was too late. Newton bounced and slid, picking up speed as he went, until he ran headlong into a boulder, and crumpled to a heap on the ground.

Horrified, Kip leapt over the side, barely keeping his footing as he ran. He skidded to a halt and bent down over Newton, who was just starting to sit up, looking about himself dazedly.

"Oh my. Lucky that rock was here. Otherwise, I would have gone on forever." Suddenly, he leapt into the air. "That's it!"

"Er, are you OK?" Kip asked.

"What? No, I don't think so." Newton winced, but he began to climb the incline again, taking large strides with his bony legs. "But I've got it, lad!"

Kip stumbled after him. "Got what?"

"Don't you see? If I hadn't hit that rock I would have gone on forever!"

"Well, until you got to the bottom."

"Exactly!"

"What?"

"Everything must keep doing exactly what it's doing unless something forces it to change! I'll call those things 'forces.'" He grinned maniacally. They had reached the road again and stood, hands on hips, panting.

"But . . . but . . . that's just not true. I mean, nothing goes on forever."

"Oh, it would, if given the chance, my boy! Try me. Show me something that changes what it's doing, and I'll show you the thing forcing it to change. The force."

Kip picked up a rock and tossed it. It flew a few feet through the air, arcing up and then back down. When it hit the ground, it rolled a few inches and stopped.

"Easy!" Newton cried. He picked up the rock and rubbed it along the ground. "The ground is rough. The ground stops it!"

"So, you're saying that if the ground were smooth, it wouldn't have stopped?" Kip couldn't imagine this.

"Now you've got it!"

Kip didn't think he did.

"Look, let's find a rougher patch of ground. The rougher the patch, the sooner it'll stop." He tossed a rock onto some grass, and it stopped immediately.

A short way away, Newton found a frozen puddle. He tossed the rock onto that, and it skid several feet before stopping. "See? The smoother it is, the farther it goes. It's the roughness that's stopping it. If we had something perfectly smooth it wouldn't ever stop. Like when things are going through the air. They go a lot farther in the air than along the ground."

"That's true. But why do they always fall?"

Newton scratched his head. "Well, that's a tough one. Something must be pulling them back down. Otherwise, they wouldn't go down."

"But they're not attached to anything."

Newton waved his hands. "That doesn't matter."

"Doesn't it? If I want to move anything I have to touch it."

"Maybe it's something invisible. I don't know, lad, I was trying to work that one out earlier and gave up."

As they walked the rest of the afternoon, Kip looked around, trying to see if there was anything that didn't obey this law, but it was exactly as Newton had said. Birds turned by flapping their wings. Loose rocks tumbling down slopes stopped when they hit other rocks. And nothing that was stationary moved without something pushing or pulling on it first. It seemed like Newton might be right.

NEWTON'S SECOND LAW

THE next day they came to a narrow rope bridge. It was guarded by two men in Prince Eric's livery. One was very large, and the other was very short.

"Halt in the name of Prince Eric!" the large one said.

Not wanting any bother, Newton and Kip knelt.

"Have either of you murdered anyone or stolen anything today?" the small one asked.

"No, sir," Kip said, while Newton rolled his eyes and huffed.

"Good, you may be on your way, then."

Kip started for the bridge, but Newton wasn't moving. He was eyeing the two guards.

"You're not very evenly sized," he commented.

The large guard raised an eyebrow. "You can be on your way now, old man."

Newton ignored him. Instead, he addressed the small guard. "Everyone must attack you first, right?" He reached out and poked him. The guard narrowed his eyes.

"Newton, come on," Kip said.

"Just Kip, if you were going to attack one of these two guards, which one would you choose?"

"Neither of them," Kip said, alarmed. "Come on, let's go before they change their minds." He turned to the guards. "Sorry, sirs."

"Answer the question!" Newton roared.

Kip sighed. "The small one, I guess. But neither." He glanced at the guards, who were eyeing each other. "Definitely neither."

"And why is that?" Newton prodded.

"Because he's smaller."

"Exactly!" Newton smiled in a self-satisfied way, bowed deeply to the two confused guards, and swept past them onto the bridge.

"I have formulated my second law!" He waved his arms excitedly, and the bridge shook. Newton gave a little hop and chuckled as the bridge quaked. Kip closed his eyes and gripped the ropes on either side. "Don't you want to hear it?"

"Yes. But please keep going."

Newton continued making his way across. "Fine, fine. You're not as excited about this as you should be."

"Sorry."

There was a long pause. Finally, Kip said, "So, what's the law?"

"I'm glad you ask! The larger the object, the more force it takes to make it change what it's doing."

That made sense, but then he thought about the large bags of feathers he'd seen merchants carrying through his village. "What about big things that aren't very heavy, though?"

"Hmmm . . . Excellent point, lad, excellent point."

They'd reached the other side of the bridge, and Kip, feeling smart for having thought of something, was warming to the topic. "Isn't it really heavier things that are harder to move?"

"Yes, yes, you're right."

"Because, some things, even if they're the same size, don't weigh the same."

"Very true. It's not about size at all, it's about how much stuff is there. The more stuff, the harder it is to move. A bag of feathers is big, but it's not very compact. There's not as much stuff there, really."

"Why not just say 'heavier things' rather than 'more stuff'?"

"I don't know, that just feels wrong to me."

"But . . . aren't they the same? The more stuff there is, the heavier it is, right?"

"I can't think of a counter example, but it just feels like there might be a place where things don't weigh anything." He looked up into the sky and pondered for a few moments.

"What? But everything weighs something."

Newton shook himself. "Eh, you're right, I don't know what I was thinking."

"I think you're right, though." Kip said. "About the law, I mean. The more stuff in something, the more force it takes to make it change what it's doing."

Kip paused, then continued, "I don't like the word 'stuff', though." His middle brother had always told him it was a bad, non-descriptive word, and that it could always be replaced with a better one.

"Well, I don't want to call it weight."

"Fine. That guy was pretty massive. Why not call it mass?"

"Kip the Wordsmith!" Newton exclaimed. "Wonderful. Just wonderful. The more mass something has, the more force shall be required to move it. By law. By royal decree." He grinned.

Kip gave a half-skip and smiled.

That evening, as they sat by the fire that Kip had built and ate the random assortment of partially edible things Newton had gathered, Newton pulled out a large leather tome and began scribbling in it.

"What's that?" Kip asked.

"Oh, just something I'm working on," Newton muttered, sucking on his quill and squinting at the pages. It was so dark that Kip wondered how he could even see to write.

"Something magical?" He had yet to see Newton do any magic and was wondering what kind of wizard he was.

"Oh yes, very magical."

"Really? Can you tell me about it?" Kip leaned forward, forgetting the slimy mushroom he had been nibbling.

"Well, all right," Newton said, setting the book down and looking up. He got a misty look on his face. "I call it—" he held his hands up in the air and spread them wide in a grand gesture, like he was writing the word in the stars, "Calculus!"

"Oh." So, not a fire spell, or something that would conjure dragons. Or get them normal food.

Oblivious to Kip's disappointment, Newton held the book out to show him. Kip saw lines and lines of calculations in tiny, neat handwriting. He doubted even his middle brother could have made sense of it.

"What's it for?" he asked.

"Well," Newton said, rubbing his hands together. "Imagine you have a sphere, and the radius is changing. . ."

Kip tuned out after that. Newton spoke long into the night, his enthusiasm only growing as he described water flowing through culverts and collecting in ponds; men on horseback, one riding north at seven miles an hour and one riding east at twelve miles an hour; and farmers wanting to build pastures of maximum area with set amounts of fencing. It all sounded very complicated to Kip, but Newton was enraptured.

Newton's Third Law

THEY walked all the next day, talking about possible third laws, but nothing came to them. Several times they had to stop, kneel, and assure a representative of Prince Eric that they had neither stolen nor murdered recently. Neither said it, but the trial was only three days away and both were beginning to worry. Late in the afternoon, a strange pressure wave passed over them, and Newton went pale.

"What was that?" Kip asked, feeling faint. Before Newton could answer, another wave hit them, and this time, neither of them could move. For several seconds, Kip felt like he was held in an iron grip, unable to breathe. He was beginning to see stars when whatever it was released him and he collapsed, coughing, to the ground. Newton only stood, a grim expression on his face.

"Leibniz."

"What?" Kip looked around.

"Oh no, lad. He's not here. He's at the capital, I expect."

"But . . ."

"It appears he's working on a spell."

"Do you think everyone in the kingdom felt it?"

"Hard to say. We're close now."

"We'd better hurry, then!"

"No point in hurrying unless we figure out a third law."

Despite Newton's words, they both picked up the pace.

The next day they walked and walked, coming up with wilder and wilder ideas, but every idea had an exception. Nothing they could think of was true for everything, all the time. None of their ideas could be called a law.

Twice more during the afternoon they were stopped in their tracks, held captive by some invisible pressure. After each of these, they grew quieter, less certain of their plan.

The next afternoon, the day before the trial, they came around a bend in the road and there it was: the capital. It gleamed, a shining collection of towers and bright red roofs, with a white limestone castle rising in the middle.

Kip couldn't believe that something so beautiful had always been here, and he might never have seen it. His father had never seen it. Neither of his brothers had ever seen it. Only Kip.

Despite his hunger and his sore feet, Kip felt light and joyful just to be there. But they still needed a third law.

The road, which they'd had almost all to themselves for most of their journey, was now filled with traffic. Horses and oxen pulled carts laden with crops towards the capital, and carts full of barrels and boxes and stacks of trade goods left

The next morning, Kip awoke to see Newton sitting on the floor, staring up at the ceiling. There were dark circles under his eyes and a haunted expression on his face.

"It's no good, Kip. I haven't thought of a third law."

"Well, let's just use one of the ones we've already thought of. The first two are so good, maybe they won't pay as much attention to the third."

Newton put his head into his hands. "No. We know those don't work."

"Maybe they won't figure it out."

"Leibniz will. He'll be there. He'll point it out. I'm not going to go in with only two laws. It's a cheat, anyway. If I'm going to cheat, I should at least do it well."

The clock outside struck nine. The trial was at ten.

"Come on, we have to go," Kip said. "We'll think of something on the way."

"No, we won't," Newton said through his hands. "I can't take any more fruit attacks."

"What?"

"He'll just curse me again. Who knows what he'll do this time? I used to like fruit."

Kip jumped out of bed and grabbed Newton's arm. "Come on, we're not giving up now. Get up or I'm going without you. I'll take credit for all your work."

"Good, yes, you go without me," Newton said.

"Of course, I'm not going without you!" Kip said. "They're your ideas, you deserve to go."

"They're stupid ideas."

Exasperated, Kip dropped Newton's arm and looked around the room for inspiration. He saw his pack. He'd completely forgotten about the apple. He dug around until he found it, then pulled it out and held it up.

"If you don't come with me right now, I'm leaving this with you."

Newton looked up and flinched.

"In fact, I'm going to follow you around throwing apples at you for the rest of your life if you don't get up off the floor and come with me right now."

Newton glared at him, then at the apple, then he shuddered.

"Fine. Fine. Put it away."

"You'll come?"

"Fine. Yes." He looked down at his robes, which were mud splattered. "I can't go to the palace looking like this."

"You should have thought of that earlier," Kip said, stuffing the apple back into his pack. "Come on, get up. Let's go."

Very reluctantly, Newton got to his feet, sighed, looked down at his robes again, and then followed Kip out of the room.

Kip's mind raced as they made their way through the streets. He looked everywhere, at people pouring water out of buckets into culverts, at children carrying chickens and women pushing carts. But nothing occurred to him. He didn't give up hope, though. He might be the youngest son, and he wasn't as strong as his eldest brother or as smart as his middle brother, but he would think of something.

28

They reached the palace, where rows of trumpeters with golden trumpets lined the bridge across the moat. Newton's face was slightly grey now, but Kip smiled at everyone and took the wizard's hand as they walked into the grand entrance hall.

The walls and floors were marble, with gold filigree and glittering white statues everywhere. The hall was crowded with lords and ladies in silk, with gold and silver and jewels at their throats and around their wrists and embroidered into their gowns and tunics. In the middle was an open space where two men and a young girl stood.

The first was clearly Prince Eric. He wore black leather and carried a gleaming sword at his side. He had a noble expression and smiled at Kip and nodded politely to Newton as they came to join the group.

The second could only be the wizard Leibniz. He wore deep green robes embroidered with gold and encrusted with tiny, glittering rubies. He also nodded and smiled at Kip, but then ignored Newton, who ignored him back.

Next to Leibniz was a girl about Kip's age. She wore a simple green tunic, belted in leather, and her brown hair was tied back in a messy knot at the base of her neck. She grinned at him, and Kip blushed and looked away.

A hush came over the crowd as the clock struck ten, and a small gold door opened behind the empty throne. The five advisors filed out, each wearing a simple white robe and carrying a piece of parchment and quill.

They arrayed themselves in a line in front of the silent crowd. The middle one stepped forward, reading from his scroll.

"By royal decree, we will now hear and pass judgement on the laws made by the candidates for the crown. Prince Eric, you may begin."

At the sound of his name, everyone in the hall took a knee. Without thinking, Kip did, too. To his surprise, he saw Newton and the others kneeling, as well. Leibniz looked like he wanted to laugh, and the girl at his side covered her mouth to suppress a giggle. Newton noticed what he was doing and, annoyed, tried to get back up again but slipped on the marble floor and fell over.

Prince Eric smiled, and several ladies in the room giggled. He turned to face the crowd.

"Thank you, ladies and gentlemen, for following the first of my three laws. It is the hardest to enforce, but a true king can do it. The second and third, of course, are that there will be no stealing and no murdering in thi—"

The girl darted forward, slipped a hand into Prince Eric's pocket, pulled out a coin and darted away, holding it up for all to see.

"Oops. Stealing." She grinned again.

"Give that back!" Prince Eric's face contorted, and he moved for her, his hand on his sword hilt. She laughed, leapt forward, and pushed him. He was so much larger, though, that her push barely impacted him, causing her to fly backwards instead, laughing and sliding away on the slick marble floor.

The idea hit Kip like a two-by-four to the back of the head. He knew what the third law should be.

Prince Eric was furious, but several noblemen had stepped forward to restrain him.

The advisor spoke again. "Thank you, Prince Eric. Unfortunately, it is clear you are unable to enforce your laws. You are disqualified."

Eric looked like he wanted to throw something at someone, but he settled for storming out of the hall. There was an uncomfortable silence before the advisor cleared his throat and continued. "Wizard Leibniz the Great, please give us your demonstration."

The great? But Kip thought Newton was Newton the Great.

Leibniz bowed. "If my assistant will return, please." The girl was playing with the coin, tossing it into the air and catching it. "Allora, please?" he said. She slipped the coin into her pocket and returned. They closed their eyes, each with their hands raised, and a crackling energy filled the hall. The pressure returned, stronger than it had been before, and for several seconds no one was able to move.

Afterwards, there was a lot of coughing and muttering and it took several minutes for the advisors to restore quiet.

"Most impressive, Wizard Leibniz. We shall check to determine whether the entire kingdom was affected, but so far it seems to be a success. And for your second law?"

Leibniz bowed. "Unfortunately, that was all I was able to accomplish. One law. Given more time I could likely make more, but, as you might guess, controlling an entire kingdom takes quite a lot of power."

They only had a single law? Kip saw Newton's head shoot up for the first time since they'd entered the hall. Hope gleamed in his eyes, and he started to look around frantically, clearly trying to think of something. Kip tugged on his robe to get his attention and when Newton looked at him, he mouthed "I've got it." Newton raised his eyebrows and looked at him in wonder.

"Wizard Newton the Lesser," the advisor said, and Newton cringed. "Do you have your laws?"

"I do," he said, straightening his back. He explained about the first law. "In summary," he said, "objects in motion will stay in motion, and objects at rest will stay at rest, unless acted upon by an unbalanced force." There was some confusion at this. No one had heard a law like this before, and no one could quite make out why one would want to have a law like that in the first place.

Everyone immediately set about trying to break this new law. Ladies kicked off their shoes and slid about the marble floors, men tossed their hats into the air, and the girl, Allora, ran around in the midst of the chaos pickpocketing people. The wizard Leibniz just smiled thinly. After a long while it was concluded that no one could break the law.

So, Newton explained about the second law. Various sized animals and boulders and bags of feathers were brought in to try to disprove it, but nowhere in the city could be found something that was more massive but easier to get moving or stop moving.

"Well, Wizard Newton the Lesser, you seem to have done well," the advisor said. "Although it does feel like you are cheating. What is the third law?"

Newton cleared his throat nervously and looked at Kip.

Kip felt himself blush as everyone in the hall turned to stare at him. He tried to think of how Newton would phrase it. "For every action, there is an equal and opposite reaction." There were a lot of confused looks, so he tried to put it into simpler terms. "You can't push on anything without it pushing back on you," Kip said. He accidentally caught Allora's eye, and she grinned at him. He blushed harder and looked away. "If I push on a wall, I can feel it pushing back on me. If a horse pulls a cart, the cart pulls back on the horse."

"Wait, wait, wait," the advisor said. "If the cart pulls back on the horse, how does anything move?"

Kip thought for a moment. That was a good question. How did things move if every force had a balancing force? Then he had it. "They aren't pulling on the same thing," he said. "The horse pulls on the cart. So, it moves the cart. The cart, though, pulls on the horse. If both forces were pulling on the cart, then the cart wouldn't move, but one is on the cart and the other is on the horse. Forces that act on different objects don't balance each other out. Only forces on the same object balance each other out."

There was much arguing about this, but eventually most people agreed this was true, and the advisors were convinced. Newton looked at Kip and glowed with pride. Kip smiled, his heart pounding.

The advisors deliberated together for a few moments, then returned to address the crowd. "We are in something of a difficult position here," one said. "The task was to make three laws which everyone would have to follow. Leibniz has clearly succeeded in the spirit of the task. He has controlled the entire kingdom, which was the true nature of the task we set. However, he has only enforced a single law. Newton, on the other hand, has formed three laws, which, it is true, no one can break. However, we are of the opinion that these were somehow already laws before Newton informed us of them. So, in some ways, he has cheated. Discovered rather than made laws. Still, is it not kingly to sense the true nature of the world? But, as king, one cannot just make laws about the way things already are."

The assembled nobles nodded wisely.

"And so, we have determined that the land must be ruled by a balance of the two. A king must know how to sense the truth of the world and work within that truth, but also a king must be able, in some instances, to impose his will upon the world. And so, we declare that Newton and Leibniz shall rule the kingdom jointly, combining their wisdom and strength."

Everyone in the hall smiled and nodded at this wise decision, except for Newton and Leibniz, who both looked like they'd been told they could eat nothing but moldy apples for the rest of their lives. Neither of them would look at the other.

Kip caught Allora's eye, and she nodded. She kicked Leibniz. Kip poked Newton.

"He's not evil at all, is he?" Kip whispered.

"Of course, he is. I told you about the apples."

"He doesn't seem that evil. How do you know him?"

"We were apprenticed together. He was always better than I was." Newton wouldn't look at him.

"But you've won, you've just bested him. Even with all his magic, you out-thought him."

Newton looked up. "I suppose I did, didn't I?"

"Yes, and look, you can be friends, can't you? You can forgive him?"

Leibniz was making his way over, looking mutinously at his apprentice, who continued kicking him every time he stopped.

"Newton," Liebniz said, in a forced voice, holding out his hand.

"Leibniz," Newton said coldly.

"Apologize," Allora hissed.

"I'm sorry," Liebniz said through gritted teeth. "About the apples."

There was silence.

Kip poked Newton. "Accept his apology."

"It's fine." Newton muttered this, but then he looked up and met Leibniz's eye. "Eh, it was pretty funny. Not a bad bit of magic."

Liebniz chuckled.

"Great!" Allora said, smiling at everyone. Kip smiled back.

Newton and Leibniz gingerly shook hands.

"Clever laws," Leibniz said finally.

"Not terrible magic," Newton said.

Leibniz smiled, and, reluctantly, Newton smiled, too.

They began to discuss each of their tricks more thoroughly, and Kip and Allora left them to it.

"He seems nice," Kip said, gesturing to Leibniz.

"Oh, he is. Just don't get him started on Calculus."

Kip stopped. "What?"

"It's this thing he's inventing." Allora picked at a thread on her sleeve.

Kip sincerely hoped that it wouldn't come up.

From then on, Leibniz and Newton ruled the kingdom together, assisted by their advisors, Kip and Allora. And, except for the Calculus thing, everyone lived happily ever after.

THE END

The Physics

(Some explanations of the concepts behind the story.)

NEWTON'S FIRST LAW

Newton's laws are widely known but also widely misunderstood. They seem obvious when you first hear them, but they actually contradict what most of us instinctively believe about the world.

Take the first law, sometimes stated like this: An object in motion will stay in motion, an object at rest will stay at rest, unless acted upon by an unbalanced force. Seems pretty basic, right?

Now ask yourself this question: When a ball is thrown, why does it come to a stop?

Most people instinctively say something like "because it runs out of force", which is wrong but fits with what we observe in the world. The truth, which Wizard Newton realized when he rolled down that hill, is the ball would have kept going forever except that gravity pulled it down, which meant it hit the ground. When it hit the ground, friction pulled it to a stop.

Newton's first law is often called The Law of Inertia. Inertia is the tendency of an object to keep doing what it's doing. Basically, something moving will keep moving unless some force stops it. The more mass something has, the more inertia it has.

We never see things move forever. This is because there's friction everywhere. If we grew up on space stations, we wouldn't have this misconception. We'd throw something, and it would sail through the air in a straight line at a constant speed until it hit something else. But here on earth, every single thing we throw or move or push or pull comes to a stop unless we keep pushing on it. Friction is so pervasive that we just don't notice it.

Let's take a moment to define some terms. There are a lot of words used in physics that are also everyday words, but they're sometimes used differently, or more precisely, in physics:

Force: A push or a pull. Some common ones include: Gravity, Friction, Tension, the Normal Force, Magnetic Forces, Electric Forces, Air Resistance, Applied Forces. I'll go into these more later, in the Problem Solving section.

Weight: Weight is a force. Weight is the pull of gravity on you. (So, weight is also often called the Gravitational Force or the Force Due to Gravity.) It is measured in 'Newtons' usually. Those are the standard units, but also if you say something weighs 12 pounds you are talking about weight. If you go to the moon, your weight will be 1/6 of what it is here on Earth. If you go into space, far enough away from any planet or moon or other massive body, you will be 'weightless,' meaning there is no force of gravity pulling on you.

Mass: How much stuff makes up an object. Not to be confused with weight. These are different, but very closely related, because the more mass something has, the heavier it will be (ie. the more weight it will have). Mass is measured in kilograms. In the everyday world, we often talk about kilograms as if they are a unit of weight, but that's actually not right. Kilograms are a unit of mass, a unit of how much stuff makes something up. Weight, on the other hand, is a measurement of how much the earth is pulling down on us. It's how heavy we are. If we go into outer space, we would be weightless, but we would still have mass. If we went to the moon, we would have less weight (because the moon pulls on us less,) but our mass would be the same. An object's mass is the same no matter where it is. To change the mass of an object, you must break a piece of it off or stick another piece on.

Velocity: How fast you're going. You can think of this as speed. It's basically speed, only it also includes direction. So, you can change your velocity by turning, even if you're still going the same speed.

Acceleration: How quickly your velocity is changing. Imagine you're driving at 30 mph. Then you push on the gas pedal and start speeding up. That feeling that you feel? That's acceleration. I saw a post on the internet yesterday that said, 'velocity is a funny thing'. It had a picture of the earth, showing how incredibly fast the earth rotates, and some smiling people having dinner, oblivious to the speed. Then it had a picture of a car driving at 60 mph and a smiling, totally calm woman driving.

Then it had a picture of a kid going down a slide. It was labelled as 3 mph or something and showed the kid's horrified face. Reading this, I was like 'noooooo'. Because the reason that kid is upset isn't that he's being a baby about such a slow velocity, and it's also not that 'velocity is weird'. It's that he's accelerating. We feel acceleration. We don't feel speed. Driving 30 mph feels the same as driving 60 mph which feels the same as being stationary. We don't feel anything until we try to speed up, slow down, or turn.

Try This: The Maze Phet Simulation

To help you understand the differences between position, velocity, and acceleration, try playing around with this Phet Simulation by the University of Colorado called 'The Maze'. (Also, a note about links: if you're reading this on a kindle without an internet browser, you can open this book instead in the kindle cloud reader, or on the kindle app on a smartphone, and then you'll be able to follow the link. Alternatively, you can just search for Phet Maze and it should come up.)

The goal here is to get the ball to the point labelled 'finish'. You can do this by controlling either the position, velocity, or acceleration. To start, make sure you've selected 'practice' in the green area and 'r' in the yellow area. Here, 'r' means "position". Then, click play. You move the ball by clicking and dragging on the blue dot above where it says "Position" in the lower right-hand corner.

Once you've scored a goal using position, keep it on 'practice' and try it with velocity ('v') instead. Then try it with

40

acceleration, 'a'. Then bump it up to Level 1 and do the same thing.

YouTube Videos:

Veritasium makes awesome videos about physics. I can't recommend them highly enough. Some good ones to watch at this point are:

The Difference Between Mass and Weight
Egg Experiment to Demonstrate Inertia

NEWTON'S SECOND LAW

Newton's second law is often stated simply as an equation:

$$F = MA$$

In the story, this was the law Newton thought of when they came to the bridge with the two differently sized guards. (Also, just as a side note, this is completely my invention. This is not how these laws were derived. The history of these laws is complicated. The idea of the second law was already known in Newton's time, but he proved some really amazing things with this idea combined with Calculus and Kepler's work on orbits and gravitation. I won't go into it here, because the math gets complicated—outside of the scope of this book—but you can read more about it here: https://science.howstuffworks.com/innovation/scientific-experiments/newton-law-of-motion2.htm., or in the history section of the Wikipedia page.)

The idea here is that acceleration is caused by force. The harder we push on something, the more it will accelerate. Meaning, the harder we push on something, the more it will speed up, slow down, or turn. Also, the more massive something is, the more force it takes to speed that thing up, slow it down, or make it turn.

Try This: Forces in One Dimension Simulation

A fun simulation to play around with to get a feel for forces and how they cause acceleration is Phet's Forces in One Dimension. You click on the object and drag to create a force on the object (caused by a little stick man).

Try creating a force, then let go and see what the object does. Try turning friction off and on (in the sidebar on the right.) Try objects of different mass. Which of the objects requires the most force? How quickly do they stop once you stop pushing on them?

NEWTON'S THIRD LAW

Newton's Third Law is also one of those things that seems obvious but is actually more complicated than it seems. It is usually stated as "For every action there is an equal and opposite reaction." This feels so commonplace, it almost sounds like "haste makes waste" or "a job worth doing is worth doing well". Let's talk about what it really means.

In the story, Allora pushes on Prince Eric and goes flying backwards. Anyone who has gone ice skating and pushed off against a wall or sat in a wheeled chair and pushed back from a table has an intuitive feel for this.

The classic misunderstanding of this law is stated in the story. How does anything move? If every force has an equal and opposite reaction force, why does anything move at all? Why don't these forces just cancel each other out?

The answer is that these forces don't cancel each other out because they don't act on the same object. When two equal forces act on the same object from opposite directions, they do of course cancel out. If you push on a box from one side and your friend pushes on the same box from the other side, if you push with the same amount of strength (force), then the box won't move. Your efforts will cancel out. That's not what Newton's Third Law is talking about.

Newton's Third Law is for what are called "action-reaction pairs". Meaning, basically, the push-back from whatever action you're taking. So, if you push a kid on a swing, you can feel the kid pushing back on you. If you kick a soccer ball, you can feel the force of the impact on your foot. If you're sitting in a wheeled office chair and you throw a heavy computer, you'll roll backwards. The two forces, the action-reaction pair, are often called "third law pairs".

This always reminds me of the joke "Chuck Norris doesn't do push-ups, he does earth-downs". Technically, we all do "earth-downs" when we do push-ups, it's just that the earth is so much bigger it doesn't notice. But we both experience the same amount of force.

YouTube Videos

Three Incorrect Laws of Motion
Best Film on Newton's Third Law. Ever.

NEWTON AND THE APPLE

The classic story of Newton is that he discovered gravity when an apple fell on his head. I always thought this was just a made-up story, but apparently Newton did say that he started thinking about gravity when he watched an apple fall. You can read this New Scientist Article: https://www.newscientist.com/blogs/culturelab/2010/01/newtons-apple-the-real-story.html for the details." I felt like any story I wrote about Newton had to include an apple in some way, and I thought it would be funny if instead of one apple falling on him, all apples fell on him.

Also, the "Newton" in this story is not meant to be a portrayal of the actual Newton. The real Newton was a genius, one of the greatest thinkers and scientists to ever live and gave humanity an incredible amount of knowledge. I hope I'm not doing him a disservice by giving his name to a genius but comically flawed fairy-tale wizard character. Here's some interesting reading about what he may have actually been like as a person: https://www.quora.com/What-was-Isaac-Newton-like-as-a-person.

This concludes the conceptual side of things. I hope you've enjoyed it! Next, for people who are interested in the math or who are taking a physics class, I'm including a section on problem solving. It assumes a basic familiarity with algebra. Feel free to skip it if you're not interested. You can still go on and try the Conceptual Practice Problems at the end if you'd like. If you enjoyed this book, check out the rest of the series on Amazon!

PROBLEM SOLVING

This section is for people who want to get into the math of doing calculations with Newton's Laws. Feel free to skip it if your main focus is the conceptual understanding. Also, in this section I'll assume a basic familiarity with Algebra. If you want to brush up on your math skills first but you're not sure where to start, check out Khan Academy's Algebra 1 Course Challenge.

Problem solving with Newton's Laws usually involves determining which forces are acting on an object and then using this to calculate the acceleration of the object. Sometimes we work backwards from the acceleration and determine the forces on an object from this.

The main tool we use for thinking about the various forces on an object is called the Free Body Diagram.

In a Free Body Diagram, we start by drawing a square to represent an object. Then we draw a dot in the middle, like this:

Then we draw all the forces acting on the object as arrows coming from the center of the object, like this:

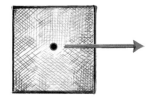

The length of the arrow represents the strength of the force. The longer the arrow, the stronger the force. It doesn't have to be super precise; there's no set length they have to be. It's more like, if you know one force is bigger than another force, you draw that arrow longer.

Now, let's go over some of the different types of forces that might be included in our diagram:

Gravity

The gravitational force is the weight of the object, or, how much the object is being pulled down by gravity. When we're on Earth we can use Newton's Second Law to calculate the force of gravity on an object. This is because gravity accelerates all objects equally.

"Acceleration" is basically how quickly an object's speed is changing. (Technically I shouldn't use the word speed, I should use the word velocity, but I'm not going to get into vectors here.) We measure speed in meters per second (m/s). Let's say I'm going 10 m/s but I'm speeding up. Two seconds later, I'm going 18 m/s. I sped up by 8 m/s, and I did that in 2 seconds. So, on average I got 4 m/s faster every second. That's acceleration.

We would call that an acceleration of 4 meters per second per second.

Note: the units for acceleration are usually written like this:

$$m/s^2$$

Going forward, though, I'm going to write it like this: m/s/s, which is read "meters per second per second." I'm choosing to write it this way for two reasons: 1. It's easier to type, and 2. I think it's clearer conceptually what m/s/s means. It's the change in the speed of an object. Meaning, it's how many meters per second (m/s) are added or subtracted every second.)

The force of gravity gets weaker as you get farther away from the Earth, or as you go higher, but around the surface of the Earth, the acceleration due to gravity is around 9.8 meters per second squared. If we want to know how much gravitational force this is, we can use Newton's Second Law:

$$F = MA$$

Here, m is the mass of the object and a is the acceleration of the object, which will be 9.8 m/s/s.

Force is measured in Newtons, which we abbreviate with a capital N. When we multiply kilograms by meters per second per second, we get Newtons.

If we had an object of mass 30 kg, we would find the force of gravity on it like this:

$$\vec{F_G} = (30 \text{ KG})*(9.8 \text{ M/S/S})$$
$$\vec{F_G} = 294 \text{ N}$$

Incidentally, we use the little subscript 'g' to indicate that it's the force of gravity on an object. Also, just so you know, 9.8 is often just written as 'g'. So, we often write the equation for the gravitational force as:

$$\vec{F_G} = MG$$

This is because:

$$F = \text{FORCE}$$
$$G = \text{GRAVITY}$$
$$\text{SO,}$$
$$\vec{F_G} = \text{FORCE DUE TO GRAVITY}$$

Here, m is the mass of the object in kilograms (not grams or any other unit. It needs to be in kilograms), and g is 9.8 m/s/s if we're on the surface of the Earth.

The Normal Force

The normal force is weirdly named. Don't think of it as "regular force". The word normal in math means perpendicular. The normal force is called that because it's a force that's always perpendicular to a surface. So, what is it? Well, it's sometimes called a "support force" because it's the force that holds things up, or supports them, when they're sitting on tables or floors. Basically, it's the force that surfaces exert on objects. For example, I have my cup of tea here. It's being pulled on by gravity as we speak, but luckily my desk is holding it up for me. That force that my desk is exerting on my cup is called the normal force.

Also, my chair is exerting a normal force on me, holding me up. My stack of Calvin and Hobbes books is exerting a normal force on my computer, holding it up. Usually, the normal force exactly equals the gravitational force, balancing it out.

Like this:

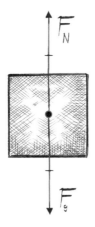

Here, we indicate that the two forces are the same strength in two ways. First, by drawing the arrows the same length, and second by drawing those little tick marks on the arrows. The tick marks indicate they are the same length. Notice also that we write the normal force as a capital F with a subscript N.

Friction

Friction is the force between two objects as they rub against one another. For example, when you push a box across a concrete floor, that's easier than pushing a box across a carpet because the concrete floor is smoother. The smoother the surface, the less friction. There are multiple types of friction, but I won't go into it here. For now, when I give you a practice problem, I'll just tell you how much friction force is being exerted. Friction is often indicated with a lowercase f. Sometimes a cursive f, like this:

Tension

Tension forces are the forces exerted by ropes and cables and things like that. When a rope pulls on an object, the rope gets stretched a little. The more stretched it is, the tauter it gets. This 'tightness' or stretch in the rope pulls on the object. It's like stretching a rubber band. The more you stretch a rubber band, the more it wants to pull back into itself.

We usually indicate tension forces like this:

$$F_T$$

F= force
T = tension

So,

F_T= tension force

Applied Forces

This is a broad category and includes things like people pushing on objects. These can be written a bunch of different ways, but here's how I like to write them:

Air Resistance

Air resistance is basically just the force of air molecules as they bounce off you. Imagine sticking your hand out the car window as it goes (hopefully someone else is driving). You can feel the force of air resistance on you. The faster you go, the stronger the air resistance is. I usually write this force like this:

Some people will write it as a frictional force. I don't like this approach, though, because I think it's misleading. Friction and air resistance work differently.

Electric and Magnetic Forces

These are super cool, but they're a huge topic and I'm not going to go into them much here. Electric forces are the forces that charges exert on each other, and magnetic forces are forces that moving charges exert on other moving charges. In general. It's complicated and totally fascinating.

Ok, now that we've got a set of forces to think about, let's draw some Free Body Diagrams. I'll give you some examples.

Free Body Diagram One

A book sitting on a table:

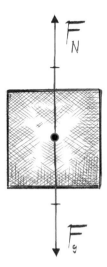

Notice that we've got the gravitational force because the book is presumably on Earth. Also, we've got the normal force because the table is holding it up. Now let's add some numbers to our diagram to make it quantitative. Let's say the mass of the book is 5 kg.

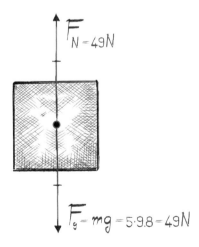

I calculated the gravitational force first, using the formula:

$$F_g = mg$$

$$= (5 \text{ kg})(9.8 \text{ m/s/s})$$
$$= 49 \text{ N}$$

and then I knew that the normal force was the same, so I just labelled it as 49 N, too.

Free Body Diagram Two

A book of 6 kg sliding over a frictionless surface at a constant speed of 4 m/s:

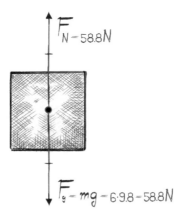

This is one that usually confuses people, because since the book is moving, they feel like there should be a force in the sideways direction. That's where Newton's First Law comes in! The book is going at a constant speed, so there doesn't need to be a force there. We only need forces to change motion.

Free Body Diagram Three

A box of 10 kg being pushed with a force of 50 N and experiencing a frictional force of 20 N:

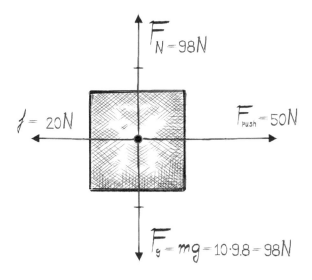

Again, I calculated the gravitational force first, then made the normal force equal to it, then drew on the applied force and the frictional force.

Free Body Diagram Four

A 0.2 kg baseball flying through the air:

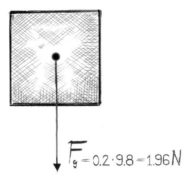

$$F_g = 0.2 \cdot 9.8 = 1.96 N$$

This one also trips people up. First off, in most cases, we ignore air resistance. This is for two reasons. The first reason is that it often doesn't exert very much force, so it wouldn't change our answer much, and the second reason is that it's really hard to calculate. It depends on a lot of tricky things about the shape of the object. So, since it doesn't have much of an effect anyway, we leave it out.

When something is flying, if we're ignoring air resistance, and if it doesn't have like wings or rockets or something making it go, then the only force acting on it is gravity. It doesn't matter whether it's going up or down or whatever. The Free Body Diagram always looks like this. That's the tricky thing to wrap your head around with Free Body Diagrams: they don't convey speed at all. They only show the forces on an object.

Ok, now let's talk about how to find the acceleration of an object.

In general, this is the process:

1. Draw the FBD with all the forces.
2. Find the net force.
3. Use F = ma to find the acceleration.

For example, imagine that you're pushing on a box to the right with 50 N, and your friend is pushing to the left with 40 N. The FBD looks like this:

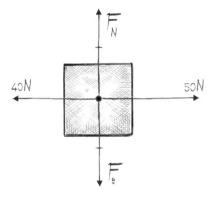

It makes sense that some of your force gets cancelled out, because you guys are working against one another. We call whatever is left over the 'net force'. In this case, the net force is 50 - 40 or 10 N.

We calculate the net force in the horizontal direction separately from the vertical direction. So, in this case, because the normal and the gravitational forces cancel out, the net force in the vertical direction is 0 N.

The net force is important because it's what causes the acceleration. (The force that gets cancelled out doesn't do anything to the box.) So, the net force is what we plug into our equation from Newton's Second Law. If the mass of the box above was 2 kg, we could find its acceleration like this:

$$F_{net} = ma$$
$$10 = 2 \cdot a$$
$$5 \, m/s^2 = a$$

Now, let's move on to a tricky type of problem, the kind where you are given the acceleration of an object and want to find either its mass or one of the forces acting on it. In general, the process looks like this:

1. Draw a FBD, label all the forces you know.
2. Use F = ma to find the net force (assuming you have the mass)
3. Think about which forces should be bigger or smaller.
4. Either add or subtract to find the forces you don't know.

(This is a little vague, but I'll do an example next.)

Finding the Frictional Force

A 7 kg box is being pushed with a force of 50 N. It is accelerating at 4 m/s/s. What is the frictional force on the box?

First, I'll draw the FBD:

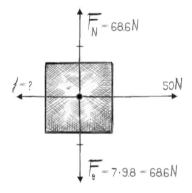

I knew that the frictional force would be smaller than the applied force, so I drew the arrow shorter.

Next, I'll use the acceleration and the mass to find the net force:

$$a = 4\,m/s^2$$
$$F_{net} = ma$$
$$= 7 \cdot 4$$
$$= 28N$$

Then I'll write an equation for the net force. The net force is the 50 N force minus the friction force, and I figured out above that the net force is 28 N.

$$50 - f = 28$$
$$+f \qquad +f$$
$$50 = 28 + f$$
$$-28 \qquad -28$$
$$\boxed{22N = f}$$

Ok, lastly, here's a classic problem called the elevator problem. Have you noticed that when you're riding in an elevator you feel lighter or heavier sometimes? Well, we call that the 'apparent weight'. Your apparent weight is just the normal force of the floor pushing up on you. Because the way you feel your weight is by how much the floor is pushing up on you. So, to find your apparent weight, you can just calculate the normal force, in the same way as we did above.

Finding Apparent Weight

You are riding upwards in an elevator. The elevator is speeding up with an acceleration of 3 m/s/s. You have a mass of 60 kg. What is your apparent weight?

Ok. So, same as before, start by finding the net force:

$$F_{net} = ma$$
$$= 60 \cdot 3$$
$$= 180N$$

Next, draw your FBD:

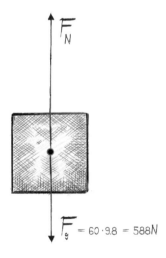

Here, I find it helpful to just imagine I'm in the elevator and ask myself whether I feel heavier or lighter. The elevator is going up and speeding up. I feel heavier. So, I make the normal force arrow longer. Also, I know that we're accelerating upwards, which means we need more force upwards to make the net force be up. So, now I can write this equation:

$$F_N - F_g = F_{net}$$

Now I'll just plug in numbers:

$$F_N - 588 = 180$$

And solve:

$$F_N = 768N$$

The normal force is 768 N, so my apparent weight is 768 N, too.

PRACTICE

(The answers are on page 75.)

1. A child and an adult are ice skating. They stand facing each other and push off from one another. Which one experiences more force, or do they experience the same force?

2. In the question above, which of them accelerates more?

3. If you kick a soccer ball with 10 N of force, how much force does it exert back on you?

4. Identify the third law pairs (the reaction forces) for each of these action forces:

   a. The gravitational force of the earth pulls a pinecone to the ground as it falls out of a tree.

   b. You push on a heavy trunk to slide it across the floor.

   c. You stand on a table. The table exerts a force on you to hold you up.

   d. You exert a force on a ball to push it into the air.

   e. You jump off a skateboard, pushing the skateboard back.

   f. A rocket shoots propellant out from its rockets.

   g. You are sitting in a canoe and push an oar against the water.

5. An air hockey table uses air to hold the puck up off the surface of the table so that it doesn't experience much friction at all (almost none). If you had a giant air hockey table and you hit the puck to get it going, what would it do? Would it come to a stop?

6. In the previous question, if you hit the puck harder, what does that change about how the puck moves?

7. Here's a tricky one: Imagine you've got a tennis ball on a string, and you're swinging it around your head. What happens if the string breaks? How does the ball move? Draw a top-view sketch of what you think it will do.

8. Here's another tricky one: If you were in a windowless box in outer-space, and you couldn't feel any acceleration or hear any sounds, would you be able to tell if you were stationary (not moving) or moving at a constant speed?

9. Ok, I guess these are all just going to be tricky: If you were in the same windowless box, but you didn't know where you were, would you be able to tell if you were floating somewhere in outer space or falling to earth?

10. The Moon and the Earth are both pulling on each other with their gravity. How does the force of the Moon on the Earth compare to the force of the Earth on the Moon?

QUANTITATIVE PRACTICE PROBLEMS

(Be sure to give units for all your answers, and directions for all vectors (forces, velocities, and accelerations.)
You can find the answers in the next section.

1. Draw qualitative (just the arrows, no numbers) Free Body Diagrams for each of the following objects:
    a. A cup sitting on a table.
    b. A hockey puck sliding along at a constant speed (assume the ice is totally smooth and frictionless).
    c. A box being pushed along at a constant speed.
    d. A rock flying through the air, moving upwards.
    e. A rock flying through the air, moving downwards.
    f. A rock flying straight up through the air, right at the highest point of its motion, hanging motionless for an instant before falling back to earth again.
    g. A box being pushed by a person so that it speeds up.
    h. A box moving to the right but slowing down because of friction.
    i. A box moving to the left but speeding up because someone is pushing on it.

2. Draw quantitative (including numbers) Free Body Diagrams for each of the following objects:
    a. A box of mass 5 kg is sitting motionless on a table.

b. A box of mass 12 kg is being pushed by a force of 30N to the right but is motionless because there is too much friction.

c. A box of mass 40 kg is being pushed to the right with a force of 100 N and is moving at a constant speed.

d. A rock of mass 3 kg is flying upwards in the air, after being thrown.

e. A rock of mass 6 kg is falling through the air after having fallen from a cliff.

f. Two friends are pushing on a box of mass 50 kg. One friend pushes to the left with a force of 100N, the other friend pushes to the right with a force of 80 N. Ignore friction.

g. Two friends are pushing on a box of mass 8 kg. One friend pushes to the right with a force of 60 N, the other friend also pushes to the right with a force of 10 N. Ignore friction.

h. A skydiver of mass 60 kg has deployed her parachute. The force of air resistance is 100 N.

i. A box (50 kg) is sliding to the right. The force of friction on the box is 50 N.

3. Use the free body diagrams you drew for question 2 to find the net force in each of these situations:

a. A box of mass 5 kg is sitting motionless on a table.

b. A box of mass 12 kg is being pushed by a force of 30N to the right but is motionless because there is too much friction.

c. A box of mass 40 kg is being pushed to the right with a force of 100 N and is moving at a constant speed.

d. A rock of mass 3 kg is flying upwards in the air, after being thrown.

e. A rock of mass 6 kg is falling through the air after having fallen from a cliff.

f. Two friends are pushing on a box of mass 50 kg. One friend pushes to the left with a force of 100N, the other friend pushes to the right with a force of 80 N. Ignore friction.

g. Two friends are pushing on a box of mass 8 kg. One friend pushes to the right with a force of 60 N, the other friend also pushes to the right with a force of 10 N. Ignore friction.

h. A skydiver of mass 60 kg has deployed her parachute. The force of air resistance is 100 N.

i. A box (50 kg) is sliding to the right. The force of friction on the box is 50 N.

4. Use the net forces you found in question 3 to find the accelerations of these objects in each of these situations:

a. A box of mass 5 kg is sitting motionless on a table.

b. A box of mass 12 kg is being pushed by a force of 30N to the right but is motionless because there is too much friction.

c. A box of mass 40 kg is being pushed to the right with a force of 100 N and is moving at a constant speed.

d. A rock of mass 3 kg is flying upwards in the air, after being thrown.

e. A rock of mass 6 kg is falling through the air after having fallen from a cliff.

f. Two friends are pushing on a box of mass 50 kg. One friend pushes to the left with a force of 100N, the other friend pushes to the right with a force of 80 N. Ignore friction.

g. Two friends are pushing on a box of mass 8 kg. One friend pushes to the right with a force of 60 N, the other friend also pushes to the right with a force of 10 N. Ignore friction.

h. A skydiver of mass 60 kg has deployed her parachute. The force of air resistance is 100 N.

i. A box (50 kg) is sliding to the right. The force of friction on the box is 50 N.

5. A child of mass 30 kg is sliding across a wood floor in his socks. He experiences a frictional force of 40 N. What is his acceleration?

6. A canoe of mass 200 kg is experiencing a friction force of 50 N from the water. What is its acceleration?

7. A rock of mass 40 kg is falling through the air. What is its acceleration? (Ignore air resistance).

8. A person of mass 70 kg is riding upwards in an elevator travelling at a constant speed. What is the normal force on them?

9. A person of mass 70 kg is riding upwards in an elevator, accelerating upwards at 1 m/s/s. What is their apparent weight?

10. A person of mass 70 kg is riding upwards in an elevator, accelerating downwards at 2 m/s/s. What is their apparent weight?

11. A person of mass 70 kg is riding downwards in an elevator. The elevator is slowing down at 5 m/s/s. What is their apparent weight?

12. A person of mass 70 kg is riding downwards in an elevator. The elevator is speeding up at 2 m/s/s. What is their apparent weight?

13. A person of mass 70 kg is riding upwards in an elevator, and the elevator is speeding up. Their apparent weight is 900 N. What is their acceleration?

14. A person of mass 70 kg is riding upwards in an elevator and the elevator is slowing down. Their apparent weight is 400 N. What is their acceleration?

15. A box of mass 30 kg is being pushed with a force of 500 N and is acceleration at 2 m/s/s. How much friction is acting on the box?

16. A sled of mass 50 kg is being pulled by a force of 60 N and is travelling at a constant speed. How much friction force is there on the sled?

17. A ball of mass 10 kg is flying through the air. What is its acceleration?

18. A plane of mass 3,000 kg is flying at a constant speed through the air. What is its acceleration?

19. What is the mass of a ball that is kicked with a force of 30 N and accelerates at 10 m/s/s?

20. What is the mass of a box that is pushed to the right with a force of 60 N and experiences a frictional force of 10 N and accelerates to the right at 3 m/s/s?

CONCEPTUAL QUESTIONS
ANSWER KEY

(Or go back to Conceptual Questions.)

1. They experience the same force (by Newton's Third Law). This is surprising because it feels intuitively like the adult should have been pushing harder. But imagine the adult pushing against a wall. However much the adult pushes on the wall, that is how much of a push they'll feel back from the wall. It's the same with the child. However much the adult pushes on the child, that's the amount of force they'll feel back. The child helps, too. It's like they create the force together. If the kid just let their arms go limp, it would be hard for the adult to push at all.

2. The child accelerates more because they are smaller (have less mass).

3. 10 N (by Newton's Third Law).

4. Answers:
   a. The pinecone pulls up on the earth as it falls.
   b. The trunk pushes back on you with the same force.
   c. You push down on the table.
   d. The ball exerts a force back on you as you throw it.
   e. The skateboard pushes you forwards with the same force.

f. The propellant pushes the rocket forward.

g. The water pushes forward on the oar (which pushes the boat forward, since you're holding the oar steady).

5. The puck travel in a straight line at a constant speed, until it hit a wall.

6. If you hit the puck harder, it just means it'll be going faster for that whole time.

7. The ball will move in a straight line, like this:

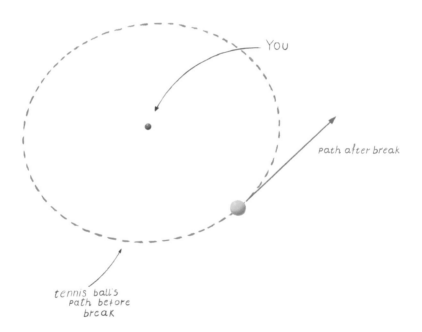

You

path after break

tennis ball's path before break

8. No, you wouldn't be able to tell. You might be stopped, or moving at 60 mph. It's a bit of a strange question, though, because if you're in space, what does speed even

mean? What are we comparing our speed to? A passing spaceship? The earth? The sun? All of those things are moving. So, it's hard to even say what our speed is, since we don't have some fixed reference point in the universe that we've all agreed is the "stationary" point.

9. No, again, you can't tell. This is why we can use those planes to simulate weightlessness. If you and the box are both falling to earth, then you're accelerating at the same rate. So, if you imagine being inside, you're still just floating inside that box. You can push off the sides and the top and float in the middle of it because it's accelerating at the same rate you are. So you feel stationary compared to it. To make it make more sense, have you seen videos of people skydiving together? Notice how they all are kind of floating next to each other? If they could only look at each other they might think they were stationary.

10. They're the same. (Newton's Third Law).

QUANTITATIVE PRACTICE PROBLEMS ANSWER KEY

Back to Practice Problems.

Answers:

1.   Free Body Diagrams:

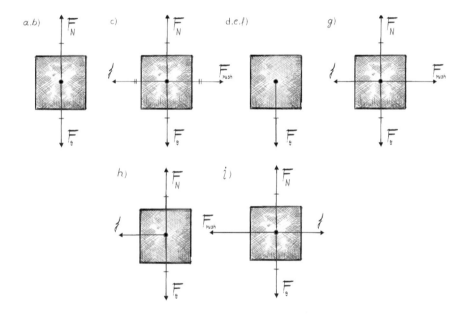

2. Quantitative free body diagrams:

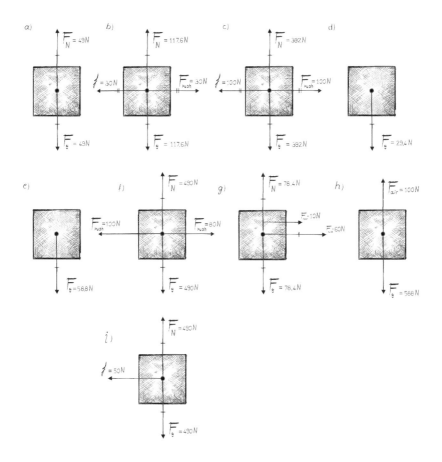

3. Net Force:
    a. 0 N

    b. 0 N

    c. 0 N

    d. 29.4 N Down

    e. 58.8 N Down

    f. 20 N Left

    g. 70 N Right

    h. 488 N Down

    i. 50 N Left

4. Acceleration:
   a. 0 m/s/s
   b. 0 m/s/s
   c. 0 m/s/s
   d. 9.8 m/s/s Down
   e. 9.8 m/s/s Down
   f. 0.4 m/s/s Left
   g. 8.75 m/s/s Right
   h. 1 m/s/s Left

5. -1.3 m/s/s (Instead of using the - sign to indicate direction, you could also say "opposite to the direction of travel of the boy.)

6. -0.25 m/s/s

7. 9.8 m/s/s Down

8. 686 N Up

9. 763 N Up

10. 546 N Up

11. 1036 N Up

12. 546 N Up

13. 3.06 m/s/s up

14. 4.09 m/s/s Down

15. -440 N (or 440 N opposite the direction of travel of the box.)

16. -60 N

17. -9.8 m/s/s

18. 0 m/s/s

19. 3 kg

20. 17 kg (rounded from 16.777...)

PRINCESS ELISE
AND THE
RIPPLE OF LIES

ONCE upon a time there lived a princess in a castle. Her mother died when she was a baby, and she was raised by her father, King Alexander.

The king didn't have much time for Princess Elise. He awoke three hours before sunrise every day and went to bed three hours after sunset. He worked tirelessly to make the kingdom into the kind of place Elise's mother had always wanted it to be: prosperous, safe, and full of happy citizens.

Elise learned early on that to spend time with her father, she had to work. From the age of three she would sit on the floor next to his desk, reading books on economics, supply chains, and military readiness, carefully sounding out words like flotilla and echelon.

At first, she would only sit silently beside his throne while he discussed issues with his advisors, but it wasn't long before she began to speak up, first to ask questions and eventually to make suggestions. As she grew, she gained a reputation for wisdom, intelligence, and the same work ethic that had earned her father so much respect.

Elise's best friend was a student named Edmond. They grew up attending classes together and would spend hours arguing political theory and exploring the castle.

OVER THE YEARS, as Elise grew into a young adult, she slowly took over more and more of the duties of running the kingdom. For a long time, all was well, until one winter the king became deathly ill. He called Elise to his bedside, taking her hand and looking at her seriously.

He cleared his throat. "You must marry before I die," he said at last. Of all the things Elise had expected, this was the furthest from her mind. She asked him to explain, but he only shook his head, saying that it was important. He was barely able to look her in the eye now. "But why?" Elise asked. He'd never mentioned anything like this before. "Am I not capable of running the kingdom on my own?"

A deep sadness came over the king, and he took her hand, squeezing it tightly. "Of course not. You are more than capable." His eyes darted away. She could see there was something he wasn't telling her.

"What is it, then?" She racked her brain, going over every law, ordinance, treaty and sub-treaty she could think of. There was nothing. No alliance that needed to be made, although perhaps there was some benefit she wasn't considering.

Her father shook his head, releasing her hand to cover a cough. The doctors swarmed around his bedside, and Elise was ushered from the room.

Two suitors arrived at the castle the very next day.

Full of worry for her father, and confusion at this strange turn of events, Elise agreed to meet them, but she had little intention of marrying.

The first suitor was tall, dark-haired, and handsome and gave her a golden dress trimmed with rubies. The second was tall, fair-haired, and handsome and gave her a silver dress decorated with spirals of emeralds.

Elise had dinner with each of the princes in turn.

On the first night, she ate with the first prince, who gave her small golden treasures and told her of his vast gold mines in the East.

On the second night, she had dinner with the second prince, who gave her jewels and silver and told her of his silver mines in the West.

On the third night, Elise was on the verge of going to see her father again to tell him she must decline the proposals, when Edmond arrived, blushing, in the throne room. He was carrying a large package, wrapped in burlap. With the gold and silver princes and all the courtiers looking on, he knelt in the center of the room, bowing his head.

"So sorry I'm late. I had to write to my brothers for a proper gift." He unwrapped the package and held up a strange green dress, made of discs of jade sewn together like fish scales.

AS SHE HAD with the other two, she had dinner with Edmond that night. He asked how she was doing, and she told him more of her father's strange demand. Together, they talked it over, trying to figure out why the king would have suggested something like this, but nothing new occurred to them.

She asked about his brothers, Archimedes and Bernoulli, who were powerful wizards living in the North, on the edge of the great sea.

They were well, Edmond said, although they had gotten reports from sailors of strange flashes of light far out to sea, and the storms on the coast had been worse than usual.

THE NEXT MORNING, Elise visited her father again and told him she wasn't ready to marry.

"But what about the prince with the gold?" the king asked.

"Is there something I should know about him?" she asked, but the king hedged, shaking his head and twisting his blankets nervously in his hands.

SLOWLY, the king recovered, and Elise gradually took on running the kingdom. Many years passed, and he never brought up his strange demand again. Until one day his health began to fail again. Sensing his death was near, he called her to his bedside. He said needed to tell her a story.

"When I was young," he began, pausing to catch his breath, "I was not a king. I was just a boy living in a village. One day a beautiful princess came riding through town, and I was entranced. I wanted to meet her. My parents and brothers urged me to forget about her. There was nothing I could do, they said. But I couldn't give up. I had to meet her. I set out for the capital, intent on making my fortune and at the very least hoping to talk to her.

"On the road one night I met a traveler who was cold and hungry, and I offered to let him share my fire and my meager supply of food. He was grateful, and when he had eaten, he revealed that he was a powerful wizard and that, because of my kindness, he was willing to make a bargain with me. He would help me become king, but only if I would agree to make him king after me by letting him marry my daughter. But what if I have no children? I asked him. He said that I would have one child: a daughter. I agreed."

The king looked down at his blankets. "I am ashamed to say that I never truly thought I would have to honor our agreement. Part of me didn't believe he could make me king, but also I just couldn't imagine that the future would ever really come. And . . . I never considered how it would affect you." He looked at her for a moment, then away again.

"He fulfilled his part of the bargain. I became a successful merchant. I met your mother, and we fell in love."

"I wish that I had made my fortune on my own, now. When I first became ill, I knew it was time to fulfill my promise to him. Soon after, he appeared. I agreed to let him meet you. But I didn't tell you. I hoped that you would simply pick him and that everything would be all right."

"The golden prince?" she asked.

"Yes. He was the golden prince. I should have told you from the beginning. When I told him you refused to marry, he flew into a rage and disappeared. I haven't heard from him since."

Elise's stomach went cold. It felt like the stone tiles were shifting under her feet. It made sense now, why her father had worked so hard. He'd wanted to feel like he deserved to be king.

"I'm sorry," the king said.

Elise nodded vaguely, but inside her chest was a storm of emotions.

Her father died that evening.

As she had learned from her father, Elise turned to work to distract herself. But even running the kingdom was full of conflict for her now.

In the back of her mind, she wondered where the wizard was, guessing it was only a matter of time of time before he returned.

Edmond was by her side every day after that, listening to her thoughts and helping where he could.

TIME PASSED, and the wizard did not appear. Eventually, Elise decided she had to make her own choices, and that she couldn't be responsible for her father's bargain. She was crowned queen, and she and Edmond were married.

Three days after the wedding, the wizard appeared.

Elise and Edmond were sitting in the empty throne room, talking. It was late at night, and rain lashed the stained-glass windows. Suddenly, the candle flames wavered and flared, and the golden prince appeared.

Elise jumped to her feet; the guards were outside. They were completely alone.

She cleared her throat, wishing she had thought of something to offer the wizard, or some way of appeasing him. Her mind raced, but the wizard spoke first.

"Thirty years ago, I gave your father everything he wanted, and in exchange I asked for one thing."

"I'm sorry—" Elise started to say, but he cut her off.

"I'm not interested in words. You're clearly just as trustworthy as your father."

Edmond stood, too, and started to speak, when the wizard whirled around, pointing a long finger at him.

Edmond's face went gray, and he collapsed.

"Until I get what was promised to me, everything you value will wither and die."

On the last word, the wizard vanished.

Elise ran desperately to Edmond. His eyes were closed, and his body was as still as if he were dead, but he was breathing. She summoned the court physician, who informed her that Edmond was apparently in a deep sleep.

She clenched her fists, angry at herself. Ignoring this problem was exactly what her father had done, and it had gone on long enough. She summoned her most trusted advisor, Peony.

Peony was short, tense, and always wore a pink ballgown. She would stare people down with her intense dark eyes, focusing on them so hard that they often forgot what they wanted to ask her and ran away.

"What do we know of this wizard?" Elise asked

Peony whipped out a leather-bound notebook, consulting it with a flourish.

"Your father told me he comes from a land far to the North. Farther north than the land of King Edmond's brothers. Across the ocean. I've plotted five different routes there and analyzed the various pluses and minuses and possible pitfalls of each, as well as the projected cost of each journey." She held up a series of charts, graphs, and figures. Elise wondered briefly when she could possibly have had time to compile this. "You'll see the route through King Edmond's lands appears to be optimal."

"Thanks, Peony, that's fantastic." As usual, Peony had read her mind. She was going to go after the wizard. She was going to fix this.

"The only variable I haven't accounted for is that I don't know how you will cross the ocean." She chewed her lip nervously, flipping through pages of her notebook.

"I'll figure that part out. I'm sure Edmond's brothers will be able to help me."

Peony nodded. "That's what I was thinking, too." "Will you rule the kingdom while I am away?"

Peony gripped her notebook so hard she nearly ripped it in half.

Her voice rose an octave. "I would be honored."

Elise suspected that by the time she got back, the kingdom might possibly be the most powerful, well-run country in the world. She just hoped Peony would be okay under the pressure while she tried to fix every single problem the country had or might ever have in the future.

"I won't let you down," Peony said.

THE GREAT ARCHIMEDES
AND BERNOULLI

Queen Elise took no one with her on her journey. She was a light and fast rider, and she didn't want to be encumbered. She wore the jade dress that Edmond had given her all those years ago, so the brothers might recognize her. It was surprisingly light and strong. She felt like an armored fish.

It took her three weeks to reach the coastal city where Edmond's brothers lived. On the morning of the twenty-first day, Elise crested a ridge and paused for a moment, looking down the steep, sandy cliffs to a white limestone castle. It looked like an enormous, delicate shell that had washed up on the sandy shore. Maybe the shell of an enormous crab, with curling white pillars like spines sprouting   throughout.

She urged her horse into a rolling canter down the winding, sandy road towards the castle, passing well-kept homes and gardens. Townspeople paused in their work to look up at her and wave.

As she approached, she began to see strange devices. First a towering pillar with what looked like a glass disk as large as a wagon wheel perched on top of it, then a strange, mechanical arm of wood with iron joints and a claw hand that extended over the smooth waters of the bay.

She stared as it began to move, extending its wooden fingers, gripping a ship around its middle like a toddler grasping a fork, and plucking the whole thing, dripping water and trailing seaweed, from the ocean. It swung smoothly to the side, flinging water in all directions, and deposited it on some stilts where a group of repairmen   were waiting.

Her mouth dropped open, and she narrowly avoided trampling some ornamental flowers. Edmond had mentioned his brothers were inventors, but he'd said it in such an offhand way she hadn't thought much about it.

The gates of the castle were open wide, and wagons full of goods clattered in and out, accompanied by more chatting, happy townspeople. She slowed, weaving around them, and arrived in the middle of a vast limestone courtyard, where she was approached immediately by a greeter holding a quill and a piece of parchment.

When she heard who Elise was, she hurriedly had her horse taken care of and brought her inside, hurrying through a maze of marble staircases until at last they arrived in an echoing octagonal room with a domed, frescoed ceiling arching high overhead, supported at each of the eight vertices by marble pillars.

Two men sat at a pair of desks, one on each side of the room.

The left side of the room was full of bookshelves, and what wall space wasn't filled with books was completely covered with scribbled mathematical formulas and geometric drawings. Behind the desk, a large man wearing a small gold crown tucked in a nest of short, curly brown hair sat writing furiously, partially on paper and partially on the desk. Three assistants surrounded him nervously. One was attempting to cut his hair but kept having to pull the sharp scissors out of the way as the man exclaimed and nodded his head to himself. The second assistant held a gold plate beneath the scissors, attempting to catch the curling snippets of hair. The third assistant hovered nearby, slipping fresh sheets of paper under the man's pencil whenever he started writing on the desk.

He did not look up when Elise was announced, but the man on the other side of the room did.

He was neatly dressed, with well-trimmed gray hair and a large mustache.

"Your sister, Queen Elise, requests an audience," the greeter announced, her words echoing against the marble.

The gray-haired man stood, his eyes widening. "Your majesty!" He glanced over her shoulder towards the door. "Did we miss a letter from you? Is Edmond with you?"

"You must be Bernoulli," Elise guessed.

He smiled and came around the desk, holding out his hand. "Indeed I am. What a pleasure to meet you finally." He glanced at his brother, who hadn't looked up. "Archimedes, our sister is here."

Archimedes' head tilted up, narrowly missing the scissors. The assistants jumped back, scrambling out of the way as he stood.

"Sister?"

"You know, Edmond's wife." "Edmond?"

"Our brother."

Archimedes looked like he was having genuine difficulty. He clasped his hands in front of him and strode forward, his

93

cream toga swirling about his pointed leather shoes. Stopping a few feet from Elise, he looked her up and down, clearly trying to place her. Something dawned in his eyes, but it wasn't recognition. Instead, he grabbed a pencil from a small holster strapped to one shoulder and made a quick note to himself on one sleeve. The rest of his toga was similarly covered in writing.

"Please excuse us," Bernoulli said. "It's wonderful to finally meet you. What brings you here?"

Elise quickly explained about Edmond and the wizard and the bargain her father had made.

Archimedes sketched a large triangle on his toga. He lifted it up and squinted at it, revealing a great deal of one leg.

Bernoulli barely even glanced at him. "Yes, we've heard reports of strange happenings out to sea. Flashes of light, disappearances. We've sent soldiers out looking for him, but they spent weeks sailing in circles to no avail."

"Well," Elise said. "I am going to find him and fix this. Any help you can give me is much appreciated."

Bernoulli's eyebrows knitted together, and he crossed his arms, tapping his long fingers together. They looked liked spider legs.

"Your majesty, I would highly advise you not to do this. We're doing all we can, but he's too powerful. It's too dangerous for you."

Archimedes was still writing, but Elise noticed his eyes occasionally darted over to them now.

"What do you think, Archimedes?" she asked.

He didn't answer, focusing more closely on his work.

Elise looked at the picture he was drawing. He had now pulled out a small device like the letter v, which looked like a pencil and a sharp metal rod attached together with a hinge, and he was using it to draw circles over the triangle.

Elise smiled, remembering frustrating hours spent trying to memorize triangle facts with Edmond. "If you're trying to draw a circle around the triangle, you need the circumcenter of the triangle," she said. "You're using the centroid, which is actually the balance point of the triangle."

Archimedes raised his eyebrows, smiling widely and making full eye contact for the first time. "Oho. Well. Very impressive." He elbowed Bernoulli in the stomach. The man gave a soft, dignified grunt, and slowly bent forward, taking small, pained sips of air.

"What's this?" Archimedes asked, pointing to a smudged formula on his right sleeve.

Elise squinted, bending forward to look at it. "The formula for the volume of a sphere."

Archimedes looked absolutely delighted. "And this?" He turned around and gestured at a large, nearly indecipherable smudge on his back.

"Er, that is a right cylinder drawn inside a regular pentagonal prism."

Archimedes drew himself up to his full height, which brought the top of his head to Bernoulli's shoulder. "All right, person who is apparently my sister because apparently I have a brother. I will help you. If you solve one more riddle for me."

"Happy to," Elise said, while Bernoulli held one hand over his eyes and shook his head in a long-suffering way.

"Is my crown made of solid gold?"

He waited a few seconds, his eyes gleaming, then he went back to his desk.

Bernoulli heaved a long sigh. "I'm so sorry, he does this to everyone." He waved a hand. "He has all these crowns made of different... it doesn't matter."

Elise considered the problem. It shouldn't be too difficult to solve. She pulled some solid gold coins out of her saddlebags and hefted them thoughtfully. She spied a set of scales on Archimedes' desk. That would help. She knew that different metals had different weights. If you had a chunk of gold and a chunk of copper that were exactly the same size and shape, they would weigh different amounts.

She could start by seeing how many gold coins it took to balance the crown. Then... Elise's thoughts trailed off. She supposed she could try to smelt the gold coins into the same shape as the crown. Maybe she could make a mold out of clay. But the crown was very irregularly shaped, and anyway it would take a long time to make a clay mold, harden it in a kiln—if they even had one for her to use—then melt down the gold, then form a new crown.

She didn't want to waste that much time. Every moment she took was a moment Edmond was in trouble.

She bit her lip, thinking. As she thought, she played with the coins in her hand, moving them around, stacking them, spreading them out flat. Then, she realized something. No matter how the coins were arranged, they had the same total volume. They took up the same amount of space.

96

She didn't need to melt the gold down and reform it, she just needed to figure out what the volume was.

But then she was stuck. She scratched her head, frowning, but nothing came to her.

"It's all right," Bernoulli said. "It's probably best if you don't worry about it. Would you like a glass of water?"

She realized she was very thirsty from all the riding, so she accepted the drink gratefully. She knew that sometimes when she was working on a hard problem, it was best to think about it for a little while and then think about something else, kind of forget about it and let her mind ponder it on its own, so she let the problem go for a moment, waiting to see if something would come to her.

"What do you know about where the wizard might be?" she asked. "There is a series of islands way out to sea," Bernoulli answered.

"We believe he is hiding there, but we can't be sure. Also, we can't find the islands anymore."

"What do you mean you can't find them anymore?"

"Every time anyone gets more than a mile from the shore, their compasses go haywire."

"How do they find their way back, then?" she asked.

"They just always end up back here, even if they're trying to go the other way."

"What about navigating by the sun or stars?" Bernoulli shrugged.

Elise took a sip of water to cover her frustration.

She focused on the glass, looking into the depths of the water, and that's when a very helpful idea popped into her mind.

Grinning, she held the glass of water up, then dropped a coin into it. It sank quickly to the bottom, a few bubbles rising around it. The level of the water in her glass raised, as the coin was now taking up some space where formerly water had been.

"Do you have a bucket I can borrow?" she asked.

One of the assistants was at her side so quickly she didn't even know where they had come from and was holding out four different shapes and sizes of buckets. She took the largest, thanking him, then asked Bernoulli to fill it halfway with water.

"I'd happily refill your glass as many times as you would like," he said, confused and a little affronted, as he filled the bucket, but Elise wasn't listening. She strode over to where Archimedes was hard at work again, plucked the crown from his head and dropped it into the bucket. Then she pulled one of his pens from his sleeve, marked the side of bucket to indicate how high the water had risen, and pulled the crown back out. She waited patiently while most of the water dripped off back into the bucket, then she placed the crown on one side of the scale, tipping it.

Next, she dropped her coins into the bucket one by one until the water had risen back up to the same level. A little water had been lost with the crown, but probably not enough to make a difference. This meant that the volume of the coins in the bucket was the same as the volume of the crown.

Grinning more to herself, she pulled the coins out, dried them on a fluffy towel thrust at her by the assistant, and placed them on the other plate of the scale. It tipped, overbalancing, the coins pulling it much farther down, the crown lifting high. She had it.

Based on her bucket measurements, she knew the coins had the same volume as the crown, so they should be pretty nearly balanced. But the coins were much heavier.

"Your crown is not made of solid gold, I'm afraid," Elise said. Archimedes whipped out a pocket watch he had hidden in his toga, clicked a button and shouted. "Eight minutes and forty-three seconds, Bernoulli! A new record!"

Bernoulli sighed heavily.

Archimedes patted her on the shoulder, the fish scales of her dress rattling.

"Took me three days in the bathtub to come up with that trick," Archimedes said, beaming at her. "You're sharp."

Elise shrugged. "Thank you. Can you help me find the wizard?"

"Of course I can!" he bellowed.

Elise sighed, then caught herself. She sounded exactly like Bernoulli.

Archimedes whipped something out of a pocket somewhere and held his hand out to her.

"Here," he said proudly, his eyes alight. As far as she could tell, there was nothing in his hand.

"Um, what it is it?"

"It is an invisible bronze ball. It gets smaller when it gets closer to the wizard. Only you can't tell by looking at it how big it is, of course, because it's invisible."

"Um..."

"The wizard is doing something that makes him hard to find, impossible to see, so I made this ball that can't be seen, just like him," Archimedes said, tapping the side of his nose conspiratorially. "However!" he shouted, holding up one finger, "Simply drop it in a bucket of water, and..."

He held his empty hand out over the bucket and opened his fingers. To Elise's surprise, there was a small splash and the water level of the bucket rose.

"Just don't lose it," Archimedes said warningly, glancing around at the floors. "I can't tell you how many of these I've made and lost."

"What!" Bernoulli exclaimed. "Is that what I've been slipping—"

Archimedes cut him off. "Anyway, that should let you find him. Now you just have to convince Bernie here to let you use his boat."

Bernoulli was still sputtering about ankle injuries as Elise turned to him.

"Your brother is in danger, and so too apparently are your soldiers and sailors. I am happy to pay you for a boat. I swear to you that if you give me some way to get to him, I will fix this."

Bernoulli's expression softened. "Very well. This way."

He whirled about, striding towards the back of the room. His foot landed on something invisible, shooting out from under him, but he caught himself on his hands, flipping himself up with surprising agility and continuing on his way. Elise followed more carefully, feeling her way and kicking several invisible balls out of the way as she went.

Bernoulli led them down a steep staircase in the back, which ended at a stone pier.

"This is the escape route in case the townspeople revolt," Archimedes said jovially. Bernoulli ignored him, gesturing instead to a small silver boat tied up and bobbing with the waves.

It looked barely large enough for one person, and too heavy to float. In the front of the boat was an emerald basin filled with still, silver water. On the water in the basin floated a tiny jade boat.

"This is a magic boat I made with the help of a powerful sorceress."

"And me," Archimedes said.

"And Archimedes helped," Bernoulli added. "I'm the whole reason it floats."

Bernoulli sighed yet again. "All boats float."

"This one, though is because of me. Don't blame me, you wanted a silver boat. Silver doesn't float, in case you've forgotten."

Bernoulli massaged a temple.

Archimedes patted Elise on the shoulder. "You must know how things float."

"Because of buoyancy," Elise said.

"Correct!" he shouted, near her ear. "And what causes buoyancy?"

"It's the same idea as the way of measuring the volume of the crown," Elise said. "There's part of the boat that's underwater. It's taking up space where water would have been." She looked up at the surrounding green waters. "If this whole bay froze solid, and then you pulled the boat up, there would be a divot in the ice where the boat was."

"Lovely visual," Bernoulli commented.

"The amount of water that it would take to fill that divot, that's the amount of water that got pushed out of the way. However much that water weighs, that's the buoyancy force on the boat."

Archimedes was nodding along sagely. "Indeed, indeed." He glanced at Bernoulli. "We should have invited her to visit earlier." To Elise, he said, "Actually, I have some more problems I'm working on. You should take a look." He glanced down at his toga, pulling on the fabric, looking for a particular equation. "Actually, take a look at this, I want to see what you think."

Elise cleared her throat and looked to Bernoulli. "I'd love to but I really need to get going."

Bernoulli nodded and took out a small silver cup, which had three stoppered holes in its sides. One hole was near the rim, the second was lower down the side, and the third was almost at the bottom of the cup. He scooped water into the cup and placed it in the basin where it hovered. He pulled the cork from the first stopper, and a slow stream of water curved out from it, splashing down into the water below.

"If you place the boat on this stream, the boat will move at this speed."

He replaced the first cork and removed the second one. Water sprayed out more quickly this time.

"Here, where the water is deeper, it flows out more quickly. If you remove this cork and place the boat on this stream, the boat will move more quickly."

Elise nodded. She knew that water that was under more pressure would spray out more quickly, if given an opening.

Again, he replaced the cork.

"The third and deepest cork, which I will not remove now, is the fastest. Using the faster speeds will drain the cup more quickly." He refilled the cup. "Use the speeds sparingly, because only I can refill the cup."

She nodded and thanked them both again. Archimedes asked her to stay and eat with them, but she shook her head, repeating that she needed to find the wizard as soon as possible.

The silver boat sank a few inches but held perfectly steady as she stepped into it. When she was seated, Archimedes handed her the bucket with the invisible ball.

"Good luck," Archimedes said, and they both smiled at her.

She moved to the front of the little boat, reached into the emerald basin, and uncorked the first cork. A small stream of water arced out of the cup. She plucked the jade boat from the surface of the water and set it on the stream. It hung there disconcertingly, and the boat began to move forward at a smooth, steady pace, barely even rocking with the waves.

She turned and waved, watching as the two of them shrunk in the distance, still arguing about something.

There was a thin tiller of white wood at the back of the boat, and when she moved it gently from side to side, the boat turned smoothly. Now she needed to know which direction to go. She pulled the tiller firmly towards her and the boat angled to the right, parallel to the shoreline. The water level in the bucket was still dropping, but more slowly now. Next, she gradually pushed the tiller farther and farther away from her, until she was traveling in exactly the opposite direction. As the boat turned, the water level lowered faster and faster, but then held steady for a moment and began to rise again. She adjusted her course until the water level was dropping its fastest, then sat back and looked around.

It was early evening now; a fog was gathering over the sea and moving in towards the black rocks and high cliffs offshore. Farther out, a bank of thick, bright fog waited for her. Fragments of it drifted inland, trailing up and over the cliffs. As the sun began to set, the water below her glowed pink, but within just a few minutes she had entered the white mass, and everything became dark and gray, eventually subsumed by the black of night.

The only light came from the basin, which glowed slightly. The water was calm at first, but as the night wore on, the small waves grew larger and larger, and soon the little boat was rocketing down one side of each giant wave and trudging up the other. She quickly lost all sense of direction and had to keep consulting the bucket to stay on course.

The air was cold and clammy, and she was soaked through with spray. The jade dress was warm, though. The stones seemed to have absorbed her body heat from the day before and now gave it back to her. It felt as if she had been sitting in the sun.

She did not sleep, and by morning she was exhausted, wishing she had let Archimedes convince her to stay for a meal because she wasn't sure how long her traveling food would last. But, as the sea calmed and the fog thinned and lifted in the morning sunlight, she began to feel a little better. Up ahead, a dark island appeared.

It was a tall rock protruding from the sea. Its sides were sheer cliffs, but she could just make out specks of green way at the top. A perilously narrow path scribbled up the side of the cliff.

At the base of the path was a small landing. She replaced the cork and tied the boat up with a grimy rope. Then she began the climb. It took her over an hour to reach the top, during which time she did not look down once. The last little bit was the worst; whoever had made the path seemed to have run out of interest by the end, and there was only a sheer rock wall with a few handholds. The handholds were dirty and slippery with sand, gravel, and little bits of rock, some of which came off in her hand.

When she reached the top, she squirmed over it, dragging herself on her belly, glad of the protection of the stone dress. She lay gasping and shaking for a moment with her eyes closed, which was when she noticed how forceful the wind was way up there. She opened her eyes cautiously.

The top of the rock was small, no more than fifteen feet in diameter. It was not flat, but sloping, with jagged black rocks poking up randomly. A giant crack ran through the middle. The heather growing over the top was still damp with dew. A few scraggly trees hung on grimly, their branches twisted by the wind. In the middle, directly over the crack, stood a circle of thick rectangular stones. In the center of these was the wizard, watching her.

"I—" she croaked out, but he lifted a corner of his black cape, whirled, and disappeared. She spent several minutes looking for him, then several more waiting to see if he would come back. But he was nowhere to be found.

The climb down the rock was worse than the climb up. She was more tired than before, and there was no way to avoid looking down. To prepare herself mentally, she lay on the top and cried for a while. Slipping and sliding and taking frequent crying breaks, she made her way back down to the little boat. The sphere had expanded again, and the bucket appeared to be fuller than before.

Again, she uncorked the cup, placed the little jade boat upon the stream, and set off. She traveled the rest of the day and all through the night. The next morning, when the fog had cleared, she saw another island. This was a large, flat rock, low and close to the sea.

When she brought her little boat up to the stone dock, she saw smooth stone paths, square pools of water, green fruit trees, and moss-covered sculptures, all chipped and overgrown. The wind whistled emptily. Dark clouds gathered overhead, and it began to rain, slowly at first and then more heavily.

In the center of the garden, she came to the remains of a large house. Only its stone foundations were left, and an immense fireplace. In the fireplace burned a roaring fire, and in front of that stood the wizard. She was ten feet away from him when he turned angrily and disappeared.

With a sigh, she sank down onto the hearth, feeling the heat from the fire warm against her face and hands.

How would she ever get near enough to him to convince him to change his mind? She sat up a little straighter, thinking of Edmond. She was making progress, she told herself. She'd already managed to find the wizard. She would just keep following him until he agreed to speak to her.

She pulled some bread from her bag, deciding to rest a few minutes before she continued, and her thoughts turned to her father. Her memories of him were now conflicted. How could he have made such a bargain? And how could he have never told her? She'd always thought he was the hardest working, most honorable person she knew, but now she saw all his work in a different light. He hadn't earned being king. He'd made a deal with a wizard. And when it came time to honor that deal, he hadn't.

What did that mean about her own claim to the throne? Could she really continue being queen, now that she knew how her father had earned the title? Maybe she really should give the throne to the wizard. But she had no idea if he would be a good king.

All these thoughts swirled through her mind as she sat by the fire, letting it warm her wet clothing and hair. No answers came to her.

THE CANYON OF
FLOW RATE

Again, she traveled all night, and when the fog cleared the next morning, a third island appeared. This island was larger than the other two, and she could see nothing but sheer black cliffs all around it. The only way inside appeared to be a jagged fissure. It was about twenty feet wide, and water flowed out of it. The walls of the fissure shot straight up and were completely blanketed in ferns. Consulting her bucket, she pointed the boat up the fissure, noticing that the water level in the cup was significantly lower than when she had started, almost down to the level of the first hole.

For almost an hour, she piloted the boat up the canyon. It curved this way and that but stayed about the same width. Up ahead, she heard a rushing noise. Rounding a bend, the canyon abruptly narrowed. It was now only about ten feet wide, and the water was flowing twice as fast. It was too fast for her boat to make any progress against the current, so she replaced the first cork and removed the second. The little stream of water shot out faster than before, and her boat picked up speed, just barely able to fight against the current. The water level in the cup was now below the first hole; she would not be able to use the first speed anymore.

Afteranother hour of traveling up the winding canyon, she rounded another bend and the walls narrowed even further. Now they were only five feet wide. She could reach out and touch them, and the water was yet again twice as fast as before. Again, her boat could make no progress against this current, so she removed the third and final cork. She was now slowly inching her way up the canyon, but she could see the water level in the cup dropping. It passed the second hole. As the water level lowered, the boat slowed down, just barely making progress.

The water was nearly gone when she rounded a bend and came to a small sandy beach. The last of the water trickled out as she leapt ashore, pulling the boat up past the waterline. She picked up the bucket and set off on a narrow dirt trail.

Soon, she came to an intersection. There were no signs, but she checked the bucket, walking a little way down each of the paths, and chose the leftmost one. At first, the path sloped upwards through a dense forest. Then she came to a small ridge and followed it a short way to the right before taking a path that switch-backed down the other side.

The forest became darker, and the trees looked older. Here, where they were sheltered from the wind, they grew to an enormous thickness and a towering height. She walked quietly, noticing that she felt hungry again, but wasn't sure if any of the berries were edible. They were strange and unfamiliar to her.

At last, she came to a clearing. In the center of it was a lake; a small cottage crouched on the shoreline. In the very center of the lake was a very strange sight. A large wooden ship floated there. The sails were ragged, and the wood looked a little green, but it floated. Elise could not see why it would be there. There was no way for it to reach the sea, no outlet from this tiny lake which it almost filled. It barely had room to move at all. On this ship stood the wizard, looking angrily down at her.

"STOP FOLLOWING ME," the wizard said. "I told you. Your father and I had a bargain. Neither of you honored that bargain. Now you must pay the price."

"I know," she said. The wizard did have a point, even if what he had done was wrong. "And I'm sorry my father didn't fulfill his promise to you. What can I do to make up for the promise that was broken?"

The wizard considered this skeptically.

"I will offer you one chance. If you complete a task for me and make me a new promise, I will wake your husband from his sleep."

"What promise?"

"That on one day a year I will be king."

She considered this. "What would you do if you were king?"

The wizard looked surprised and not quite ready for the question. He opened his mouth and closed it again. Then he muttered something about maybe throwing a ball. She raised her eyebrows.

"What about the rest of the year?" she asked. "Would you be willing to use your magic to help the kingdom?"

He considered this. "Could I live in the castle? Maybe . . . in a very tall tower . . . that leans ominously to one side?"

One of her eyebrows raised even higher. Now that she was finally talking to him, the wizard wasn't at all like she'd expected. She wasn't sure it was wise or responsible to give the kingdom to this person, even if it was only one day a year, but he had been promised much more. And there might be huge benefits to having a wizard in court.

"I'm sure we could build something like that."

He gave a little excited hop, clicking his boots together. "What is the task?" Elise asked.

He gestured to the trapped galleon below him. "You must free my boat and get it back out to the ocean."

She eyed it thoughtfully. "How did it get there?"

"A storm. I was shipwrecked here. I don't know how it happened, though, because I was asleep."

"I'll do my best," Elise said. She didn't know how she would accomplish this, but she knew that even things that seemed impossible could be figured out, if one kept trying.

The lake was in a large, tree-filled valley, the sides of which were sheer rock rising a hundred feet into the air. Had the storm been so powerful it had lifted the boat over those walls? And why, if the wizard was so powerful, could he not free it himself?

She sat on a log to think. The wizard extended a ramp from his boat to the shore, crossed it, and went into his cabin. Maybe she could dismantle the ship and carry it, piece by piece, to the dock. Although, there was no way the ship would fit through the narrow canyon. Could she build some sort of rigging to lift the whole ship over the walls? Maybe she could secretly build a replica of the ship out on the ocean somewhere, then destroy this one. Except, she didn't know anything about shipbuilding. The ship bobbed in front of her, tauntingly.

A twig cracked and she turned to see the wizard walking towards her, carrying a tray laden with food.

He said to her, "I'll give you a sandwich if you give me one." "Give you back one of your own sandwiches? Sure," she said.

He set to eating surprisingly ravenously. When they finished, he went back inside his cottage. She continued to contemplate the ship. She could probably use logs to roll it along. It wouldn't be impossible to get it to the base of one of the cliffs. Then maybe she could build some sort of lifting device with pulleys. She needed rope and an ax. She asked, and the wizard had both, but the rope looked old and frayed, and there wasn't enough of it, anyway. She would have to make rope.

She gathered grass all that afternoon. In the evening, she wove thick cords with it. For five days, she gathered grass during the day and wove it into rope in the evening. The wizard continued to bring her food and watch her progress without comment. He always offered her food with the condition that he have some, too. She wondered about this, and finally decided to ask.

"I was shipwrecked here as a young man," he explained. I was trapped here a year until a water fairy took pity on me and granted me magic powers to help me escape. But fairies don't like just giving gifts. They like their jokes. She gave me magic powers, but with the condition that I could never do anything for myself without bargaining for it with someone else. Anything I wanted, I had to trade another for it. I've been that way ever since."

Elise's eyes softened. "How do you survive? Can you not even eat or sleep without bargaining for it?"

"I've found ways to work around that. Bargains. But I've found that even without food I do not die." He sank into heavy silence, and she didn't press him further, contemplating what that must be like for him. She had a hard time imagining what it would be like to not be able to do anything for oneself. Horrible, probably.

When there was enough rope, Elise began to gather logs. She worked for four days setting up the transportation system. When everything was ready, she looped the ropes around trees, tying them securely to the ship. Then she positioned the logs and began to pull. The ship slowly rose out of the water, rolling along the logs she had painstakingly smoothed with the ax. It moved about ten feet, but then one of the ropes snapped, and the ship slid all the way back into the water with a great splash.

QUEEN ELISE DISCOVERS A MANOMETER

Frustrated, Elise decided to take a break for the rest of the day and go for a swim. She took off the jade dress and wore just her cotton undergarments. The water was transparent turquoise and cold but refreshing. Usually, she liked to swim near the surface, but this time she decided to swim deeper and explore.

The underside of the ship was coated in barnacles, except for some long scratches in the sides. The grooves weren't deep enough to sink it, but it looked like it had been clawed by a giant animal.

Elise was puzzled but couldn't look at them long before she had to return to the surface. As she stood waist deep in the water, she licked her lips—salty. The water was not fresh water at all, but ocean water. This was surprising because as far as she could tell, the little lake was landlocked; it didn't even have a stream connecting it to the ocean.

Come to think of it, the water was exceptionally clean for still water. No bugs or slime—it was a lot more like running water than stagnant. Maybe there was an underground stream. Diving down again, she examined the bottom closely, peering through the clear water.

The lake was much deeper than she'd expected. At the end of a short shelf, the bottom dropped off, plunging deeper than she could see. She came up for another breath and dove down deeper, quickly, as far as she could go. It kept going. She swam down fifteen feet before she reached the bottom. And here it didn't end but curved into a horizontal tunnel.

Desperate for breath, she shot back to the surface, gulped in air for a few minutes, and dove down again, this time following the tunnel a short way. It became very dark. Low on air again, she turned to head back to the surface, but realized she couldn't see a thing. She didn't know where the path to the surface was. Panicked, she began swimming as fast as she could, looking for a wall to guide her back. Then she saw a ray of light and swam frantically towards it, following it up and up and finally surfacing at last, gasping.

She was no longer in the lake.

The ocean waves crashed somewhere below her. The sun was hotter and brighter. She swam to the edge of a small pool—like a very large tide pool—and clambered out onto some rocks to rest. She was on a shelf overlooking the ocean. It was above the water level— although she didn't know if it was high tide or low at the moment. The wind blew little ripples across the water of the pool she had emerged from. A connecting tunnel. Somehow, the wizard's ship must have been forced through the tunnel by the storm.

She wrapped her arms around her knees and thought. How to get it back out, then? She watched the water speculatively for a few minutes and then smiled, remembering something she'd read as a young child. She dove back into the pool, swam carefully through the tunnel, and popped back out on the other side.

The logs she had collected were still sitting there, waiting for her to have a use for them. She immediately set-to with the ax.

QUEEN ELISE BUILDS ARCHIMEDES' SCREW

The wizard came out later, watched her work for a few minutes, but said only, "New plan?" She nodded, too out of breath from chopping to answer.

It took her seven days to build the little aqueduct—a system of hollowed-out logs to convey water away from the lake. Then came the tricky part. She had saved the largest log for last. This she hollowed out, partially with the axe, partially by burning it out. While it was burning, she used another log to carve a corkscrew. It took her a whole day to get the corkscrew shaped well enough that it would fit inside the hollowed-out log, but finally it worked. She fitted a handle to the top of it.

She placed one end of the screw in the water, the other end extended over her aqueduct. When she turned the screw, it lifted water out of the lake and deposited it in the logs so that it was carried over a small hill about a hundred feet away.

As the water was emptied, the boat sank deeper and deeper into the hole. The wizard seemed confused as to how this was helpful, but didn't say anything, just went inside his cottage to take a nap. When only a few feet of water remained at the bottom of a fifteen-foot rock hole, Elise loaded the screw into the ship. Then, she rigged up a system of pulleys to pull the ship through the tunnel.

Lastly, she repositioned her screw, only this time she thrust one end into the ocean. The top extended over the empty hole. Careful not to pour water on the boat, she refilled the tunnel, and the ship rose to the surface. She tied up the ship and swam back through the tunnel.

The wizard had apparently just come out of his cabin and was staring at the lake.

"Did you sink my boat?"

She grinned. "I have completed the task."

"What? How?" The wizard looked around, as if expecting to see the boat hidden behind a tree somewhere. "Where is it?"

"It's tied up on the outside of the island. I think it'll be ready to go as soon as it's high tide."

The wizard looked like he was having trouble believing his ears. Since it didn't look like he was going to say anything, she went on. "I agree to your terms. You can be king once a year for one day, as long as you promise to stay on as the court wizard and help the kingdom during the rest of the year."

The wizard grinned, spinning around, and clicking his heels again. "Fantastic. I'll gather my things."

The wizard had just a few things to pack, and then together they swam through the tunnel to get to the ship.

They made a quick trip across the ocean, docking in a small town where they sold the ship and purchased some new horses. From there it was only a few days' ride back to the castle.

Peony was beside herself with relief when they arrived. She had hidden Edmond away in a back room, refused to let anyone see him, and had pretended to be acting on his orders.

"But I gave you authority when I left," Queen Elise said.

"Yes, but you were gone for weeks, Majesty. The people would never let me rule forever. It was starting to look like you were never coming back, and I needed a contingency plan."

"Which was?"

"I was prepared to tell the people that King Edmond was fine, hide him from everyone, have you declared dead, have him remarry, fake a new heir to the throne, and then fake Edmond's death to hide the evidence," she said grimly.

"Well … I …" As often happened with Peony, the queen didn't really know what to say. "I'm glad you had a plan," she finished at last.

When Edmond awoke, he was overjoyed to see Elise safe and sound, and understandably skeptical of the addition of the wizard at court. But Elise was adamant that he had been promised the kingdom, and that giving him one day per year was a small price to pay to have a wizard around.

The king and queen were always careful of what they promised him, and for his part, the wizard proved to be a competent ruler, so much so that when they went on vacations, they often left him and Peony in charge. There were a few memorable and unfortunate occasions where things did not go quite as smoothly as planned—the entire royal court once spent a few weeks as chipmunks—but for the most part the system worked well. And, by and large, everyone lived happily ever after.

THE END

This concludes the story portion of the book; I hope you liked it! If you'd like to read some more about some of the concepts in the story, read on!

ARCHIMEDES: THE CELEBRITY MATHEMATICIAN OF ANCIENT GREECE

Edmond's two older brothers in the story, Archimedes and Bernoulli, were famous scientists in real life.

In fact, Archimedes is one of the most famous mathematicians of all time. He was already a celebrity when he was alive, although not for his mathematics. He was a Greek, born in 287 BCE, and lived in Syracuse, Italy for most of his life. He was good friends with—or possibly a cousin of—the king, King Hieron II. Archimedes' obsession was pure mathematics. He was most proud of the theorems he created, his favorite being the relationship between the surface areas and volumes of cylinders and spheres, which he liked so much he had them inscribed on his tomb.

But what he was most famous for were his war machines. In his time, Syracuse was under attack from the Romans, and King Hieron II convinced Archimedes to create devices to fight them off.

It's not clear whether some of these accounts are exaggerated or apocryphal, but some describe him using super-powered catapults, systems of mirrors to burn down attacking ships, and great claws that would grab whole ships and lift them out of the water.

But for Archimedes, all that was much, much less important than his mathematical theories. Most of what we know of him and his work comes from his books: On Plane Equilibriums (two books), Quadrature of the Parabola, On the Sphere and Cylinder (two books), On Spirals, On Conoids and Spheroids, On Floating Bodies (two books), Measurements of a Circle, and The Sandreckoner.

In The Sandreckoner, he attempts to calculate the number of grains of sand needed to fill the universe. To do this, he had to invent his own number system. The Greek system at the time used 27 letters and you could only use it to count up to 10,000 (10,000 was called a "myriad".) So, he invented a number system to count higher, and in the process discovered one of the fundamental laws of exponents $(x^a x^b = x^{a+b})$.

But King Hieron convinced him to build practical things, too. So, Archimedes invented the compound pulley, which can let a single person lift whole ships on their own. Possibly most famously in our time, he is the inventor of the field of hydrostatics, investigating how and why objects float, and how different liquids interact.

As part of this, he figured out a cool trick for measuring how much volume an object has (how much space it takes up).

A CLEVER TRICK FOR MEASURING VOLUME

The story goes that one time when King Hieron II gave a metal worker some gold to make a crown, he suspected the man might have mixed some silver into it and kept some of the gold for himself. He asked Archimedes if he could figure out if the crown was actually pure gold. This seemed like it would be possible, since they knew the density of gold (density being how much stuff is packed into an object. The denser an object is, the more stuff is crammed into a smaller space, and the heavier it is.) Except, the crown was so irregularly shaped that they couldn't figure out its volume.

The story goes that Archimedes was taking a bath (it was apparently hard to get Archimedes to leave his work and take a bath, and he would often still be writing mathematical formulas while bathing) when he noticed that when he got into the bath the water level in the tub rose. This made him realize that he could figure out the volume of an object by submerging it in water and measuring how much water it displaced.

For example, if you have a pool:

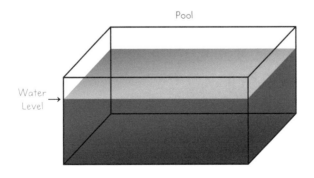

Pool

Water Level →

And you put a beach ball in it:

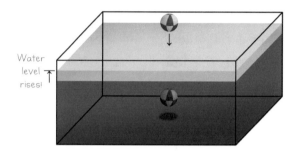

The water level rises by an amount that's exactly equal to the volume of the ball. The bigger the ball, the higher the level of the water.

TRY THIS: PHET DENSITY SIMULATION

To play around with a cool simulation and see how density affects a submerged object, go to this website:

https://phet.colorado.edu/en/simulations/density (or, just google "phet density simulation".

The part of the story about noticing the water level is probably true, but the next part is probably apocryphal. The story is that he leapt from the bath and ran naked down the streets shouting "Eureka!"

He measured the volume of the crown, and then, comparing it to its weight, found that the crown had indeed been diluted with silver.

The magical bronze ball Archimedes gives Elise in the story represents this technique he invented for measuring volume. Elise submerges the ball in the bucket and then watches the water level rise and fall. When the water level goes up, the ball is bigger, when the water level goes down, the ball is smaller, meaning she was getting closer to the wizard.

ARCHIMEDES' PRINCIPLE

This brings us to something called Archimedes' Principle, which tells us how and why things float. Basically, when we put an object underwater, we are pushing some of the water up and out of the way. That water wants to get back down, so it pushes down on the rest of the water, which pushes up on the ball. This is called the buoyancy force.

The more water something displaces, the more buoyancy force there will be on it.

The boat in the story floats because of the force of buoyancy. The weight of water the boat displaces has to be exactly equal to the weight of the boat for it to float. When the queen steps into the boat, the boat will sink a little farther into the water. This is because it needs to displace more water for the buoyancy force to be strong enough to lift both the boat and the queen.

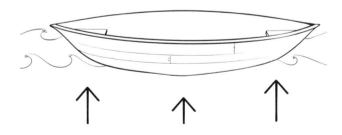

EDMOND'S other brother in the story, Bernoulli, represents the famous Swiss scientist and mathematician Daniel Bernoulli, who was born in the Netherlands in 1700. Bernoulli is the creator of Bernoulli's Principle, which relates the speed, pressure, and depth of a fluid. It's extremely useful for figuring out how much air or water pressure there will be if you go up higher or down lower in a fluid (or in the air), or if the speed of wind or water will change.

Like Archimedes, Bernoulli loved mathematics, and wanted to study it in school. His father, though, who was also a mathematician, wanted him to study business so that he would earn more money. Bernoulli refused, and they compromised. Bernoulli agreed to study medicine and become a doctor, as long as his father would teach him mathematics.

The magic cup in the story illustrates one feature of Bernoulli's Principle: the deeper you go underwater, the greater the pressure is. So, if you have a container of liquid with holes in the side, the water will come out faster from the lower holes than the upper holes, because there is a greater difference in pressure between the inside and the outside when you're closer to the bottom.

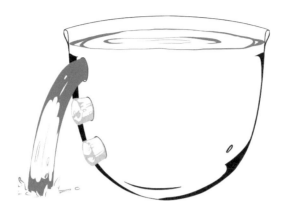

Here, Bernoulli's study of medicine became useful. He found that if you had a pipe with water flowing in it and you wanted to know the pressure of the fluid, you could poke a little hole in it with a straw and see how high the water rose. The higher the pressure in the pipe, the higher the water would rise in the straw.

Horrifyingly, this quickly became used to measure peoples' blood pressure (they would actually poke little glass tubes into people and see how high their blood rose in the tube) and it wasn't until 1896 (over 100 years later) that our current, non-painful, method was invented.

TRY THIS: PHET PRESSURE SIMULATION

On Google, search 'Phet Under Pressure". Here you can play around with the idea of water pressure and how depth and container shape affect (or don't affect!) it.

FLOW RATE

Another idea closely linked with Bernoulli's Principle is the idea of flow rate. When the queen comes to the third island, she has to guide her boat up a canyon that becomes narrower and narrower. In the canyon, there is a certain amount of water flowing. When the canyon is wide, the water can flow slowly. But when the canyon gets narrower, all that water has to make it through less space, so it has to go faster. (To put it in more science-y terms, the volume of water flowing through any point must be the same.)

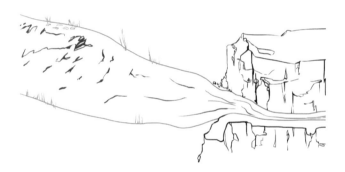

YOU CAN EXPERIMENT with the concept of flow rate yourself. Try putting your thumb over the end of a hose, partially blocking the flow of water. You'll see that the water sprays out much faster. This is because you've given it a smaller space to flow through, so it has to speed up.

THE MANOMETER

When Elise finally catches up with the wizard and he asks her to free his boat from where it is trapped, she goes for a swim, investigating the lake where the boat is.

Elise discovers during her swim that the little lake is connected to the outside water by a tunnel. The tunnel illustrates an interesting thing, which is that the water level in either end of the tunnel would have to be the same, because both ends have to be balanced. The tunnel is a sort of natural manometer, which is a device for measuring pressure. In simplest form, a manometer is a u-shaped tube. If you fill it with water, the water levels will balance on either side. If you connect one end to something with a higher pressure, it will cause the water on the other side to rise (very similar to Bernoulli's blood pressure measuring technique).

ARCHIMEDES' SCREW

ONCE SHE DISCOVERS there is a tunnel to the outside, she uses something called Archimedes' Screw (another of Archimedes' cool inventions!) to empty the water out.

ARCHIMEDES' screw is a way of moving water (or sand or grain, lots of things) from one place to another, and it works in an interesting way. Imagine in the diagram above that the screw isn't turning. As long as the seal between the walls and the blades is good, the water won't leak out. Because of the way the loop works, to get to the next lower point, the water would have to go up. It would have to go over the central pole. (The key here is that the screw only works when it's at an angle like this. It wouldn't work at all if it were vertical, because all the water would run out. But, because it's at an angle, the water would have to flow up to get to the next low point.)

Once we can see that the water is trapped, now let's think about what happens as we rotate the screw. As we rotate it, the water gets pushed up the incline. It still stays in the lowest portion of its little space, but the lowest portion moves up the tube as the screw rotates. All you have to do is rotate the screw and the water is lifted through it.

IF YOU WOULD LIKE to experiment with fluid mechanics in your everyday life, here are some things you can try:

You may have seen this one before, it's a classic, but it's really interesting. Take a straw, hold it straight up and down, and stick it halfway underwater like you normally would. Then, put your finger over the top so it's plugging one end of the straw. Then, lift your straw out of the water. You'll notice that the water stays inside the straw.

This amazed me when I was a kid, but it amazes me even more now that I understand what's happening. You might think that the water is just stuck inside or something, but really what's happening is that the air under the straw is pushing up on it.

Normally, when both ends of the straw are open, the air is pushing on the top part, too, so it balances out, but when we cover the top with our finger, now the air is only pushing on the bottom, and it's powerful enough to hold the water up.

We call the force of the atmosphere 'atmospheric pressure' and because we're feeling it all the time, we don't notice it, but it's incredibly powerful.

If you're interested in learning more about this, try searching YouTube for the video 'Space Straw' by Vsauce.

To play with more of the invisible but powerful effects of air pressure, try searching for 'vortex cannon project' which tells you how to build a device that will make toroidal (donut-shaped) air pressure missiles. To see a cool illustration of this, find Physics Girl's 'Crazy Pool Vortex' video on YouTube.

Another simple illustration of fluid mechanics that you can do is to get a paper or plastic cup, poke three holes in it at various depths, and then fill it with water. You'll see that the water coming out of the lower holes goes faster. But the distance each stream goes can be surprising. Try experimenting with different depths and differently sized holes.

THIS CONCLUDES the conceptual side of things. I hope you've enjoyed it! Next, for people who are interested in the math or who are taking a physics class, I'm including a section on problem solving. It assumes a basic familiarity with Algebra. Feel free to skip it if you're not interested. You can go on and try the Conceptual Practice Problems at the end if you'd like!

PROBLEM SOLVING

I t's been said that math is the language of the universe, so I wanted to include some math here for anyone who was interested.

My goal with these books is to give you plenty of options so that you can adapt what's here to whatever is most helpful and fun for you.

Feel free to skip this section if your main focus is the conceptual understanding.

One thing to know when reading about math: it takes a lot more time than reading usually does. When I'm reading about math, I have to pause a lot, reread, and think about things. It usually takes me a few times before I really start to get it. I usually have to try out a few problems on my own, too, before it fully makes sense.

Feel free to just read straight through, enjoying whatever is interesting or sticks out, and skip anything that doesn't interest you. You can always come back to it later.

In this section I'll assume a basic familiarity with Algebra. If you want to brush up on your math skills first but you aren't sure where to start, check out Khan Academy's Algebra 1 Course Challenge.

CALCULATIONS WITH DENSITY

The first concept we need to cover in order to understand the math behind fluid mechanics, is density. Density is just how much stuff there is in an object. By 'stuff' I mean mass. The more mass an object has crammed into a smaller space, the higher its density is.

For example, if you have a slice of cake, and you squish it into a ball in your hands, you're increasing its density, because its mass is the same, but its volume has gotten smaller.

Here is the equation for density:

$$\rho = \frac{m}{V}$$

ρ (the Greek letter rho, pronounced 'row') is the density of an object, in kilograms per cubic meter (kg/m^3)

m is the mass of the object, in kilograms (kg)

V is the volume of the object, in cubic meters (m^3)

IF WE KNOW the density and mass of an object, we can find its volume, or if we know its volume and mass, we can find its density. (Or, if we know the density and volume, we can find its mass.)

FOR EXAMPLE:

WATER HAS a density of approximately 1,000 kg/m3. How much space does 500 kg of water take up?

We simply plug 1,000 in for ρ and 500 in for m and solve for V. It's a bit tricky because the V is in the denominator, so we have to multiply by it first and then divide by rho.

$$\rho = \frac{m}{V}$$

$$1{,}000 = \frac{500}{V}$$
$$1{,}000V = 500$$
$$V = \frac{500}{1000} = 0.5 \text{ m}^3$$

PRESSURE

Pressure is interesting. Fundamentally, when we say something is under pressure, we mean that it's submerged in some fluid and that fluid is pressing in on it from all directions. (Or maybe a fluid is held in a container and is pressing outwards in all directions.)

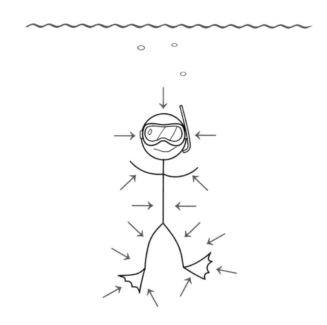

In the case of air pressure, air is made up of molecules, and air pressure is the force of those air molecules bouncing off an object.

Because pressure is exerted over an area, instead of measuring the force from a fluid in Newtons like we usually would, we talk about the amount of force per area, instead. So, pressure is measured in Newtons of force per square meter (N/m²). Another name for this unit is the Pascal (Pa). 1 Pascal is 1 N/m².

What's crazy is the sheer amount of pressure air puts on us at all times. We don't even notice it unless there's a breeze, but the average amount of air pressure at sea level with a temperature of 15 degrees Celsius is 101,325 Pa. Which means that if you have a piece of plywood that is 1 square meter (meaning a square that has a length of 1 meter on each side) then the force on one side of that plywood is 101,325 Newtons.

For comparison, an average 60 kg person weighs about 588 Newtons. So, this is like the force of 172 people standing on this piece of plywood.

Why don't we feel this? Because pressure is exerted in all directions. In the case of the plywood, it's like there are 172 people standing on both sides of it. So, the force in one direction is the same as the force in the other direction.

Because atmospheric pressure is so large, we actually have another unit we sometimes use to measure it: the atmosphere (atm). 1 atm of pressure is equal to 101,325 Pascals.

One of the main calculations we do with pressure is calculate the force on something due to the pressure, like I showed you above in   the case of the piece of plywood. The equation we use looks like this:

$$P = \frac{F}{A}$$

P = pressure in Pascals

F = the force in newtons

A = the area of the surface in square meters

If we know any two of these three quantities, we can use this equation to find the third.

For example, if we know the pressure and the area, we can find the force:

If you build submarine with a window that is half a square meter, how much force will be exerted on it by the water outside when the water pressure is 250,000 Pa?

First, we list out our variables:

F = ?
P= 250,000 Pa
A = 0.5 m²

Next, we plug the numbers we know into our formula:

$$P = \frac{F}{A}$$
$$0,000 = \frac{F}{0.5}$$

Then we solve by multiplying by 0.5 on both sides:

$$0.5 \cdot 250,000 = F$$
$$125,000 = F$$

The force is 125,000 Newtons!

CALCULATING WATER PRESSURE AT A GIVEN DEPTH

The deeper underwater we go (or under any fluid) the greater the pressure is. What's interesting is that the pressure is exactly equal to the weight of the water above you. This makes sense because when you're underwater all the water above you is pressing down on you— you're basically holding it all up.

We can use this idea to figure out an equation that helps us calculate the pressure at a given depth.

First, let's imagine a square piece of plywood submerged underwater, like this:

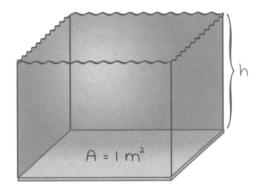

To calculate the weight of the water above it, we need to know its volume. That way, we can use its volume and the density of water (1000 kg/m3) to find its mass.

The volume of a rectangular prism like this is base area x height. So,

$$V = A * h$$

Now we also know that:

$$\rho = \frac{m}{V}$$

Multiplying by V on both sides gives us:

$$\rho V = m$$

Since we know that the volume is A*h, we can plug that in for V:

$$\rho A h = m$$

So, the mass of the water above the plywood is rho*A*h. To find its weight, we multiply it by 9.8 if we're on Earth, using this formula:

$$F_g = mg$$

So, the weight of the water is:

$$\rho A h * g$$

$$Or$$

$$F = \rho A h g$$

LASTLY, we know we want an expression for pressure, not Force, so let's divide both sides of this equation by A (because pressure is F/A)

$$\frac{F}{A} = \frac{\rho A h g}{A}$$

And simplify to make it:

$$P = \rho g h$$

This is our equation for the pressure at a given depth! is the density of the fluid, g is 9.8 (the acceleration due to gravity) and h is the height (or depth) of the fluid.

ONE LAST THING, we can't forget about air pressure! Whatever the pressure is underwater, we have to add on the pressure from the air above it, too:

$$P = \rho g h + P_0$$

The P with the little 0 subscript (which is pronounced "P naught" because 'naught' is a fancy word for nothing, or 0) represents the initial pressure.

CALCULATING THE SPEED OF A FLUID IN A PIPE

I talked about the idea of flow rate earlier, but now let's see how to actually do some calculations with it!

So far, we've talked about how, when water is flowing through a pipe (or a canyon), and then that pipe becomes narrower, the water has to speed up.

This is because there is a certain amount of water flowing through the pipe, and if that pipe changes, the same total amount of water still has to be flowing through it at every point (because all the water that goes through one point will also go through every other point, and if less is going through in one spot, it'll get backed up.

Imagine a crowd of people walking through a hallway. If there's a narrower spot, the people will have to go through it faster, because otherwise you'll get a crowd of people backing up in front of it.)

It turns out that, because the total amount of water flowing through each point is the same, we can set up this cool equation

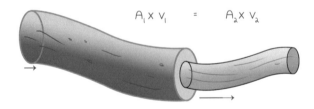

This equation is often written like this:

$$A_1 v_1 = A_2 v_2$$

Here, A stands for Area, and it means the cross-sectional area of the pipe (the area of the shape you'd get if you took a knife and took a circular slice out of one of the pipes above). The v stands for velocity, and it means the speed of the fluid in that part of the pipe. The little subscripts stand for the two different parts of the pipe.

Why is this true? Well, it turns out that if you multiply area by velocity, you get a speed that is the total volume of water through any point. I imagine it like this:

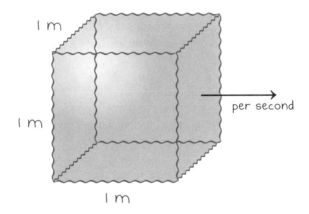

Here, you have a cubic meter of water flowing along. The number of these cubes that flow through a point every second is called the "volume flow rate."

Here's an example of how this works:

If water is flowing through a pipe that has an area of 6 m² at a rate of 2 m/s, what speed will it be traveling at if the area shrinks to 3 m²?

First I'll write out what I'm given:

$$A_1 = 6$$
$$v_1 = 2$$

$$A_2 = 3$$
$$v_2 = ?$$

Then I'll write out my formula:

$$A_1 v_1 = A_2 v_2$$

I'll plug in what I know:

$$6 * 2 = 3 * v_2$$

I'll multiply the numbers on the left side together:

$$12 = 3 * v_2$$

And divide both sides by 3 to solve for the speed.

$$4 = v_2$$

So, the speed of the water in the narrower part of the pipe is 4 m/s.

TWO WAYS TO FIND THE BUOYANCY FORCE OF AN OBJECT

FINDING THE BUOYANCY FOR FLOATING OBJECTS

When you see an object is floating, you automatically know a very useful piece of information about it. You know that the object is completely held up by the water underneath it. It's not sinking; gravity isn't pulling it down into the water, which means that the buoyancy force is exactly canceling out the weight.

So, rather than finding the buoyancy force directly, we can just figure out the weight of the object, and that will be the same as the buoyancy force.

In book one of the Fairy Tale Physics series, Newton's Laws: A Fairy Tale, we learned how to find the weight of an object using this equation:

$$F_g = mg$$

Fg is the weight of the object in Newtons
m is the mass of the object in kilograms
g is the acceleration due to gravity (9.8 m/s² on Earth)

Now we'll use the exact same equation to find the buoyancy force on a floating object!

An Example:

A toy sailboat with a mass of 3 kilograms is floating on a pond.

What is the buoyancy for acting on it?

Because I am told that the sailboat is floating, and there aren't any other forces mentioned, I know that the buoyancy force equals the force from gravity. So, I'll use the equation above to find the force:

$$F_g = mg$$

$$= 3 * 9.8$$

$$= 29.4 \, N$$

So, the weight of the boat is 29.4 N, and the buoyancy force is also 29.4 N.

FINDING THE BUOYANCY FOR SINKING OBJECTS

When an object sinks, we know that the buoyancy force isn't enough to hold the object up. This means that we have to get a little fancier with how we find the buoyancy force on the object.

This is where Archimedes' Principle comes in. We saw earlier that the reason for the buoyancy force is that when you submerge an object underwater you are moving the water out of the way and up. That lifted water is pushing back down, trying to get back down. The weight of the water displaced is exactly equal to the buoyancy force.

So, to find the buoyancy force on a sinking object, all we have to do is find out the weight of the water it is displacing.

Here's what we're going to do:

1. Find the volume of water that is displaced (maybe you already know it, or maybe you'll have to figure it out. For all the problems in this book, I'll give you the volume.)
2. Know that the volume of the object is the same as the volume of water displaced
3. Use the volume of the water to find its mass
4. Use the mass to find its weight
5. Because of Archimedes' Principle, we know that the weight of the water is the buoyancy force, so we're done!

Whew! That's a lot of steps. Let's walk through them one at a time. First, if we already know the volume of the water displaced, we're going to take it one step further and find the mass. To do that, we're going to go back to our old friend, then density equation:

$$\rho = \frac{m}{V}$$

We know that the density of water is about $1,000 \text{ kg/m}^3$, so we can plug that into our equation if our object is submerged in water.

$$F_g = mg$$

What's super cool, though, is that rather than do all the steps every time we want to find the buoyancy force, we can actually just put these two equations together, making them one single equation. It's kind of like building a machine to solve problems for us.

This is some fancy algebra, but here's how it works. First, we rearrange the first equation by multiplying by V on both sides (if you haven't taken algebra yet and you're interested, check out my book Algebra 1: Part 1: Exponents and Operations.)

$$\rho = \frac{m}{V}$$
$$\rho V = m$$

Notice that what this equation says is that rho times V is the same thing as m (because an equals sign means that two things are equal). What I'm going to do next is rewrite the Fg equation, but since rho times V is the same as m, I'm going to write instead of m:

$$F_g = mg$$
$$F_g = \rho V g$$

And now we have made a shortcut to finding buoyancy! This equation will give us the buoyancy force on an object.

$$F_B = \rho V g$$

F_B is the buoyance force on an object
Rho is the density of the liquid
V is the volume of the object
g is the acceleration due to gravity (9.8 m/s² on Earth)

HERE'S an example of how we use this equation:

A 75 KG diver has a volume of 0.07 m³. What is the buoyancy force acting on them when they are completely submerged underwater?

WE'RE GIVEN the mass here, but that's actually a trick. We only need to know the volume, and the density of the water they're swimming in, which we'll assume is regular water, so about 1,000 kg/m³.

We'll plug 0.07 in for the volume, 1,000 in for the density, and 9.8 in for g:

$$F_B = \rho V g$$
$$F_B = 1,000 * 0.07 * 9.8$$
$$F_B = 686 \ N$$

This concludes the math section! Thanks for coming along with me! The next few chapters have some conceptual and then mathematical practice problems.

CONCEPTUAL PRACTICE PROBLEMS

1. If you were at the bottom of a swimming pool filled with olive oil, would you feel more or less pressure than if you were at the bottom of a swimming pool filled with water?

2. If you are floating on an air mattress in a pool, and you for some reason have a giant boulder on the air mattress with you, and you push the boulder off so that it falls into the pool and sinks to the bottom, will the water level of the pool rise or lower?

3. If an object has sunk to the bottom of a lake, does it still experience a buoyancy force?

4. Kitchen sinks often have detachable faucets where you can click a button so that the faucet head becomes a sprayer, shooting water out quickly in a bunch of little streams. Can you explain what is happening here and how this works? Is the water coming from the pipes in the wall going faster? What conclusion could you draw about the total area of the little holes compared to the area of the main faucet opening?

5. What is Archimedes' principle?

6. If you are swimming in an underwater cave, and you see a side passage and swim into it, and the cave goes

perfectly horizontally, but you're now surrounded by rock, does the water pressure you experience change at all?

7. What factors influence how much pressure you experience when you're underwater?

8. If you know that in a particular part of a river, the water speed slows down, what can you guess about the size of the river at that point?

9. If you see three objects all floating in a lake, partially submerged, is there a way you could tell just by looking at them which one has the highest density?

10. If an object is fully submerged underwater, what do we know about the volume of the water displaced by the object?

11. You take two drinking glasses, one skinny and the other wide, and pour water into them until the liquid is 2 inches deep in each. How does the water pressure at the bottom of the skinny one compare to that at the bottom of the wide glass?

12. You take two identical drinking glasses. You pour water into one and olive oil (which is less dense than water) into the other, filling them both to the same height. How does the pressure at the bottom of the glass with the water compare to the pressure at the bottom of the glass with the oil?

13. If you take a marble and submerge it in a bowl of water, just under the surface of the water, how does the

buoyancy force on it compare to what it would be if you let it sink to the bottom?

14. You have two identical glasses of water, both filled with the same amount of water, and you drop two different objects into the glasses (one in each glass). You notice that the water levels in the glasses rise the same amount. What can you conclude about the properties of the two objects you dropped into the glasses?

15. You take two paper cups and poke one hole in the side of each. In the first cup, you poke the hole up high, and in the second cup you poke it down low near the bottom. Then you fill both cups with water. How does the speed of the water exiting the first cup compare to the speed of the water exiting the second cup?

CONCEPTUAL PRACTICE PROBLEMS ANSWER KEY

1. Because olive oil is less dense than water, the pressure at the bottom of a pool filled with olive oil will be less than that of a pool filled with water. (Pressure depends on the weight of the fluid above you, plus the weight of the atmosphere. Because the olive oil is less dense, it weighs less.)

2. This one is a tricky one! There are several competing ideas at play here. The first thing to consider is that if you push the boulder off into the pool, now it's taking up space in the pool, displacing an amount of water equal to its volume. However, what is happening when the boulder is on the air mattress? Well, it's causing the air mattress to sink lower into the water. So, when the boulder falls off the air mattress, the air mattress rises, causing the water level to lower. Which of these is greater? Which has more of an effect? Well, when the boulder is on the air mattress, the amount of water being displaced is equal to its mass (because the air mattress is having to displace enough water to keep that boulder lifted above the water – that's a lot of work the air mattress is doing!) When the boulder falls into the water, the amount of water displaced is no longer enough to keep it floating, which is why it sinks. So, when the boulder

sinks, the amount of water displaced is less, so the water level lowers! A concise way to say this is that when the boulder is on the air mattress, the volume of water displaced is equal to its mass, but when it's in the water the volume displaced is equal to its volume. Because the boulder is denser than water, the amount displaced by its mass is greater.

3. If an object has sunk to the bottom of a lake, it does experience a buoyancy force, just not enough to keep it floating.

4. The water coming from the pipes in the wall isn't traveling any faster. What is happening is that the total amount of area available for the water to flow out of is smaller, so the water must speed up to go through the smaller holes.

5. Archimedes' Principle states that the buoyancy force on an object is equal to the weight of the fluid displaced.

6. The water pressure does not change at all. The pressure experienced only depends on the depth of the water (assuming that there aren't any currents in this cave - flowing water would change the pressure.) So, if you don't swim up or down but only horizontally, the pressure you experience would stay the same.

7. When you're underwater, the pressure you experience depends on how deep you are. It would also be different if you were on a different planet with different gravity, or if you were swimming in something other than

water (the denser the fluid, the greater the pressure would be).

8. If the water speed of the river decreases, you can guess that happened because the cross-sectional area of the river increases (maybe it becomes deeper or wider).

9. You can tell which of the objects has the most density by seeing which is the most submerged. The more of the object that is underwater, the greater its density.

10. If an object is fully submerged underwater, then the volume of the water displaced is exactly equal to its own volume.

11. The water pressure is the same at the bottom of each glass. The size and shape of the container doesn't matter. All that matters is the depth of the water.

12. The pressure at the bottom of the glass with the olive oil is less than that at the bottom of the glass with the water. Because olive oil is less dense than water, it weighs less, so an equal amount of olive oil will cause less pressure than water.

13. As long as the marble is fully submerged, it doesn't matter whether it's at the top or the bottom of the fluid. The amount of water displaced it equal to its volume, so its buoyancy force is the same in either place.

14. We know that the two objects must have the same volume. Regardless of their shapes, if they are displacing

the same amount of water, they must have the same volumes.

15. The speed of the water exiting the second cup (with the lower hole) will be faster than the speed of the water exiting the first cup. This is because the water pressure is greater at the bottom, which means the water will be forced out at a greater speed.

QUANTITATIVE PRACTICE PROBLEMS

1. Atmospheric pressure is around 101,325 Pascals (N/m^2). If you have a piece of plywood that has an area of 1 square meter, how much force is the atmosphere exerting on each side?

2. If your palm has an area of 0.008 m^2, how much force is the atmosphere exerting on it?

3. What is the pressure exerted on you when you are swimming 2 m below the surface of a pool? (Including atmospheric pressure.)

4. What is the pressure exerted on the sides of a submarine when it is at a depth of 600 m below the surface of the ocean? (Ocean water has a density of 1036 kg/m^3 on average.)

5. How deep underwater (density of 1,000 kg/m^3) do you have to go before the pressure exerted on you is twice what it is on dry land (meaning, the pressure that is just from the atmosphere.)

6. The density of milk is around 1,035 kg/m^3. If you filled a pool with milk and swam 2 meters down to the bottom, what pressure would you feel?

7. If a hose has a cross-sectional area of 0.0007 square meters and the water is traveling at a speed of 2 m/s, how fast will it be traveling if you cover half of the opening?

8. If a water pipe has a cross-sectional area of 0.05 m² and the water is traveling with a speed of 3.4 m/s, how fast will it be traveling if it flows into a wider pipe that has an area of 0.1 m².

9. A duck of mass 4 kg is floating on the surface of a lake, what is the buoyancy force on the duck?

10. A sailboat has a mass of 3,000 kg. What is the buoyancy force on it when it is floating, without any passengers?

11. If you load 5 passengers into the boat from question 12, and each person has a mass of 60 kg, what is the buoyancy force on the sailboat now? (Assuming it remains floating.)

12. A glass ball of mass 9 kg and volume .0003 m³ is dropped into a lake (the density of the lake water is approximately 1,000 kg/m³) and sinks to the bottom. What is the force of buoyancy on the marble as it sinks?

13. A shark has a volume of 2.5 m³. What is the force of buoyancy on the shark as it swims beneath the surface of the ocean? (Ocean water has a density of 1036 kg/m³ on average.)

14. A submarine has a volume of 15,000 cubic meters. What is the buoyancy force on it when it is fully submerged in ocean water (1036 kg/m³)?

15. If a person has a volume of 0.062 m³, how much buoyancy force acts on them when they are swimming underwater (1000 kg/m³)?

QUANTITATIVE PRACTICE PROBLEMS ANSWER KEY

1. 101,325 N

2. 810.6 N

3. 120,925 Pa

4. 6,193,005 Pa

5. About 10.3 m

6. 121,611 Pa

7. 4 m/s

8. 1.7 m/s

9. 39.2 N

10. 29,400 N

11. 32,340 N

12. 2.94 N

13. 25,382 N

14. 152,292,000 N

15. 607.6 N

LIGHT:
A FAIRY TALE

King John, Fourteen Portraits, and a Sorceress

ONCE upon a time, there was a young prince named John who had just been crowned King of Amrath. The new king was an orphan, raised by maids and butlers and looked after by his steward, Griselda, who had managed the kingdom until John came of age. Taking the throne was terrible news, both for the citizens of Amrath, who just wanted to go about plowing their fields and treating their goats' hoof rot. And for John himself, who only wanted, in an abstract way, to slay dragons and rescue princesses. In fact, the idea of being king was so terrible to him that John avoided the throne room as much as possible. This was partly because there was nothing fun to do there, and partly because of the fourteen enormous portraits of his forebears looming down at him from high up on the walls.

Today, however, the portraits were not on his mind.

John stood on the parapet overlooking the crowd in the square below.

Most of them were screaming, but not all of them were demanding his execution. Some of them wanted him thrown in prison. Others were focused on throwing rotten vegetables at him.

The crown on John's head was cold, the metal biting into his scalp. Someone down below had quite an arm, having hurled a potato which smacked into his jaw. The new king stumbled and reached up to keep his crown from tumbling. Standing next to him, Griselda shifted her weight to the other foot.

John wished he hadn't spent the week before his coronation reading gossip about the nobles. He wished he hadn't spent years before becoming king reading adventure stories about young princes who saved kingdoms from dragons. If only there were a dragon around. That was why no one liked him. He needed to kill a dragon. Maybe he could find one. Or declare war. He'd tried that, though, and the neighboring kingdom had ignored him, and the troops had refused to march.

He took a deep breath. He was now King John XV and as he looked down at his subjects, he saw their faces contorted with anger and contempt. He looked at Griselda, who smiled encouragingly but without a lot of confidence. John considered giving up. But then he remembered the story of Prince Henry III, who rode dragons and burnt his enemies to a crisp while rescuing maidens and increasing the economic production of the kingdom. He thought of King John XII, his great-grandmother (yes, his own great-grandmother was named after a man; the naming tradition really was unfortunate for the women of the family). She had ridden into battle with the wild men in the north, driving them back. She hadn't given up, even when she'd been captured and beheaded. He wished he could have met her. She could have told him what to do now.

John readjusted his crown, squared his shoulders, and approached the end of the parapet, dodging a carrot as it sailed past. He planted his feet on the golden circle where his father had stood to announce his birth, only days before both he and John's mother had become ill and died. John cleared his throat, and the sound, magnified as if by magic, echoed off the perfectly designed walls of the square. The furious shouting quieted to an angry muttering.

He opened his mouth, not knowing what he was going to say, but just then the sun came out from behind a cloud and shone straight in his face, blinding him. The crowd gasped, and a hush settled over the square. The new king stood bathed in a ray of sunlight, not daring to believe his luck. John struggled not to blink, but to stare stoically into the sun with what he hoped was a kingly expression on his face.

"Since the death of my parents, dark times have fallen on our land," he said. "Steward Griselda has done an admirable job, but a kingdom needs a king." That last line came from The Adventures of King Edward the Relentless. "I will be a light in the darkness. I will illuminate the darkest corners of our kingdom." He could feel the sunbeam starting to fade. Time to wrap it up. "Light is coming to Amrath." He turned and walked away from the parapet just as the cloud moved back over the sun. Behind him, the crowd explode into talk. Griselda's gaze landed on him. He grinned.

Then he tripped on the carpeting. His crown tumbled off his head, but he caught it, tucked it under his arm, and looked around to see if anyone had noticed. The soldiers lining the walls stared straight ahead. Someone laughed, but it was quickly turned into a cough.

The next few weeks did not go as King John had hoped. He commissioned several statues of himself to be put up around the kingdom, got himself a sword-fighting teacher, and rode out into the woods looking for dragons and was nearly mauled by a boar. The peasants, briefly impressed by what had appeared to be an act of the divine during his speech, rapidly returned to their grumbling, and the square outside the palace collected protesters again.

One evening, feeling morose and deciding that the most heroic place to be morose was the throne room, King John XV went and lay prone on the carpeting, looking up at his heroic, judgmental ancestors.

"I know I'm doing a terrible job," he said defensively.

To his surprise, someone answered. "Yes, you are."

King John had heard of people hallucinating conversations with portraits or statues or even things like bedside tables or chamber pots—you'd be surprised how good the advice of a hallucinated chamber pot can be—but he'd never experienced it himself. Still, at this point John was up for anything.

"Yes, oh glorious ancestors! What must I do?" This was what people said in the sorts of books he liked to read.

Then he saw the woman standing underneath the portraits.

"Oh, I'm sorry, I didn't see you there." On second thought, that was probably too apologetic a thing for a king to have said, and John wished he hadn't said it, but it was too late now. At least it was polite. And it was entirely possible that she was a hallucination as well. It was probably best to be polite to hallucinations.

The—possibly hallucinated—woman was old, with a hunched back and short, thick fingers. She clutched a lumpy grey candle in one hand.

"I heard of your speech, young king," she said. Her voice was soft now, barely above a whisper. "I can teach you to be a light in the darkness, if you wish."

John didn't think she could teach him any of things he had in mind. Like troll-wrestling. On the other hand, this was often the way things started in stories, so he went along with it.

"What do I have to do?" After all, maybe she was a powerful sorceress. She looked like a powerful sorceress. Maybe it was better to check. "Are you a powerful sorceress?" he asked quickly.

She blinked. "Maybe." For a moment, her image wavered, and John thought he saw a young woman with long, white hair and pointed ears, glowing with a bright purple and white aura. But it must have been a trick of the light because a moment later the vision was gone.

The old woman cleared her throat and held up the candle. "Take this candle. Go to the top of the highest tower and light it. You will learn all you need to learn."

John reached out for the candle, but just as his fingers touched it, she pulled back. "Take care, though. Do not let the candle burn all the way to the end."

John nodded solemnly, but immediately decided he would let the candle burn all the way to the end, just to see what would happen.

"Thank you, great sorceress," he said. When he looked up from the candle, she was gone, and he was alone in the throne room. Except, of course, for the horrible portraits on the walls.

Immediately, King John climbed the rickety, winding stairs—all three hundred and seven of them—to the top of the tallest tower. Disconcertingly, the tower tended to sway and, as it was a windy evening, there was more than a slight wobble. Luckily, despite his many failings, John was at least totally unafraid of heights. He'd always hoped it would come in handy for dragon riding someday. If he ever found a dragon.

For ten or fifteen minutes, King John stood lost in thought at the top of the tower, imagining what it would be like to ride a dragon, but then he remembered why he was there. He took out the candle and realized he hadn't brought any matches. (Matches had been invented by King John III, who had also invented heated carriage seats and GPS. To be fair, GPS was simply Gregory Pontius Samson, a local mapmaker whom King John III had employed to lead him around town because he was always getting lost. But still. The matches were a useful invention.)

Annoyed with himself for forgetting the matches, John trudged back down the three hundred and seven stairs, found a packet in a kitchen drawer, got distracted taste-testing mince pies for forty-five minutes, drank several pints of ale with the disconsolate cook who had recently broken off his engagement to the baker, took a two-hour nap, then returned to the top of the tower.

By now it was quite late.

Looking down, he noticed a large crowd still occupied the square. The square was called Proclamation Square, but John had recently come to think of it as Protestor Square. The protestors were waving torches, and John could hear faint shouts. He was going to have to do something about the unrest soon. He'd heard what happened to kings when peasants got too angry.

Well, he had this candle now, given to him by a powerful sorceress. That was something. John took a deep breath. His stomach, full of mince pies and ale, strained and groaned.

King John set the candle upright in the center of the tower, squishing it around until its waxy bottom was well-stuck to the sandstone. Then he struck a match and held the flame to the wick. The fire changed color as the wick caught, burning with a diamond-like brilliance. John felt as if the light shone straight through him; he could feel it illuminating his bones with its white, shining light. He looked around and saw that all the color had gone from the world. It shone in black and white with every shade of grey shimmering in between.

He could see straight through the tower beneath him, down through every step, down to the kitchens beneath. He could see the bones and the eyeballs of the cook from above, could see his heart and his stomach—also full of mince pies. Beneath the cook were more flag stones, and storerooms, and a thief sneaking through a culvert John hadn't known existed. He turned to see the rest of the castle, and there was the throne room with the portraits on the walls. There was something behind them that he couldn't quite make out. John made a mental note to check later.

He could see every maid and butler and swordsman in the entire castle. He could see the femurs of the protestors down in the square.

For several hours, John simply sat and gazed at the strange view he had on the world. It didn't seem to be wearing off, and the candle didn't seem to be burning down at all, which surprised him. Then, he began to wonder. While entertaining, he wasn't sure what he was supposed to be learning from this. How was this supposed to help him be a better king? He turned to look at the candle.

"Oh, great candle, help me to be a light for my people, teach me to illuminate my kingdom."

There was a faint pop and suddenly John was speeding through the air. If he'd had time to think about it, he'd have noticed that he wasn't feeling the wind in his hair because he didn't have any hair. But he didn't. He was moving too quickly.

He sped in a straight line, hurtling over the rooftops of the town. He saw he was approaching a tree and tried to close his eyes. That was when he noticed that he didn't have eyes. He still didn't notice the hair, though. He tried to flail his arms and legs, to turn or slow himself, and discovered he didn't have those, either. For some reason that came as a relief. At least they wouldn't be injured when he crashed into the tree.

He collided with a single, large maple leaf and felt himself divide. Part of himself absorbed into the leaf, and part of himself bounced off. His mind stayed with the part that bounced, and he felt different. Less. But just as fast. He hit another leaf and bounced off that, too, this time losing nothing. Then he hit the trunk, and that was a different story. The last of himself soaked into the trunk, and he was gone.

There was another faint pop, and John found himself standing at the top of the tower again. He immediately fell over.

When at last he was able to push himself up to a seat, and, to his relief, found that he again had arms and legs and eyeballs (he still hadn't noticed the hair, although that was back, too). He saw that the candle had gone out, and that it was a quarter of an inch shorter.

"What in the world was that?" John mused aloud, not expecting an answer.

"You asked to be light," a sonorous voice proclaimed.

John whirled around and saw not one but five ghosts floating above the other side of the tower. One of them was trying to hide behind the others, but as they were all transparent it wasn't working. In fact, John found himself staring at that one in particular. He had a shock of pearly white hair.

"That's Snell. Don't mind him," one of the others said.

"Er," said John, and left it at that.

The six of them stood staring at one another. One of the ghosts coughed politely. Two of them swung their arms. Snell

174

looked at his shoes, and the one directly in front of him attempted to whistle but failed utterly.

"Excuse me," John said. "My name is John. King John the Fifteenth. Pleased to meet you; welcome to Amrath."

The ghosts looked relieved, and the one closest smiled, held out his hand, then withdrew it sheepishly. "You'll have to excuse us. We're not used to being transparent." He cleared his throat. "Or incorporeal."

John waved a hand as if it were a trivial matter, and the ghost, who had a crazy cloud of white hair floating around his head, continued.

"We are the five light mages. Or we were. The witch has trapped us here in this candle, forcing us to do her bidding."

"Oh, I'm so sorry to hear that," John said, feeling bad and wondering if it was still ethical for him to ask for their help in improving his kingdom. He'd just wanted some magical help; he didn't want to enslave anybody. "Is there any way for me to free you?"

"If you burn the candle all the way to its end, we will be freed."

Well, he'd been planning on doing that anyway, so that was convenient. "Well, of course; I'll do that immediately then, shall I?" He could figure out something else for his kingdom. John moved to light the candle, and all five ghosts shot forward in alarm, their transparent arms raised.

"Wait!"

"What is it?" John asked.

The ghost with the crazy hair continued, "This candle contains the five of us and two dark secrets. If you burn it, you will let them out, too."

"Well, that can't do that much harm, can it?"

"It will kill you."

"Oh." Now John felt really uncomfortable. There were five of them imprisoned. If he didn't let them out, they would all die in there, he assumed. But if he let them out, then he would die. Was his life worth the life of five mages? He was a king, that had to count for something, but he wasn't a very good king, and to be honest he didn't think he'd amount to much. The five light mages had probably done more for the world. But he didn't want to die, and that outweighed most other arguments in his mind.

He thought of King John V, who had sacrificed himself to save the small village of Oenwaith, which made John feel guilty. Then it occurred to him that someone else could light the candle, and then he felt really guilty and tried to pretend to himself that he hadn't thought of it.

"It's all right," the ghost with the crazy hair said. "You don't have to die. We can teach you to become a light mage, too. Then you can light the candle safely and free us."

John perked up at this. Becoming a powerful mage was exactly the kind of thing he'd had in mind when the sorceress had given him the candle. "Great!"

"It won't be easy," a dapper ghost behind the crazy-haired one said.

"Oh, that's fine," John said, smiling.

"No, really. It's going to be really hard."

"Oh, I'm sure it'll be ok."

"No, no. It's very dangerous." The other ghosts nodded. Even Snell.

"Awesome. I'm in." John grinned widely.

The ghosts glanced at each other.

"Very well," the crazy-haired one said. "To be a mage you must control the light. To control it, you must understand it. I will be your first teacher. My name is Albert Einstein, and I will teach you to ride the light."

ALBERT EINSTEIN AND THE SPEED OF LIGHT

John's grin became even wider, and his mouth opened several inches. He looked at the other ghosts to make sure they weren't joking. They all looked deadly serious. "Can we start now?" John asked.

Einstein glanced at the others. They shrugged. "All right. Let's begin."

John punched the air and jumped a few feet, then tried to appear as if he was taking things seriously.

The ghost of Einstein moved forward, reaching a misty hand towards the candle. A spark leapt from his fingers to the wick and light flared. Einstein lifted his hands, and time stopped.

All sound had ceased. Only John and Einstein could move. The ghosts hung like frozen clouds behind them. Between Einstein and John was a glowing yellow orb.

"This is a photon," Einstein said. "A particle of light."
"Awesome. How do I ride it?" John asked.

"By holding on tightly. I've stopped time, so you can get on. Otherwise, it moves far too fast. I'll float along next to you as you go."

Following Einstein's instructions, John climbed aboard the glowing particle. It was bright white and pulsed with energy.

"All right," Einstein said. "Have you got a good hold?"

John wasn't sure what he meant, because there was literally nothing to hold on to, but he didn't want to be a difficult student, so he nodded.

"Good. All right, I'll start time again. But slowly. Otherwise, you'd be on the other side of the kingdom in about a hundredth of a second."

"A hundred seconds?"

"No. One second chopped into a hundred pieces. Take one of those."

"Wow."

"Yes."

John was about to say something else, but Einstein clapped his hands together and the beam of light shot off into the night, with John clinging to it.

It was much smoother than riding a horse, strangely. It didn't jostle or turn or speed up or slow down at all. In fact, once John got used to it, it was a fairly boring ride. Einstein came up next to him.

"Seems like you're getting the hang of it."

"How do I make it go faster?"

"You can't."

"Turn?"

"You can't."

"This is it?"

They were fast approaching the ground.

"No, this is only the beginning."

John felt the photon impact the ground with a shudder, but the light only dimmed, and a second later they were shooting away in a slightly different direction.

"I thought you said we couldn't turn!" John yelled.

"You can't turn light, no, but it does bounce off things quite well."

"Why is it dimmer?"

"Some of it was absorbed into the ground."

"I'm still going just as fast, though."

"Indeed. You've lost energy, but you're not any slower. Just dimmer. And your color is different."

John hadn't noticed, but it was true.

He crashed into a boulder, and the light winked out. Gasping, he found himself again at the top of the tower.

The ghosts were still standing where they'd left them.

"I hope this doesn't get boring for you," John said. "You can go down to the kitchens, or, er, something. If you want."

"You were gone less than a second. We don't get bored that easily," the dapper one said.

"Oh, right."

Einstein reappeared.

"All right, not bad for your first try. Now it's time for your first challenge. To move on to your next teacher, you must turn your photon pink. You must then successfully return to the top of the tower, still astride your light beam."

"But . . . that was just my first try."

180

"So?"

"Don't you have more to teach me?"

"You'll find that there is actually very little to teach. The difficult part is not knowing but doing."

"Do I get any more practice first?"

"No."

"Are you going to give me any hints?"

"No."

"Pointers?"

"No."

"Will you slow time down for me again?"

"I'm not here to make it easy for you. Being a light mage is difficult, and most of it you have to do for yourself."

John didn't think this was how training was supposed to work, but it didn't seem like he was going to change Einstein's mind. He still wanted to be a light mage, so he thought hard about the challenge. Normally he would have taken a good long nap before trying to think this hard, but, for the first time he could remember, he didn't want to waste time. He didn't want to distract himself by reading an adventurous tale about dragons, either. He wanted to think.

So, John sat down on the cold flagstones and thought. How was he going to turn the light pink? Well, he'd turned it brown. That was pretty close. But why did it change color? It lost something when it hit the ground. Whatever that was had turned it brown. Was it something about how he'd hit the ground?

"Remember that light is what you use to see," Snell whispered. The others turned to glare at him, and he blushed.

Why did that matter? He used light to see, yes. Then he started to put it together. If he used light to see, then if he saw something pink, he must be seeing pink light! To turn the light pink, all he had to do was bounce off something pink. The rose garden was not far away. There were pink roses there.

He stood up in excitement and looked out over the ramparts. There were the roses. Now all he had to do was figure out how to get back. But light always went straight. The only way to turn was to bounce off something. The other things he'd sort of glanced off as he'd hit them. That gave him an idea.

Without stopping to second guess himself, John grabbed the candle, pointed it at the rose, and lit the wick.

The photon appeared, picking John up as it went past him. Time slowed down as he pulled himself up onto it and they shot towards the rose. There was no controlling or changing it now; all John could do was watch. They hit the rose dead on, exactly as John had hoped; the light beneath him dimmed and glowed pink, and they bounced straight back towards the tower.

The candle still hung in midair where John had let go of it. It hadn't even had time to fall yet. They crashed straight back into it, the light absorbing into the candle's dark surface, and John fell to the ground.

"Well done," Einstein said, sounding surprised and impressed.

"You slowed time for me," John said.

"I most certainly didn't."

"But it went so slow," John said, confused.

Einstein's eyebrows lifted into his white hair. "You must have slowed it yourself." He paused and looked at John more carefully. "Perhaps you are more suited to this than I realized."

No one had ever told John he was well-suited to something. Ever. It was an amazing feeling, and John wasn't sure how to take it, so he changed the subject.

"So, what's next then?"

The other ghosts, still looking at John with curiosity, stepped aside to reveal Snell.

SNELL AND THE LAW OF REFRACTION

Snell looked so shy and uncomfortable. Wishing to put him at ease, John chose his words carefully. "Will you tell me more about how to ride the light?" he asked gently.

"No," Snell said, and his voice, though quiet, was sure. "I will teach you to *be* the light."

Without making eye contact, Snell moved forward and gestured to the candle. "Focus your attention on the wick."

John stared at the wick.

"No," Snell said, his annoyance making him quieter. "Focus on the wick until nothing exists but the wick."

"And me, right?"

"No. Just the wick."

Again, John felt he'd been given instructions that made no sense. But he would try to follow them. He stared at the wick. Other things, like thoughts and sounds and his own breath kept distracting him, but he focused on the wick. Suddenly, it ignited. Immediately, John shot through the air, crashing into things, losing energy as he did so, and then he was gone. And then he was back on the tower.

"You were supposed to stop time," Snell said.

"I've only done it the once," John grumbled.

"Yes. So clearly you know how to do it."

John wanted to complain that Snell hadn't told him to stop time, nor had anyone ever told him how to do it, but again, he didn't want to be a bad student.

"Ok. Sorry. I'll try again."

The second time was quicker. He focused on the wick, letting everything else drop away, and suddenly he was a beam of light, shooting out into the darkness, and then he was nothing, and then he was back at the tower.

"Sorry," John said. "It was too fast."

"Again," Snell said.

"Sorry," John said. "I wasn't ready for it."

"Again," Snell said.

"Sorry," John said. "I forgot that time."

He wasn't even sure what he was supposed to be doing. All he knew was that he wanted to see what happened when he was the light.

The next time the candle lit, everything froze.

"Finally," John tried to say, but found that he couldn't talk. He was a glowing orb.

"Finally," Snell said. "Now, notice that you are white now, but that you are actually made up of more than that."

John looked at himself, and realized that, yes, he was in fact all colors.

"White light is really all the colors combined."

Ah, John thought, that explained the rose.

"When you hit something, some of those colors are absorbed, the other colors bounce off. Like in the rose. Now, go into the ocean."

John would have protested, but, as a photon, he had no way to protest. So, he pointed himself towards the ocean and then he started time again. Or he tried to. It didn't work. "Start!" he thought to himself. "Go!"

He willed himself forward, straining with everything he had, but nothing worked.

"This is impossible," he thought. Time started again, and he zipped off. An instant later he hit the surface of the water, and something strange happened.

At first, he thought time had slowed down again, but it hadn't. Everything around him was still going the same speed it had been before, but he had slowed down. He thought Einstein had said he couldn't change speed. The other strange thing that happened was that he turned. Deeper into the water.

Then he hit a turtle; the last of his energy was absorbed, and he was back on top of the tower, corporeal once again.

"All right," Snell said.

"What was that? I thought you said I couldn't change speed," he said to Einstein.

"I said you couldn't go any faster. It can't go faster. But it can slow down."

"Hey," Snell said. "You had your turn. You could have explained it then."

Einstein lifted he hands and floated off. Snell addressed John.

"Light goes more slowly through some things than others."

"Like what?"

"Like glass, and water. Diamonds. It's fastest when going through nothing. Almost as fast when going through air."

"Ok, but how do you explain my turn?" John wondered if this was something that only he could do. That would be super cool.

"It's very simple," Snell said, dashing John's hopes. "Imagine you're sliding down a ramp headfirst."

John wondered where that had come from, but he did as he was told.

"Now, imagine the right side of the ramp is covered in honey."

John wondered what kind of town Snell had lived in before being imprisoned in the candle, and whether ramps with honey on them were a normal thing there.

"What's happening?" Snell asked.

I'm rethinking my life choices, was what John wanted to say, but he didn't. Instead, he tried to pretend. He felt his right side sticking in the honey, felt it grabbing onto him as he slid. And he felt himself turn towards the honey side.

"I'm turning," he said.

"Exactly," Snell said. "Usually, I use a broom as an example, but I thought this might be more relatable."

John blinked. "So . . . you thought a honey slide would be the most relatable thing for me?"

Snell shrugged. "I don't know a lot about kings."

John decided to let this slide. Then, he giggled at his own pun, but only internally as he didn't want to offend Snell.

"Light turns when it goes from one medium to another. If it goes into something where it goes slower, it turns to go deeper into the medium. If it goes into a medium where it's faster, it leaves at a shallower angle."

"Ok."

"So, make me a rainbow."

"What?"

"Turn yourself into a beam of light and then make yourself into a rainbow. That is your task."

"But . . ."

Snell moved to the far side of the tower and crouched down out of the wind. A transparent deck of cards appeared in his hands, and he began playing solitaire.

"Okay," John muttered to himself. "I'm light. I am made up of all the colors. So . . ." he raised his voice and shouted at Snell, "is it a trick question? Am I already a rainbow?"

Snell gave him a look and turned back to his cards.

Darn. "Also, I turn when I go from a place where I'm fast to a place where I'm slow. How does that help? If I turn, all of me must turn." He sighed. "Ok, different idea. When are there rainbows? When it's rainy. Ok, well, that makes sense if water makes me turn."

John leaned his elbows on the wall and propped his forehead on his hands. The stones were hard and cold under his elbows. "But just shining light into water doesn't make a rainbow. Some stones also make rainbows. Do I have any of those?"

Excitedly, John jumped up and ran down the steps. He bumped into a soldier who said something to him, but John was too excited. Strangely, he could hear the soldier jogging after him as he ran towards the royal vault. When he reached the door, he had to fumble around for his keys, giving the soldier time to catch up.

"Sir, I'm sorry to interrupt, sir—"

"Oh, don't worry, it's fine," John said, trying a ruby key in the lock. No good. He frowned. Was it the emerald one?

"No, sir, it's not just that; it's the peasants, sir."

"Oh?" No, it was definitely the iron one. A serious looking key for a serious thing like a vault. He slotted it into the keyhole and smiled when it clicked into place.

"They're . . . they're attacking the castle, sir."

"What?"

"Er, well, they've been . . ."

"Not too happy with me, no. I understand," John said, but his mind was still on rainbows. Were those crystals still here?

"I assume you'd like us to barricade the doors?"

"Yes, yes. Defend the cast—" John looked up. "Wait, did you say the peasants are attacking the castle?"

The soldier sighed in relief. "Yes, sir."

"Why?"

"It's the protesters, sir. They've gotten out of hand. What would you like us to do?"

John stroked his chin, wishing he had a beard. He didn't blame the peasants. He'd been a terrible king. If they could just wait a little longer, he would be a light mage and then he could

188

fix everything. In the meantime, he didn't want his soldiers killing them. It wasn't their fault.

"Defend the castle, but don't hurt any of them."

"Er, what sir?"

"Can you keep them out without hurting them?"

"Well, maybe, but if they start lighting things on fire or—It looks like they're bringing in a battering ram. The castle doors are solid but they're not impenetrable."

"Well, just hold them off as long as you can, all right?"

"If we can't, sir?"

"Come get me. I'll be on the north tower. Let them in if you have to; tell them I'll be down shortly, but don't hurt any of them, all right?"

"Er . . ."

John realized he might have to be commanding here. "That's an order!"

The man gave a curt nod. "Right. Of course, sir." He hurried off down the corridor.

Glad to be rid of the distraction, John let himself into the vault. There were piles of gold and silver and jewels. Maybe if he gave some of these to the peasants, they'd be less angry, he thought. It wasn't a terrible plan. Although, most of his plans didn't turn out well, so he probably shouldn't have a lot of confidence in this one.

He held up a diamond. Faint glints of color shone through it, almost rainbows but not quite right. He knocked over a pile of gold as he moved to the back of the vault. There at the far end was a pile of grubby crystals. King John the Fourth had been a fortune teller and had liked having what he called 'mystical stones' around. That was one ancestor John wasn't completely intimidated by.

He held up a crystal and grinned when he saw the rainbow pattern shining through it. He noticed how the light went straight from the candle burning in the wall sconce, through the crystal, and made a sharp bend right as it passed through, splitting into a rainbow.

"Oh, each of the colors bends a different amount," he muttered to himself. "Cool."

He sprinted back up the stairs of the tower, the crystal held tightly in his fist. His leg muscles were burning, and his breath came in gasps. This was already more exercise than King John had had in the last three weeks put together.

When John at last reached the top of the tower, the ghosts were all playing a card game, except Einstein who was pouting in the corner, having lost several hands in a row.

"I've got it!" John shouted. He grabbed the candle, focused on the wick, and immediately shot off into the night, dropping the crystal.

When he appeared back on the rooftop, he was relieved to see the crystal was unharmed. He tried again, this time more carefully. He managed to slow time enough to turn, aligning himself with the crystal, and this time, when he shot off into the darkness, he split into a magnificent rainbow before hurtling off in all directions.

"Correct," was all Snell said.

"Now it's our turn," the dapper ghost said, rubbing his palms together.

THE WAVE NATURE OF LIGHT

"I am Louis de Broglie," the dapper one said. He pointed to the ghosts beside him. "This is Thomas Young and James Clerk Maxwell, and we will each show you what you are."

"I thought I was a person," John said.

"We mean when you're light," de Broglie said.

"Aren't I light then?" John asked.

"Yes and no," de Broglie said. "Young Thomas will demonstrate."

"I hate it when you call me that," Thomas Young said.

"But your name lends itself to it so well," de Broglie said.

"Exactly, you think I haven't heard it a million times before?"

De Broglie didn't respond, so Young turned to John.

"You've probably been thinking of yourself as similar to that potato that hit you in the head earlier today," Young began.

"You saw that?"

"Yes," Young said, and John winced. "Anyway, light is much more than a potato."

"I would imagine."

"No, you wouldn't," Snell interjected.

For someone so quiet, he was suddenly very cranky, John thought. Maybe he was hungry. If ghosts could even be hungry.

"For this demonstration, you will need a piece of parchment."

After another long jog down the tower and back up again, John presented Young with the parchment.

"Excellent. Now cut two slits in it, extremely close together."

John stared at him for a few seconds, then, grudgingly, ran back down the stairs, got a knife, and ran back up again. He cut two slits in the paper, about an inch apart.

"I said extremely close together!" Young said. "So close you can barely tell they are two cuts."

It took almost fifteen tries for John to get it right.

When at last Young was satisfied, he addressed John. "Now, if you were a potato, a very tiny potato, and you were thrown at these slits, what would happen?"

"I'd go through one of them."

"Exactly."

John waited for him to elaborate.

Young smiled in a very self-satisfied way. "Now, if you travel towards these slits as a beam of light, what do you think will happen?"

"Er, I'll go through one of them?"

"See! You are thinking of yourself as a potato!"

John didn't think that logically followed.

"Try it," Young said.

Obligingly, John took the candle, which was beginning to look significantly shorter. Again, he concentrated on the wick, and again he found himself a glowing orb of light. He slowed time and directed himself at the slits that Young held aloft.

John approached the slits; ten feet away, then five, then two, then only a few inches. When he hit the slits, though, a very strange thing happened. He passed through both at once. And that wasn't all. Strangely, he felt himself overlapping. He was in many places at once, every place at once, and he found that there were parts of himself that, when they overlapped, made more of himself, and other places that, when he overlapped with himself, he disappeared.

This made no sense at all to him, so when he reappeared in human form, he looked suspiciously at the three ghosts in front of him.

"What was that?"

"See, definitely not a potato," Young said.

John felt he'd have to agree with that.

"Although technically potatoes can do that, too," de Broglie said.

"Don't confuse him," Young snapped back.

De Broglie lifted his hands. "I am simply attempting to be accurate."

"Well, you'll have your turn. We'll get there." Young turned to John. "Bring us a bowl of water."

John felt his leg muscles protest. "Is there anything else you'll need? Anything else I should get while I'm down there?"

"I don't think so."

"You're absolutely sure?"

"I can think of nothing else I might require."

John moved slowly to the stairs, glancing back over his shoulder a few times, but none of the ghosts thought of anything or moved to stop him.

Somewhere off in a distant part of the castle he could hear an ominous pounding, but he didn't give it too much thought.

He returned with a large bowl of water, only half of which he'd spilled on himself. Young instructed him make ripples in it with his fingertips.

"See how they expand outwards from your finger when you wiggle it?"

John nodded.

"Light is like that."

"Like water?"

"No, like the wave in water."

"Does it do the same thing but with air, then?"

"No," Maxwell interjected. "That's my bit. It's made of something else. It doesn't need water or air or anything at all to travel through."

"Wait your turn, Maxwell," Young admonished. "Now, John, make ripples with both your fingers at once." John did so. The waves bounced along, and where they overlapped, they made strange, complicated patterns.

"Those patterns," Young said, "are exactly what we see when light passes through two very narrow, very closely spaced slits. Or even though a single narrow slit. That is how we know that light is not like a potato."

Among other ways, John thought. But he was impressed.

"My turn," de Broglie interrupted. "Light is a wave, as is everything else."

"What?" John said, flabbergasted.

"Yes, technically nothing is a potato. Or, just a potato, rather."

This was too much for John, so he just nodded politely.

"Well, that was me. You're up, Maxwell."

194

Maxwell grinned and stepped up to John, who was still completely confused. "I fear I will only confuse you more, but you asked an important question earlier. You asked if light travelled through air."

At least he was at the point where he could ask intelligent questions, John thought. That was something.

"What does it travel through?" he asked.

"It doesn't need anything to travel through. It is its own thing. It is made up of two parts. These two parts change, and in changing, create one another. So, light is first one then the other, and in this way, it travels along through the universe, the fastest thing in the universe."

"Oh. I see." He didn't really, but he doubted it would get clearer.

Just then an enormous crash came from below. John looked down and realized the front gates were on fire and had just collapsed, bashed in by a large battering ram, which was also on fire. The townspeople were now storming in over it, shouting and throwing things. He'd better do something. The soldiers were still under orders not to hurt anyone.

"What is my final test?" John asked. "I need to free you now, before things down there get any worse."

"Oh. No final test," Young said.

"What?"

"We didn't get around to making one up."

"But you've been standing around playing cards all night."

"You don't need one. You can burn the candle all the way to the end now."

"But what if I'm not ready?"

195

"Then letting us free will kill you."

"Er, isn't there some way for me to practice first?"

"No."

John twiddled his thumbs. Down below, the people were inside the castle now, ransacking and setting things on fire. It seemed unlikely that he could sneak out past them. And he did want to free the five light mages. It was an opportunity to do a real heroic deed. Too good to pass up.

"What do I have to do?"

"You must be stronger than the candle. So, light it, but don't let it transform you. Use what you know about light to keep yourself human."

John didn't give himself time to think. He picked up the box of matches and the grubby, melted end of the candle and lit the wick.

Again, the white, clear flame blossomed on the end, and John felt its pull as it tried to transform him. He sensed the waves of energy coming off it, even with his eyes shut tightly. He found that, even with his eyes closed, he could see everything.

The candle glowed brighter, but John held on, willing himself to stay human. Underneath the light, he began to sense something else. A darkness. Two dark shapes, struggling to get out. The candle was burning down. John tipped it slightly to the side so that the wax ran onto the stones below. At last, it was so short that he couldn't hold it anymore and he set it on the cobble stones. The light grew brighter and brighter, shining through him with a horrible intensity, but he held on to himself.

"I am a potato," he thought.

The candle went out. And the first dark thing crept out from it. It was a shadowy image—his parents, leaning over the edge of his cradle, smiling at himself as a baby. A servant girl came in. She brought them goblets of wine. Wait, he recognized that face. It was Griselda. He wanted to cry out to his parents, to warn them, but they drank the wine and fell to the ground. Griselda gathered up the cups and left.

There were tears in John's eyes. He was in a dark realm; there was nothing to hear or see now. He sensed somewhere the last nub of wax that had been the candle, but that was it. The ghosts were gone. John wanted to run. He wanted to find Griselda, imprison her, have her executed for her treason. Then he would order the soldiers to repel the invasion. He would put down the revolt and take control of the kingdom, as he should have done in the first place.

But he stayed. There was one dark thing left in the candle, and if he didn't release it the mages would remain trapped. He had promised to free them, and he needed to know what the final secret was. He focused his attention on the candle and waited.

The secret that crawled out was old. Many hundreds of years old. It had been trapped in the candle much longer than any of the five ghosts and much, much longer than the previous secret. John wanted to turn away as it came out. Its sightless eyes passed over him; its teeth glinted in the blackness. But John watched and waited. He saw his parents, then their parents, then their parents, looking just like they did in the portraits on the walls. They flashed one by one before his eyes, all the way back to King John the First. This King John grew younger; the crown disappeared from his forehead. As John watched, he saw his ancestor was not a prince, but an advisor to some other king and queen. He watched his ancestor betray this king and queen, watched the throne be taken from them. But a little daughter remained. She was snuck out of the castle, in the arms of a maid, and hidden away in the forest. This little girl grew up, had a child. That child grew up and had children in turn. Their children had children, all living in a tiny village in a forest at the edge of the kingdom. Until John saw Griselda.

The secret faded away into mist, and light returned. John stood on the top of the tallest tower, swaying. He was dimly aware of the faint sounds of a battle raging far below him.

He turned and saw the ghosts were no longer ghosts but men; powerful mages who stood before him.

"Thank you for freeing us," Young said.

"Yes, you did well," Maxwell said, his moustache twitching.

"Indeed, quite well," de Broglie said.

"You are now truly a light mage," Einstein said.

There was a pause in which Einstein elbowed Snell.

"Good job," Snell muttered.

There was an uncomfortable silence, then Einstein broke in. "Now, would you like our help quelling this rebellion?"

John considered this. He felt the new power he had over the light, and he knew these five powerful mages would help him. He could rule the kingdom, maybe make it better than any of his ancestors had before him. But then he thought of Griselda.

Because of her, he had grown up without parents, with no one to teach him how to be a king. But she had also protected him, helped him, taught him things herself. And she, too, had been wronged, many years ago, by his own ancestors. John didn't think he could forgive her, but he knew he was not a very good king. Griselda had been a good leader; she had ruled the kingdom well in his stead. And now he had learned that she was in some ways the rightful queen. It was her family, many generations ago, who were the true rulers of Amrath.

John knew what he had to do.

Without saying anything, he descended the steps of the tower for the last time. He went straight to the throne room, where the soldiers stood in a line, their spears pointed at the villagers, who were attempting to break through.

John held up his hands, and light shone from them. White light shot from his fingers and illuminated every corner of the throne room. The soldiers and villagers alike turned to stare at him, their eyes dazzling. Out of the corner of his eye, John saw Griselda enter the room.

"Good people of Amrath," John began. As they were currently looting and burning the castle, this form of address confused them. "I am sorry. I've been a terrible king. However, I've just learned that I'm not actually the rightful king. Griselda is. Or queen rather. No need to continue that terrible tradition."

Griselda stared at him, her mouth open. The townspeople weren't sure what to do.

John removed his crown, walked over to Griselda, and placed it on her head. Some of the townspeople put down their weapons. Someone clapped uncertainly.

"Griselda will be a much better queen for you than I was."

There was some more polite, confused clapping. John turned to Griselda.

"Um, your turn. How do we get them to leave?"

Griselda shook herself and straightened her shoulders. "Well, thank you, everyone, for coming," she said. The townspeople looked even more confused. "Tomorrow I'll hold court here in the throne room to hear your grievances. Please come back tomorrow."

There was some grumbling, but this seemed fair. Griselda had always been popular. The peasants picked up their pitchforks and left.

When they were alone, John turned to Griselda.

"I saw what you did," he said, and Griselda looked down at the floor.

"I'm so sorry," she said. "I've wanted to tell you."

At that instant, there was a loud pop, and the sorceress appeared. No longer did she appear as an old woman. Now she was young with a strangely ancient face, glowing with bright purple light.

"Your family have all been terrible for this kingdom. Griselda didn't know what she was doing. I poisoned those goblets and gave them to her to give to your parents," the sorceress admitted. "I wanted you out of the way, too, but Griselda, when she learned what I'd done, wouldn't hear of it. She protected you. She insisted I give you a chance to learn the truth."

"Is this true?" John asked.

Griselda nodded.

John, relieved that he hadn't just given the kingdom to a murderer, sighed. "Well, good. You'll make a much better king—queen—than I would have. I didn't really want to be king anyway."

"Thank you," Griselda said. "I'm sorry. Even though I didn't know what I was doing. I still have wished every day that I hadn't done it."

"Thank you for giving me the opportunity to learn the truth," John said and felt pleased with himself. That was something a noble knight in a story might have said.

John smiled at Griselda, who smiled back.

Einstein appeared behind them, wheezing. "Those are terrible stairs," he gasped. "No wonder you complained so much."

The other light mages filed in behind him, eyeing the sorceress warily.

"And we were simply descending," de Broglie said. "The ascension must be even more arduous."

"We were stuck in a candle for several hundred years," Snell said, pointing to John. "He's been out walking around."

John laughed. He was no longer King John the Fifteenth, or even Prince John. Now he was just John. Well, John the light mage. Rider of the light. And dragons. If he could find any.

That same evening, John and the sorceress and the light mages helped Griselda take down the fourteen portraits on the wall, revealing behind them a large painting of a nice-looking family. Griselda's ancestors.

From then on, Queen Griselda ruled Amrath wisely and well. The kingdom flourished, and she was known far and wide as the greatest ruler the kingdom had ever had. She had help, though, from her six court mages, who travelled the kingdom, bringing light and truth wherever they went. John moved the portraits of his ancestors to a little-used summer cottage and visited them occasionally. And everyone lived happily ever after.

THE END

THE PHYSICS

THE SPEED OF LIGHT

PART of the inspiration for this story comes from a famous story about Albert Einstein. Einstein was famous for his thought experiments, where he would, without doing any calculations, imagine something, and see what ideas popped out. In one of these thought experiments, he imagined that he was riding a beam of light, and from there all these amazing ideas about time dilation came out. That's how special relativity was born.

But before you get into any of that, you need to know the basics. The first thing you must know is that the speed of light is, as far as we know, the fastest anything in the universe can go. In a vacuum, (meaning in empty space), light travels at approximately 300,000,000 meters per second (m/s), or 186,000 miles per second. We call this speed "c".

The whole circumference of the earth is about 25,000 miles. So, if it were able to curve, light could go all the way around the earth nearly 8 times in one second.

The distance from the Earth to the moon is about 239,000 miles, meaning it takes light less than two seconds to get there.

 ## TRY THIS:

There are a lot of fun things to think about here, in terms of whether the speed of light is the fastest anything can go. Try watching this minute physics video and see what you think of his argument: How to Break the Speed of Light.

Is the dot of the laser pointer really breaking the speed of light? Can you think of any other ways of trying to break the speed of light?

After you've thought about it, watch this Veritasium video: Will This go Faster than Light?

This Vsauce video, too, talks about some of the same ideas, in a really entertaining way: What is The Speed of Dark?

COLOR

Now let's talk about some of the properties of light. First off, what is color? Well, basically, different colors of light are different energies of light.

We need to talk about some properties of waves at this point. Specifically, frequency and wavelength. I'm going to get into a little math here. You can skip over this part if math isn't your thing or you haven't taken algebra, and the following stuff will still make sense. Having the math just gives a deeper understanding.

Because light is a wave, it has a wavelength. A wave is just a repeating pattern, and the wavelength is the distance that it takes for that pattern to repeat. For example, in this wave:

The wavelength is the distance from one peak to the next:

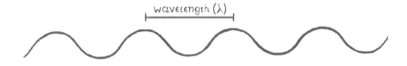

The wavelength is the distance the wave goes before it starts to repeat the same pattern over again. Notice the symbol in parentheses after the word wavelength. That is the Greek letter lambda, and it is the symbol we use to represent wavelength.

Because light is a wave, it has a wavelength. The wavelength of visible light is so short that it's measured in nanometers (nm). There are 1,000,000,000 nanometers in one meter.

Light also has a frequency. Frequency is just how quickly a wave repeats. It is measured in cycles per second. Does it take one second for the wave to go down and back up again? If so, the frequency is one, because the wave goes through one cycle each second. If it takes half a second for the wave to go down and back up again, then the frequency is two. (Because the wave travels through two cycles in one second.)

In physics, the unit we use to measure frequency is the Hertz (Hz), pronounced "hurts". If a wave has a frequency of 2 Hz, it means that it goes through two cycles every second.

The speed, frequency, and wavelength are all related. This makes sense, because speed is just how much distance we travel in a given amount of time. Speed is how many meters something travels every second. Wavelength is the distance travelled in each cycle, and frequency is how many of those cycles we go through every second. So, if I multiply them together, I get the speed. This gives us this equation:

$$V = \lambda \cdot f$$

Here, v stands for velocity, which is measured in meters per second (m/s), lambda stands for wavelength, which is measured in meters (m), and f stands for frequency, which is measured in Hertz (Hz). So, the speed of a wave is equal to its wavelength multiplied by its frequency.

For light waves—and sound waves, and many other types of waves—because the velocity is generally constant, the frequency and wavelength are related. The higher the frequency, the shorter the wavelength. (In math, we would say that wavelength and frequency are 'inversely proportional'.)

OK, now that we've got those math fundamentals out of the way, we can talk about the fun stuff. Different colors of light are different frequencies of light. It's exactly the same as sound. Sound is also a wave (although a different type). With sound, the higher the frequency, the higher the pitch. The lower the frequency, the lower the pitch.

Similarly, with light, different frequencies/wavelengths give us different colors.

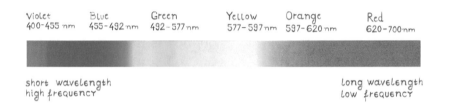

You can see that red light is made up of lower frequencies than blue light. The figure above is called the 'visible spectrum' because it's the wavelengths and colors that we can see. However, this spectrum keeps going. Past the red side is light with even longer wavelengths and lower frequencies. Once we go past red, we get to infrared light, then microwaves, then radio waves. All of these are just light waves that we can't see.

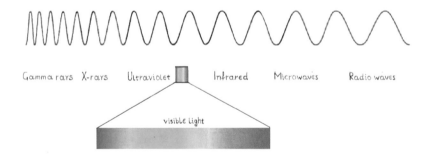

On the other side, past the blue part of the spectrum, we get to light with even shorter wavelengths and higher frequencies. These are ultraviolet light, then x-rays, then gamma rays. You might have heard these called "electromagnetic radiation," but that's just another name for light rays.

The way we see and perceive color is fascinating. First off, white light is a mixture of all the colors of light. Different objects absorb different colors of light. White objects reflect all (or most) of the colors, which is why white or light-colored cars don't get as hot in the sun as dark-colored cars do. Green objects absorb all the wavelengths of light except green. The green light gets reflected, and that's what we see.

So, color is really a process of subtraction. If you see something orange, it means that every color except orange was absorbed by that object.

REFLECTION

Here's a fun brain teaser. How tall of a mirror do you need to have to be able to see all of yourself in it at once? (Meaning, if you're six feet tall, how tall does your mirror need to be? Can it be any size?) I'll tell you how reflection works first, then you can think about it a little before I give you the answer.

So, we already know that light travels in a straight line. In the story, I had John riding the light in straight lines, and then bouncing off various objects. He wasn't totally clear how that was working because it was all happening too fast, but he had a sense that he was sort of glancing off things.

Here's how it works: it depends on what angle you hit something at. If you hit it at a very shallow angle, you'll bounce off at a shallow angle. If you hit it near dead-on, then you'll bounce out the same way, too. If you hit a surface exactly dead on, you'll bounce back exactly the way you came.

The way we say this in physics is "The angle of incidence equals the angle of reflection." The "angle of incidence" is a fancy way of saying the angle you hit something at. The only slightly weird part about this is how we measure the angles. You'd think we'd measure them from the surface, but we don't. We measure the angles from something called a "Normal Line". See the picture below to get a better idea of what I mean by this:

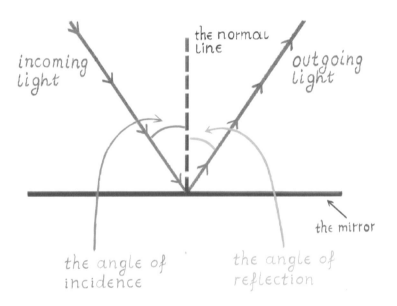

See how the incoming light comes down, hits the mirror, and then bounces off again? The dotted line is the normal line. In math, the word normal means perpendicular (or something that intersects at a right angle, a 90-degree angle). So, a normal line is just a line that is perpendicular to the mirror or surface we're talking about.

Now, the other piece of the puzzle you need to figure out the mirror brainteaser I gave you is that for us to see something, light has to go from the object, bounce off the mirror, and hit our eye.

I'll give you the answer on the next page, so think about it for a second before you continue if you want to.

Ok, here's someone standing in front of a mirror:

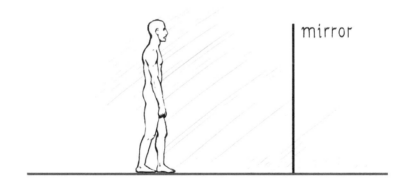

To make this easier, I'm just going to pretend their eyes are basically at the exact top of their head. Now, they can see their eyes by looking straight ahead, right? Light bounces off their eyes, goes straight to the mirror, then bounces back to their eyes again, like so:

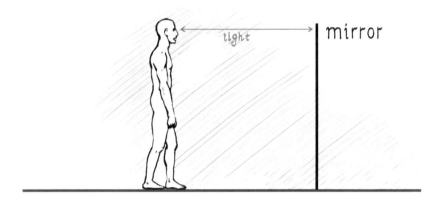

But what about their feet? How do they see their feet? Light has to bounce off their feet, bounce off the mirror, and then bounce into their eyes, like this:

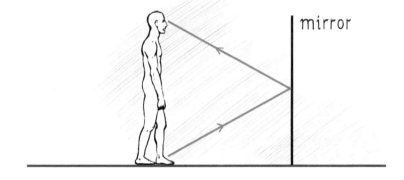

The place where the light from their feet bounces off the mirror is exactly in the midpoint of the mirror. If we wanted to be really fancy, we could prove this with geometry, like this:

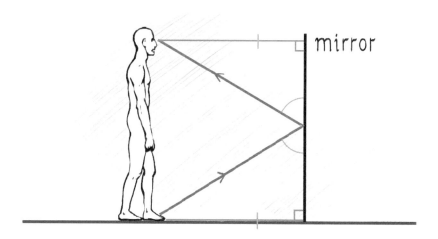

(You can ignore this part if you haven't taken geometry.) Here's the fancy geometry proof, though: the two blue triangles are the same. They each have a ninety-degree angle. Also, the two angles where the light bounces off are the same (because we know that's how light works). Also, this person's feet are the same distance from the mirror as their face is (assuming they're standing up straight). We know that if two triangles have two angles the same and one side that's the same, then they are the exact same shape (we call this being 'congruent' in math). So, therefore, the remaining sides must be the same:

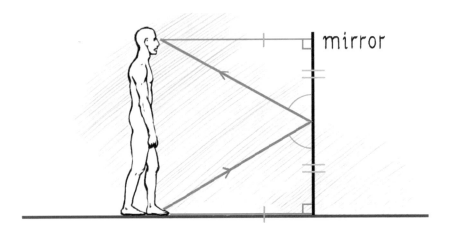

Meaning, the light from their feet hits the mirror in the exact middle. Their shins, by the same argument, are reflected a little higher on the mirror than that. Their arms are somewhere in between their feet and their head.

So, they never need to use the bottom half of the mirror at all. So, the answer to the riddle is that you only need a mirror that is half as tall as you are to see your whole self. This seems crazy, but it's true.

Also, here's another counter-intuitive thing. If you back up while you're looking at a mirror, will you be able to see more of yourself? Think about it, maybe draw some pictures, then go try it.

SNELL AND THE LAW OF REFRACTION

Willebrord Snell was born in 1580 in the Netherlands, and he gave us the law of refraction, which tells us how light bends as it goes through different mediums.

In the story, when John is a beam of light, he shoots from the air into the water. He finds that when he hits the water he turns deeper into the water. This bending of the light beam is called "refraction".

This bending happens because light travels at different speeds in different mediums. For example, when it travels through water, it only travels at approximately 225,563,909 m/s instead if 300,000,000 m/s.

In physics, we keep track of this with something called the "index of refraction" or "n". The speed of light in a vacuum (which we call 'c') divided by the speed of light in the medium, gives us the index of refraction. Here's the equation:

$$\frac{c}{v} = n$$

The bigger the value of 'n', the slower the speed of light in that medium. For example, diamond has an index of refraction of about 2.417. Water has an index of refraction of about 1.33. So, light travels more slowly through diamond than through water.

The example I gave in the story for why light bends when it travels though different mediums was the honey on the slide, but more common examples involve lawn mowing or vacuuming. For example, imagine you're vacuuming across a carpet, but there's a hardwood floor or a tile floor or something next to you. Imaging that you push the vacuum onto the floor, like this:

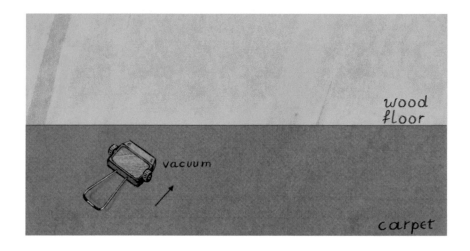

Notice that the left-hand wheel will hit first. The wheels slide more easily on the wood floor than on the carpet, so for that split-second when the left wheel is on the wood floor and the right wheel is on the carpet, the left side will be going faster, so you'll turn to the right.

Light does the exact same thing. Let's take a look at a beam of light entering a pool:

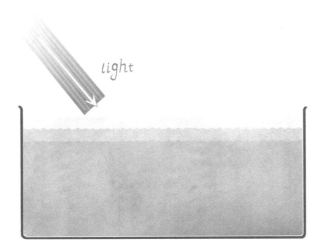

Here, I've drawn the light beam really wide, just to exaggerate the effect. Notice that the bottom side of the light beam is hitting the water before the top side. The light will travel more slowly in the water, so now the bottom side is going to slow down, kind of like it's dragging on the light beam, turning it more deeply into the water.

This refraction is responsible for all kinds of optical illusions. Like, if you put a pencil into a glass of water so that it's half submerged, you'll notice that the top half of the pencil doesn't appear to line up with the bottom half of the pencil.

Snell's Law gives us a way to calculate exactly how much a beam of light will bend upon going into a new medium. Here's the equation:

$$n_1 \, Sin \, \theta_1 = n_2 \, Sin \, \theta_2$$

Where:

n_1 = index of refraction of 1st medium

θ_1 = angle of incidence

n_2 = index of refraction of 2nd medium

θ_2 = angle of refraction

You may already know this, but the circle with the line through it is the Greek letter "theta" which we use to represent any angle. Again, we measure all the angles against the normal line.

This equation allows us to calculate the angle that a light beam will travel at when it enters a new medium. See the picture below for a more visual representation of what this equation means:

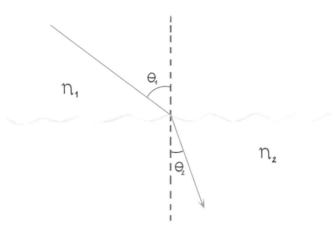

In this picture, I'm imagining a beam of light travelling from air into water. N_1 would be the index of refraction of air (1), and n_2 would be the index of refraction of water (1.33). If I knew the angle of incidence, I could then use the equation to calculate the angle of refraction.

TRY THIS

You can get a feel for this by trying out the Phet Simulation from the University of Colorado called Bending Light. Try clicking on the 'prisms' one at the bottom and play around with some of the prisms. Also, try turning on reflections. When light goes into a new medium, some of it goes in but some of it reflects, too. This simulation ignores that unless you turn on reflections.

ELECTROMAGNETIC WAVES

In 1801, Thomas Young performed an extremely famous experiment which is usually today called "Young's Double Slit Experiment". In the story, I had Young demonstrate this for John, and you can try this, too, if you have a laser pointer. Just cut two slits close together (as close as possible; around a millimeter apart) and shine the light at them. What you should see on the other side is something like this:

This was an amazing result, because if light were a particle (or a potato), it wouldn't do this. The pattern should have looked like this:

If light were made up of particles, then the pattern of light would have just been two bright spots, one behind each of the slits. Here's why this happens: as light goes through a slit, it acts just like a water wave going through a hole in a wall. The water waves would move outwards, like ripples on a pond:

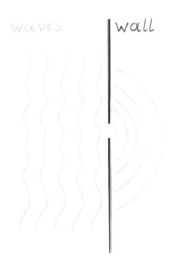

This (the way that waves expand out from their source) is called diffraction. Weirdly, light does the same thing. If the slit is narrow enough, the light diffracts outwards as it passes through. If we have two slits, the waves bump into each other as they expand, like this:

Where the waves overlap, we get a complicated pattern of new waves, which is called an 'interference pattern'. The same thing happens with light, which is why we get the alternating bright and dark spots, rather than just two bright spots, and it was evidence for light being more than just a particle.

Even more weirdly, light is not the only thing that does this. All particles do this. Now we're getting into quantum mechanics, but electrons have been demonstrated to do this, too. Technically, all matter can be described as waves, or having wave-like properties.

Einstein contributed to this idea with his paper on the photoelectric effect in 1904, which demonstrated how light can knock electrons loose from metal, and de Broglie is credited with this equation (the de Broglie equation), which gives the relationship between the momentum of any piece of matter and its wavelength:

$$p = \frac{h}{\lambda}$$

Here, p stands for the momentum of a particle, h is something called Planck's Constant, which is 6.6x10^-34, and lambda is the wavelength of the particle. So, you could technically calculate your own wavelength.

Once we knew that light behaved like a wave, people were confused because light travels through space and, as far as we knew, there wasn't anything out there to travel through. All other waves we know of, like water waves or sound waves or vibrations in the ground, they all need some medium to travel through. This is why in space you can't hear anything. There's no air for the sound to travel through. But light from the sun gets to us just fine.

Initially, in the late 1800's, people guessed that there must be something out there for light to travel through. They called this the "luminiferous aether", which is an awesome name. (Also, it's sometimes spelled 'ether'.) They thought that maybe space was full of this stuff, and that light was propagating through it.

However, in 1887 a very famous experiment, the Michelson-Morely experiment, showed that this was not the case. (Basically, because the earth is shooting around the sun, we should be travelling really quickly through this magical ether. It would be kind of like sitting in the middle of a river with the water flowing around you. Boats travelling upriver should be slower than boats travelling across the river. Similarly, light flowing in the opposite direction as the ether should have been slower than light travelling with the ether or across the current. Michelson and Morely basically set up a race between two light beams, one travelling with the expected "current" and one travelling across the "current," and they tied.)

So, if light wasn't travelling through ether, how was it getting through the vacuum of space? Well, the answer is pretty insane, and it has to do with electricity and magnets.

Magnets have something around them called a magnetic field. You can see the effects of this field when magnets attract pieces of metal. Also, charges, like static electricity, have fields around them. You can see this when a sock sticks to another sock after coming out of the dryer. The socks are charged, and so they attract (or repel, depending on the charge).

In 1865, James Clerk Maxwell published a paper entitled "A Dynamical Theory of the Electromagnetic Field". In this paper, he described one of the most amazing physics discoveries ever made. (Maxwell is often described as one of the greatest physicists of all time, ranked after only Newton and Einstein.) These are his equations:

$$\nabla \cdot E = \frac{\rho}{\varepsilon_0}$$

$$\nabla \cdot B = 0$$

$$\nabla \times E = -\frac{\partial B}{\partial t}$$

$$\nabla \times B = \mu_0 \left(J + \varepsilon_0 \frac{\partial E}{\partial t} \right)$$

You may have seen people wearing t-shirts with these equations on them. This is because they're amazing. You need to have taken Calculus to understand them, and that's beyond the scope of what I want to cover here, but basically, what they mean is that if you change a magnetic field, that change creates an electric field. This is how hydroelectric power works. And wind power. Both of these just use forces in nature to turn a turbine. The spinning part usually has a magnet of some kind on it inside a coil of wires. The spinning magnet creates a changing magnetic field. This changing magnetic field creates an electric field, which pushes electrons (charges) around, which creates current.

But the fun doesn't end there. He also demonstrated that a changing electric field also creates a magnetic field. This is how electromagnets work. And how those old Morse code tapping devices worked. If you put a current through a coil of wire, and then change that current, a magnetic field gets created. The magnetic field acts exactly like there was a magnet there inside the coil of wire.

OK, now for the really insane part. Light is basically just those two things combined. A changing magnetic field creates a changing electric field which creates a changing magnetic field. And so on and so on forever. And it's the fastest thing in the universe, and it travels billions of miles through the vacuum of space, totally unassisted by any medium. And we use it to see.

The speed of light can be calculated using constants that were derived from electric and magnetic equations. I don't know how amazing anyone else thinks that is, but I was totally blown away when I learned that.

That is why light is called an electromagnetic wave. Because it is a wave that is made up of changing electric and magnetic fields.

And that's about it. Light is an electromagnetic wave which propagates incredibly quickly. The different colors we see are the different energies/wavelengths/frequencies of light, and there are lot more that we can't see. Radio waves are also light, as are x-rays and microwaves. All of these light rays travel in straight lines, but they slow down when they enter different mediums, which causes them to bend or reflect.

The constancy of the speed of light is also the jumping off point for the theory of relativity, and the wave nature of light is a jumping off point for quantum physics, both of which I'll tackle in other fairy tales.

Conceptual Practice Questions

1. If you shine red light onto a blue piece of paper, what color will the piece of paper appear to be?

2. Why does a mirror swap left and right but not up and down? (Meaning, if you look at yourself in the mirror, your right hand becomes your mirror image's left hand.)

3. If you see an image of a person reflected off a car window, how can you tell where they are?

4. Why can we see through glass?

5. Why is it hard to tell exactly where something underwater is, if you're looking at it from above the water?

6. When light travels from diamond into air, does it bend further from the normal, or closer to the normal?

7. If you put a diamond underwater, does light bend more or less when going from the water into the diamond, compared to how much it bent when it went from air into the diamond?

8. What are some examples of waves in everyday life?

Conceptual Questions Answer Key

1. It will appear black. The blue paper reflects blue light and absorbs red light. So, if you only shine red light on it all the light will be absorbed, and it will appear black.

2. This is a little bit of a trick question. It is more about the way the terms left and right work, rather than anything about mirrors. The mirror doesn't really swap side-to-side. Your hand closer to the right side of the mirror is still closer to what (from your perspective) is the right side of the mirror. What's happened is that the image of yourself in front of you has been turned around. So, from your image's perspective, what was your right hand is now their left hand.

3. Imagine tracing a straight line from your eyes straight to where you see the image on the window. Then, based on the angle that the surface is at, remembering that the angle it comes in at has to be the same as the angle it bounces off at, imagine tracing a line in the new direction.

4. We can see through glass because light travels through it.

5. It's hard to locate things underwater if you're above the water because the light leaving the water bends. Our eyes assume that the light went in a straight line (because that's what it usually does) so we think it came from a different place than it actually did.

6. When light travels from diamond into air, it is travelling from a slower medium to a faster medium, so it bends away from the normal.

7. When you put the diamond underwater, the light bends less because the speed difference between water and diamond is less than the speed difference between air and diamond.

8. Water waves, sound waves, vibrations through floors/walls. Also, if you take a jump rope and flick it and watch the bump travel along the rope, that's a wave. Earthquakes are waves travelling through the ground.

GRAVITY: A FAIRY TALE

Chapter One:
Too Many Kitchens

ONCE upon a time, there was a girl called Worry. On the day Worry was born, her fairy godmother appeared, pronounced her name, and then promptly disappeared. She was never heard from again.

This caused many problems for Worry.

Worry grew up in a magic castle, a school for those named by the fairies. It was run by the last remaining Scholar Knight, a formidable woman named Fortitude Knightward.

"Fort for short," she said briskly whenever she introduced herself.

However, because Worry apparently no longer had a fairy godmother, she was not allowed to use magic.

Her sister, Hope, was allowed to use magic. She had a fairy godmother, a pink sparkly, kindly one named Rose who baked her sugar cookies every time she faced a challenge.

Hope always shared the cookies.

For several years, Fort taught Hope how to use magic, and Worry wandered the castle alone.

When Worry was five years old, she ran away, determined to find her fairy godmother. She set out with a great deal of confidence and almost no supplies. The first night, she ran out of both food and water. Soaked by unexpected rain, she huddled under a tree, shivering.

Over the chattering of her teeth, she heard something approaching through the woods. She caught the flash of an eye and what looked like fangs in the moonlight.

Her heart thundering, her hands shaking, she stared at the darkness where she'd seen the eye, pressing her back against the tree.

A wildcat materialized out of the darkness. Its eyes locked on her and it lowered its head, crouching and slinking towards her. She swung her empty bag at it and ran. It snarled, its paws tangled in the straps, and then gave chase. She threw herself through the forest, stumbling over fallen logs and scrambling through clumps of ferns, the cat right on her heels, until she careened over a cliff.

For a brief moment she felt weightless. She caught a glimpse of moonlight through a gap in the clouds, then tumbled several feet onto the rocky shore below. She heard the creature's claws scrape the stones of the cliff as it leapt after her. Closing her eyes, she curled herself into a tiny ball, bracing for impact.

Fortitude Knightward appeared in a burst of glowing light, wielding a silver sword, fighting back the creature.

Worry's arm burned with pain, but she watched in awe as Fort swung her sword in a glittering arc with one hand, sending out spirals of glowing green light with the other. Fort's fairy godmother, Fern, darted this way and that, directing the energy.

At last, the creature ran. Fort turned, barely out of breath, and knelt by Worry's side.

"I'm sorry, Worry," she said, not meeting her eyes as she bent over Worry's arm, gently healing it. "I know this is hard for you."

Worry gasped and swallowed back tears. Her throat was thick. She'd made a mess. Just like usual. She hadn't found her fairy godmother; she hadn't even lasted a single night out alone.

She wanted to do what her sister could do. She knew she could do it, if they would only give her the chance.

But maybe there's something wrong with me, she thought. She wasn't like Hope. Hope was always optimistic, always helping people, lifting them up. She was always working hard. If she'd run away from home, she would have thought to bring supplies. What good was worrying to anyone, anyway?

Fort cleared her throat.

"I've been thinking. There are so many enchanted objects in the castle, and . . . I just don't have time to care for them. Would you . . . maybe . . . be willing to do that?"

234

Worry looked up suspiciously. The ache in her arm dulled, but her heart burned in her chest. *She's just trying to make me feel better.*

But Fort's expression was earnest.

It was true, there were a lot of enchanted objects in the castle, with no one to take care of them.

A lot of them were very interesting.

"Could I have my own keys?" She pointed to the iron ring hanging from Fort's belt.

Fort pursed her lips.

"Just to a few places?" Worry pressed. "Like the libraries?"

"I . . . suppose . . . as caretaker, you'd need to have your own set. To just a few places."

Worry sat up, barely noticing the pain in her arm now. There were several places in the castle she'd been curious about. More than one locked door. There was a whole room of hats, each with different magical properties. Fort had told them not to touch them, but . . . if she were caretaker . . .

Fort tilted her head, smiling at her as if reading her thoughts. She gripped Worry's shoulder, then patted it a few times.

"Very good. Well. Should we make our way back home, then?"

Worry stood, brushing some of the mud and leaves off her clothes, and nodded.

Fort gave her shoulder another firm, approving pat. She conjured a glowing ball of light and led the way along the dark beach.

Worry stared at the glowing sphere, her heart aching.

Someday, she vowed, she would go looking for her fairy godmother again. And when she did, she would be prepared.

If the only thing she could do was take care of the castle's enchanted objects, then that's what she would do.

And, for seven years, that's what Worry did.

The castle was clearly trying to be helpful. A gold-embossed sign affixed to the castle wall read "Restroom" with an arrow pointing to the left. But Worry knew better than to believe it.

She continued down the stone passage. Another sign pointing to the right read "Definitely a bathroom." It pointed to a kitchen.

A herd of silverware galloped past, pursued by a soup ladle. She turned left to avoid the Infinite Loop Corridor and cut through the Hall of Mirrors.

This was an enormous stone room with a vaulted ceiling lit by floating chandeliers. The walls were hung with ancient silver mirrors of all shapes and sizes. One showed what she'd looked like three days ago, another what she might look like in thirty years, another what she absolutely would never look like (today an iguana blinked back at her.) Honestly, it was slightly disappointing to know she'd never be an iguana.

In one corner, a tiny spoon brandished a toothpick at her from the edges of the labyrinth it had built out of corks. In the center was its prized possession, a single olive.

She paused to rummage in her pockets. Where was it? No, that was the pocket where she kept her coin collection. That was the pocket with the copies she'd made of Fortitude Knightward's keys (the ones Fort *hadn't* shared with her). That was her telescope pouch. And her leather sheath holding the maps she'd sketched of the castle, including its many secret passageways.

Ah. There it is.

The spoon danced right and left, ducking and weaving as she approached. When she bent down, it skittered away, crouching behind the tiny cork wall.

She placed the object at the entrance and moved back. The spoon darted out again but stopped when it saw her gift. Another olive. It poked the olive a few times, then did a little hopping dance, scooted it onto its head, and carted it off. Worry giggled and continued on her way.

Unfortunately, the bathroom she was most familiar with had also become a kitchen now.

She frowned, scratching the back of her head and surveying the clean new tile and copper pots hanging from the ceiling.

A crash echoed down the hallway, followed by a wail of frustration.

Worry sprinted down the hall and slid around the corner. Her sister lay collapsed on the ground.

Hope sprawled face-up, her silver hair covering her face, her pink gown pooled around her. Her fairy godmother, Rose, flitted around trailing pink sparkles.

"Marvelous, Hope, just marvelous," the fairy said, in her high, warm voice. "You're doing so well. That was amazing, darling."

Hope groaned. "It's still a kitchen."

"Oh, yes, I do see that, but it's an absolutely lovely one. Would you look at that oven! You could roast five turkeys in there!"

"I'm the worst student ever," Hope moaned.

"Well now, dear, I don't think that's quite—"

"Technically, you're the best student," Worry said.

Hope sat up, her shoulders sagging. "Oh, hey, Worry. That's kind of you, but . . . I just can't get any of this right."

"I mean, technically you're the only student, so right off the bat you're automatically the best. But even despite that, you know you're doing great. Even Fort says so."

Hope shrugged and looked down at her hands clasped in her lap. "Thanks. And I'm sorry, I shouldn't be complaining."

Worry contemplated her sister.

"How long have you been working on this?"

"Oh . . . umm . . ."

Worry turned to Rose. "How long has she been working on this?"

"Eleven hours and fourteen minutes!" Rose said brightly.

Worry took her sister's hand and hauled her to her feet. "Time for a break, then."

Her stomach twinged. She really needed to find an actual bathroom.

"You don't happen to know if there's a bathroom still left around here, do you?"

Hope slumped. "No! They keep turning into kitchens! All of them!" She glared at the gleaming copper fittings and well-stocked spice rack. "This one was so close, but it flipped at the last minute. I don't know what's wrong with this castle." She paused. "Or me."

Worry hesitated for a moment, then forged ahead. "Let me help."

Hope froze, glanced at her, then looked up and down the hall. "You can't." She said it flatly. It was the answer she always gave.

"You said you almost had it, though," Worry said, sensing an opportunity. "Rose is here. And you'd be doing most of it. I'd just help. A tiny, tiny amount."

Rose clenched her wand. "You're really not allowed. Not without a fairy godmother." She flitted anxiously back and forth. "But . . . it might be fine. Yes, I think so . . . Perhaps I should ask someone. But that could take weeks to hear back . . . No, I'm sure it's . . . fine."

Hope chewed her lips. She gave the kitchen a resentful look. "Okay, let's do it. But only help a little."

"Of course."

"And don't tell Fort."

"Never."

Hope wiped her palms on her skirts and rolled her shoulders.

"Wonderful!" Rose trilled. "Teamwork! The most noble and . . . and . . . well, that's wonderful. Assuming it doesn't go horribly awry. Which it shouldn't. I think."

Worry's heart pounded. She was going to do actual magic. She could do it; she knew she could. All this keeping her back, refusing to train her, it was silly. She mimicked Hope, rolling her shoulders and cracking her neck.

Hope whispered some quick instructions. Worry moved to stand next to her sister, and they faced the kitchen together. Rose hovered between them.

Together, they lifted their hands. Worry's fingertips tingled. Her sister's hands were full of glowing spheres of pink light. There, at the ends of her own fingertips, were tiny blue sparkles. Worry's mouth opened in wonder, which turned to a grin as she caught sight of her sister's excited smile. Hope lifted her eyebrows and together they turned back to their task. Worry's stomach felt like a hot air balloon, warm and glowing and lifting up into the stars.

"What do you think you're doing?!" The shriek pierced her concentration, and the sparkles winked out.

She whirled around to see Fortitude Knightward striding towards them, looking livid.

Her green skirts snapped around her long legs. Her black hair, a cloud of tight curls, bobbed along with her. The leather scabbard belted to her waist swung wildly, its silver pommel and bright emerald flashing.

"What are you—how many times have I warned—" Her gaze sliced through them. Fern hovered calmly above Fort's head. "I can't believe—I just can't—Do you know what tomorrow night is?"

Hope hung her head, staring at the floor. "I'm so sorry, Fort. I . . . I forgot. I've been trying to fix—"

Fort made a strangled sound and took a few deep breaths. When she spoke again, her voice was clenched. "You are . . . working . . . very hard, Hope. I know it isn't easy. It's not easy to be the last of the Scholar Knights. I . . . I know it is a great deal of pressure. Believe me."

Worry couldn't help herself. "Please let me help, Fort. I know I can do it."

Fort massaged her temple, closed her eyes briefly, and then knelt to meet Worry's gaze. "I know you want to help. That's very noble of you. But . . ."

Fort paused, tilting her head, her eyes glazing over. "Did I . . . no . . . yes, I fixed that . . ." She shook her head. "Sorry, there's a lot on my mind."

She took a deep breath. "Where was I? Right. Like I said, the syzygy starts tomorrow. The alignment of the three moons. There hasn't been one since right before my time." A haunted look passed over Fort's face. "You know that the last time, it was nearly the end of the Scholar Knights."

"What happened, Fort?" Hope whispered.

Fort shook her head. "It's better not to . . . not to say. There were only a few knights left, after." She straightened. "But that is why you must be careful. You and I are all that remains."

"Let us help, Fort," Hope said, and Worry was grateful her sister had included her.

"Thank you, but no. I have been preparing for this for years. I have many defenses ready, and I've put out a call for help. You are children. You are very talented, Hope." At this, Hope straightened, her face glowed. "But you aren't ready. And you, Worry, I'm sorry. I know you want to help, and I do wish I could teach you. But you don't have a fairy godmother. You can't be a Scholar Knight. You'll never be one."

Worry's stomach curled into a tight, cold ball.

"Please, both of you. The best you can do is to stay out of the way. Go to your rooms. Lock your doors and let no one in. The syzygy will occur every night at midnight for three nights, as the red moon joins the others. You must stay inside until it's over."

Hope nodded. "Of course, Fort. We'll do that." She elbowed Worry, who gave a reluctant nod. "It'll be okay, Fort."

"Thank you, Hope."

Fort rose in a quick, fluid motion, glancing down the hall.

"Um, Fort?" Worry asked.

"Hmm?"

Worry pointed at the kitchen.

"Right." She gave a quick nod, pointed a single arm straight at the room, and curled her fingers as if gripping an invisible ball. A tight knot of green light appeared in her fist, hovered for a moment, and then, with a rushing sound much like a toilet flushing, shot into the kitchen and exploded.

The castle shook and Worry stumbled. When she regained her footing, she looked up. Where before there had been an open archway into a kitchen, there was now a tiny, understated brown door with a brass plaque reading "Restroom."

"Thanks, Fort!" Worry shouted as she pushed the door open and dashed inside. The door was still warm from Fort's magic.

Someday, Worry thought. *Someday I'll be able to do that, too.*

242

Writing Prompt:

Gravity is a complex topic that took many very smart people hundreds of years to figure out. And there's still so much we don't know about it!

Over the course of this story, we'll learn what scientists currently know about how gravity works. We'll learn about orbits, tides, and the scientists who investigated them (and the many misunderstandings and misconceptions they had along the way.)

To start, think about what you know about gravity so far. Spend 5 minutes journalling about whichever of these questions interests you the most: What is gravity? Is there gravity in space? What about on the moon? Do different things fall at different speeds, and if so, why? Does the Earth experience gravity? Does gravity always point down? What does gravity feel like? What does it mean to be weightless?

Chapter Two:
The Tapestry of
Travesties

WORRY strode the short distance across her room and paused at the open window. Dark waves lapped the shore far below. Shards of light from the castle's many windows glittered off the water. The night sky was clear and star filled.

On a balcony below, Worry could just make out Fort pacing back and forth, pausing every so often to bend down and peer through her long brass telescope. It was pointed straight at the moons. The blue and the green moons were already nearly aligned. Day and night they hung in the same place in the sky, like the multicolored eyes of a giant. The red moon lifted above the horizon and slowly rose to meet them. Worry shivered.

I can't just hide in my room.

"Fort told you to stay here, huh?" Kepler asked.

The silvery, translucent ghost-cat wound around her ankles, causing goose bumps to rise on her arms. He had a sharp, pointed moustache and beard and wore a ghostly white, puffy collar.

"Yeah." Worry propped her elbows on the window ledge and rested her chin on her fists.

Kepler hopped up to join her on the sill, his tail flicking back and forth. "I'm sorry. I know you want to help."

Her shoulders slumped and she thrust her hands into her pockets. "I just want to do something."

Kepler glanced around the room. Every shelf was crammed with magical objects in various stages of repair. There were also several large piles on the floor.

"You could always organize your room."

Worry followed his gaze. "What? Why would I do that? It's perfect. Look at all this awesome stuff."

She pulled a hat out of the middle of a pile, setting off a minor avalanche. Something popped, and the smell of burned marshmallows filled the room.

She put the hat on her head, and it turned into a wide-brimmed sun hat from which tiny raindrops fell, speckling her face.

"Ah yes. Of course. Very silly of me," Kepler said.

"I just hate not knowing what's going on," Worry continued as water dripped off her chin onto her clothes. "I'm tired of being . . . just the person who's around but not doing anything. The person who doesn't know what's going on. Who can't do magic and doesn't know what's happening and isn't allowed to help."

Kepler was silent for several moments. At last, he cleared his throat. "That is very hard." He paused again and appeared to be debating whether to tell her something.

"What are you thinking?" she asked.

"Oh nothing. Only . . . You're not the only one who doesn't know everything."

"I'm sorry, Kepler. I suppose no one tells you much, either."

He cleared his throat again. "Oh, that's not what I—I know a great many things."

Worry nodded, and the rain changed to little swirls of wind, tugging at her hair.

"No," Kepler said. He sounded like he was choosing his words very carefully. "I was actually referring to Fortitude."

Worry lifted an eyebrow. "Fort's a Scholar Knight. She knew the past scholars. She knows more than anyone else. She has the keys to every room in the castle." Although, to be fair, Worry now had all the keys, too.

Kepler scrunched up his face and ran his ghostly paws over his whiskers and moustache.

"Sometimes, we think we know things, but we don't," he said, his voice strained.

Worry returned the hat to its pile. "Is there something Fort doesn't know?"

Kepler's eyes got big. He opened and closed his mouth a few times.

"Did you know that a group of jellyfish is called a smack?" he said at last.

"Huh," Worry said. She was used to Kepler's tendency to inform her of various sea facts. "Nope. I suppose Fort doesn't know that. Er . . . is there a reason she should?"

A spider scuttled across the floor, and Kepler pounced on it. The spider paused, shivered, then continued its scuttling. He batted at it with his transparent paws, then frowned. Smoothing his moustache, he glanced back at Worry, then trotted over to the door. With a single quick glance at her and a raise of his eyebrows, he darted through it.

"Kepler?" she whispered. Having never had another cat, Worry wasn't sure if this was how they usually acted. She crossed the room and placed a palm on the door, leaning her ear towards it.

Fort said to stay inside.

Worry flipped the latch, turned the knob, and slipped out into the hall.

The ghost cat had his back towards her and was staring intently up the hall. He leapt up, spun around, clapped his paws, and trotted off down the passage. He paused at the end, glancing back at her. Confused, she followed him.

They wound through the cavernous halls, past five or six new kitchens, a cluster of teapots cuddled together and snoring in an armchair, and a sign pointing down a cobwebby set of stairs that read "Definitely Not a Dungeon". Kepler continued muttering sea facts to himself. At last, he stopped right in the middle of a passage. He turned around three times, then stared up at her looking frustrated.

"Where are we going, Kepler?"

"A . . . we're going to . . . a . . . a mantis shrimp can punch so hard it breaks . . . it breaks . . . glass."

"That . . . that is pretty impressive."

Kepler's eyes were wide and pleading, though, so she knelt.

"Did you know . . . that many species of fish . . . use the . . . the ceiling to navigate?" he said.

247

"The ceiling? Don't you mean the sky?"

Kepler gave the tiniest of nods. He meowed. "There's a way for you to get what you want," he said again. "Everyone wants . . . to be a fish. There are so many species of fish. Clown fish are protected by anemones. But anemones would sting other . . . fish. And sometimes there are caves that go to ceilings."

Worry frowned. What was a cave that went to a ceiling? "You mean like a tower? Like . . . the old Astronomy Tower?"

Kepler immediately turned and ran in the other direction, sprinting off down the tunnel, his tail held high.

That was weird, she thought. She chewed the inside of her cheek. Why would he want her to go to the old Astronomy tower?

At least I'd be doing something besides sitting around. Fort would be angry, that was for sure. It was also the one place in the castle Worry had not been able to explore. The door to it was sealed with magic. But maybe there was a way. Or maybe Worry was going to cause something awful to happen. But maybe that thought was just a worry.

Her thoughts were getting staircase-y. And not like a grand entrance to a ballroom or a steep purposeful set of stairs up to an attic full of delightful piles of interesting objects. More like a twisting, narrow, rickety set where every third board was rotten.

She needed to know how badly this could turn out. And for that, she needed to visit the Tapestry of Travesties. Some books said it showed warnings for the future, some said it showed whatever you feared most. Some said it tried to scare

248

you for its own amusement. When one couldn't get information, though, one could at least get harbingers of doom.

Worry felt that whatever its motives, it was better to have at least some information about what might be coming. But she tended to pay more attention to the ways things could go wrong than most people.

Her footsteps echoed in the empty halls, and she shivered. Silver symbols on the stone walls lit up as she passed, illuminating her path. Stars and planets, ancient bits of poetry.

She imagined what it would have been like, back when the halls were crowded with students and their fairy godmothers. All taking classes and learning to be knights. All with names like Courage or Elegance or Charity.

Even if I had a fairy godmother, would anyone want a knight named Worry? It was a familiar, well-worn thought. Did the world really need a champion to defend anxious thoughts? To remind people to stare out windows and imagine all the ways a possible course of action could go wrong?

She trailed her fingers across one of the thick tapestries as she passed. It depicted a dragon reading a cookbook.

The Tapestry of Travesties lurked at the end of its own dark hallway. As Worry approached, threads lifted like the heads of curious snakes, then began furiously weaving and arranging.

She clasped her hands, the keys clanking in their little sack as she brushed them. The only sound was the whisper of threads.

An image emerged. She saw herself standing alone on an unfamiliar cliff, her shoulders tense with fear, her hands balled into fists. Before her was a wide chasm, apparently bottomless (she knew this because a tiny label in cursive read 'Bottomless Pit of Despair'). On the other side of the chasm a many-spired castle loomed, leaning to one side as if it might topple over, its windows all stained glass.

The only way to cross the chasm appeared to be a series of pendulums, giant boulders swinging towards her and away like the weights of grandfather clocks.

How strange, Worry thought.

As she watched, the threads that made up her tiny figure pulled themselves free, and Worry saw herself leap for the first pendulum. She landed on the swinging weight, but her hands slipped, and she tumbled into the chasm, her arms flailing wildly, a look of terror on her face as she fell and fell and fell.

Where was this chasm? She'd never seen anything like it. Was this what would happen if she tried to sneak into the tower? She threaded her fingers together and chewed the inside of her cheek.

Worry could easily see all the ways this could go wrong. What if a horrible monster had been imprisoned in the tower? What if she got caught? She shivered.

"I won't sneak in," she whispered to herself. "I'll talk to Fort about it again. It's better to be honest with her."

She turned around to see Hope crouching behind a statue of a gargoyle, watching her.

Chapter Three
The Forbidden Gateway

"**OH, HEY**..." Worry said. Hope moved out from behind the statue, glanced over her shoulder, then lifted an eyebrow at her sister. "What are you doing out here?" she whispered.

"What are *you* doing out?" Worry countered.

"Following you."

"But how did you know I was out if you weren't out already?"

Hope lifted a finger and opened her mouth, but then deflated. "Okay. I left to get some books."

"You're *still* studying? I thought you were going to take a break."

"I mean, yeah, but . . . I just needed to read a little more about what went wrong the last time I transfigured the . . . But anyway, I saw you and Kepler. So, I followed you. What are you doing? Fort said to stay in our rooms."

Worry chewed the inside of her cheek and swung her arms at her sides. She'd need magic to get in the door, anyway. Maybe she could convince Hope to help.

"I . . . I was thinking about . . . maybe . . . possibly, trying to explore the old Astronomy Tower."

Hope's eyes widened, and she rested a hand on the head of the gargoyle, but she said nothing.

Worry pressed on. "I mean, what's the difference, really, between being locked in our rooms vs. locked in the Astronomy Tower?

"Fort knowing where we are."

"Okay, yeah. But . . . I don't know. Kepler said there are things Fort doesn't know, and then hinted I should go to the tower. Or . . . I think he did."

She raised her delicate eyebrows and pursed her lips.

"I don't know," Worry went on. "It may be a terrible idea but—"

"Perfect, let's go."

Worry nearly fell over. "What?"

Hope gathered her sparkly pink skirts in one hand and turned to go. "I can't study anymore. I'm losing my mind. I can't sit around memorizing spell conjugations and waiting for some nameless horror that Fort won't explain."

"You don't think maybe we should wait for a night that's not . . . apocalyptic?"

"Probably." Hope strode down the darkened hallway, her heels clacking and the glowing silver poetry swirling and rearranging around her. "But I have a good feeling about this. Something good's going to happen, and things can't stay like this. If I see one more kitchen . . ." She raised her voice menacingly, and a doorway that had appeared up ahead hurriedly vanished.

Worry stumbled as she ran after her. Kepler reappeared, trotting excitedly at her side and muttering about dolphins.

The door to the Astronomy Tower was made of highly polished gray stone that looked like it was filled with smoke. Subtle colors shifted and swirled just under the surface. The only light was the faint, ghostly illumination, like moonlight, that Kepler gave off as he wove in and out of their legs.

"What's in here, Kepler?" Worry breathed.

"When threatened, sea cucumbers can eject their internal organs to entangle or distract predators," he whispered back.

"That's how I feel, too," Hope said.

Worry glanced at her sister. "Do you still want to do this?"

Her sister's face was determined as she nodded. "Yes."

Worry scanned the door, but there wasn't a knob or a latch or a knocker anywhere.

Hope reached out and placed her palm flat on the surface.

The smoke boiled and shifted under her hand, and Hope snatched it back.

Worry hunched her shoulders. She'd placed her own hands on that door many times, and nothing like that had ever happened.

Hope gasped and Worry's jealousy immediately vanished.

Words were forming on the door's surface.

> If you'd enter the tower, first stop and conspire. Like a password,
> just a pause-word, is all that's required.
>
> An anchor, an albatross, a pendulum bob.
> The pull of a planet,
> A _____ on one's mind,
> A 'hold on' homophone.

Hope frowned.

"It's a riddle," Worry said.

"What do you think?" Hope said, scratching her head.

Worry read through the riddle a few times. "Hmm . . . I think . . . I think it's a bunch of clues that all hint at the same word . . ."

She sat cross-legged, propping her elbows on her knees and resting her chin in her hands and settled down to think.

Chapter Four:
The Astronomy Tower

WORRY scratched her head. Some of the clues were words she didn't know, but she focused on what she did know.

"A _ _ _ _ _ on one's mind," she muttered. That was something she related to. A worry on one's mind?

She snapped her fingers. "I think I've got it."

Hope's face glowed. "Fantastic! What is it?"

"Weight. The word weight. A weight on one's mind. I can't remember what a homophone is, though."

"It's a word that sounds like another word. Something that sounds like 'hold on'? Oh, wait!" Hope laughed, and the bright tinkling sound echoed through the empty cavern.

They stared at the door. Hope placed her palm flat on it again. "Weight," she said firmly, and Worry felt a tingle of magic as the light around Hope dimmed and a few of her sparkles winked out.

She's so confident, Worry thought, feeling small and slightly useless. It wasn't just that Hope could do magic. She

256

knew so many things that Worry didn't. *She deserves to do magic. She'll do good things with it.*

The grey stone dissolved, leaving the archway open.

With nervous glances at each other, they entered the tower.

They found themselves in a large, circular room dominated by a staircase that spiraled up a central column. Directly in front of them was an ornate wooden door with a heavy iron latch and—to Worry's great excitement—a keyhole.

"Hang on," she said, reaching for her bag of keys, but Hope looked longingly up the staircase.

"I'm curious how high it goes. Maybe we can see the syzygy from here."

"Just one second!" Worry said, unable to help herself. She rifled through her keys, quickly trying out a few that were of matching size and shape to the keyhole. None fit.

"Come on!" Hope urged, tugging playfully at Worry's arm.

They set off at a run up the spiraling stone staircase. The walls were hung with chalk boards, their mathematical sketches covered in thick layers of dust. Worry caught glimpses of planets, of dashed lines and hastily marked angles. Numbers were scribbled everywhere.

It wasn't long before they slowed to a jog, and then a walk, and soon they were staggering, panting and out of breath.

"How . . . high . . . can this . . . tower . . . possibly be?" Hope gasped.

"It . . . doesn't look . . . this high . . . from the outside," Worry panted.

They collapsed and lay gasping.

"Where'd Kepler go?" Worry asked finally.

Hope shrugged. "Probably got bored with all this climbing."

They continued staggering upwards. Worry's legs burned and sweat poured down her cheeks.

Up and up and up they went. How long, Worry wasn't sure. The continual spiraling made her dizzy, and the diagrams on the walls blurred together.

Eventually, Worry noticed something strange.

"Do you feel . . . lighter?" she asked Hope.

Hope was flushed, her silver hair damp with sweat and sticking to her head. She paused, catching her breath. "I feel shaky."

Worry attempted a bit of a jump. Her legs felt like pudding, but she could swear she was a little lighter, that she hung in the air a little longer than usual. "I really think I'm lighter."

Hope closed her eyes and rested her forehead against the wall. "It's so nice and cold." She pushed herself up. "Let's keep going. I think we're almost there."

Worry looked at the smooth stone walls, looking exactly like they had at the bottom. "What makes you say that?"

"I don't know, I just feel it."

"I think you're right," Hope said a few minutes later. She gave a slight hop. "We're definitely lighter."

"Interesting," Worry said. "I wonder why . . ."

They continued climbing. With every loop around the smooth stone, they felt lighter and lighter. As they neared the

258

top, they were taking large jumps and nearly flying up the stairs.

Why has Fort been keeping this from us?

Worry made another leap, expecting to see yet more stone around the bend, but abruptly the hall ended, and she flew out into an infinite, star-filled void. She gasped and grabbed the door frame, barely keeping herself from flying out into nothingness.

She grabbed Hope's arm as she flew past. Her sister yelped and grabbed a fistful of Worry's tunic with her free hand, pulling herself back down.

Gently, they landed on the stone surface of the tower.

They stood on an exposed platform, with only the flimsiest of guard rails around its edges. The ground was lost in thick mists far below, and above were millions of stars, like a great dome overhead. At the peak of that dome were the three moons, bathing the tower in their colorful light.

Worry tightened her grip on the door frame, glad of anything sturdy and solid to hold onto, but Hope took a tentative step towards the middle. She was nearly floating, and her step sent her gliding upwards, only just barely did she slowly drift back down. She craned her head back, staring up at the three moons as they moved into alignment, the red moon in front, blocking out the other two.

The colors shifted, and everything went red.

Worry kept her hand clamped on the door frame; her mouth open as she stared at the scene. Her sister's hair glowed red as she hopped up and floated back down, giggling.

"Worry, you have to try this!"

Worry glanced around, then pulled off her belt, tying one end to the door latch and gripping the other end firmly. She took a few steps towards Hope, bouncing upwards.

The stars glittered overhead, so much more brightly and intensely than they appeared from the ground. Worry gave an experimental jump, staring up at the moon as she did, feeling like it was drawing her towards it. What a strange feeling to be so light!

A shadow passed over the red moon. Worry's grip on her belt tightened, and she squinted.

"Worry, try this!" Hope did a little hop and a spin, somersaulting in midair.

"Hope, did you see—"

There it was again.

The shadow was getting bigger and bigger, and now Worry could see talons and great, scaly wings. Bulging amethyst eyes with red pupils. A blast of fire bloomed around the tower, filling the air with acrid smoke.

Worry lunged for her sister, grabbed her hand and yanked her back towards the door with all her strength.

Hope yelped, and the wind roared around them.

Heavy, muscular scales crashed into Worry's back and she lost her grip on the belt. She and Hope went flying towards the edge of the tower, their hands still interlocked.

A blast of flame shot over their heads, missing them by inches.

Worry made a grab for the railing, but with a horrible swooping of her stomach, she went over the edge.

Hope's grip on her hand tightened, and with a jolt pulled her to a stop. Worry looked up to see Hope holding onto the railing she'd missed. Hope swung Worry around, flinging her back towards the doorway.

Worry crashed into the chest of the enormous dragon perched on the tower, its mouth agape and dripping flames, its leathery wings extended, beating the air.

She drifted slowly towards its feet, then propelled herself directly between its scaly, tree-trunk-like legs. Its jaws closed in the space where she'd been only a moment ago, and she heard its teeth clang against the stone.

Pushing off the ground, she flew towards the doorway, shooting straight through it, passing a glowing comet of pink light trailing fairy dust heading the other way.

Worry spun around, grabbing the end of her belt again, wishing it were longer, and prepared to leap out to get Hope.

Hope's fairy godmother, the tiny Rose, shot past the dragon, who roared. The sound crushed in on Worry's ears. She flinched, but there on the edge of the tower, she could just see her sister's small, pale hands gripping the railing as she hung off the end of the tower. It was lucky the gravity was so low, otherwise she might already have fallen.

Rose flitted this way and that, tapping the beast with her wand and darting out of the reach of its claws. "Oh my, oh no. Stop it," she said, punctuating each exclamation with a rap of her wand. It swiped at her as if she were a mosquito, batting her away.

The dragon shot another jet of flame at Hope, and one of her hands lost its grip.

It reared its head for another blast, but Worry leapt out, still clutching the end of her belt. She grabbed one of the bags of coins and hurled it at the dragon's shoulders. It pinged off its back, and the dragon spun, its purple irises widening, the pupil contracting to a tiny, enraged pinpoint as it glared at Worry.

It opened its jaws, and Worry leapt upwards with all her strength. A blast of flame went just beneath her.

She heaved as hard as she could on the belt and went shooting back down and to the side, another blast of flame just missing her.

Around the side of the creature, Worry could just make out Hope's tiny hands, both back on the railing, as she edged her way around towards the door. *Faster, Hope.*

The sparkling pink fairy was back, heading straight for the dragon's eyes. She gave a tiny, high-pitched war shriek, but it batted her away again.

Hope was halfway around the tower now.

"Jump!" Worry yelled. "Hope, jump!"

Worry crouched; her muscles taut as she prepared to leap towards wherever Hope ended up. She'd catch her and pull them both back to safety.

She pulled another bag of coins off her belt and hurled it towards the dragon. It sailed straight into its mouth.

The dragon's eyes widened; its talons scraped at its neck. It coughed a few times, then in a great, fiery belch, the bag of coins sailed back up, the fiery remnants of the bag disintegrating and the hot coins spewing everywhere. It hacked again, pounding its chest with its talons, and belched up more flames.

Hope came flying up over the railing, overshooting a little and heading for just above the doorway. Worry leapt upwards to meet her.

They timed it perfectly. Hope wrapped her arms around Worry's stomach, and Worry yanked as hard as she could on her belt-anchor, pulling them back towards the doorway.

It was so close. Three feet, then one foot. Worry pulled them towards it as hard as she could. They were going to make it, she knew it.

Something jerked them backwards.

Worry pulled harder and harder, but she couldn't help herself. She risked a glance behind her. The dragon had a talon wrapped around Hope's ankle. She felt her sister's grip slip a few inches.

"Hold on!" Worry yelled, but even as she did, Hope slipped again. Worry let go of the belt with one hand, grabbing the shoulder of Hope's gown with the other.

Rose flitted this way and that, tapping ineffectually on the dragon and shouting at it.

But it was no use. The dragon yanked Hope out of Worry's grasp, and in a great rush of leathery wings lifted off the tower with her dangling from its claws.

Worry leapt after her sister, but just missed her tiny pink satin slippers as she was lifted away into the night.

Worry flailed her arms, just managing to avoid shooting over the edge of the tower. She stood, breathing heavily, heart pounding, as she watched the dragon stealing her sister away. They were heading straight for the red moon.

"Hope!" she yelled. But her voice was lost in the rush of wind. Worry pulled at her hair, grabbing everything out of her belt and dumping it out and letting it drift to the ground. There had to be something. Something. She had to do something.

Next to her, a tiny distraught figure flitted this way and that, trailing bursts of sparkling fairy dust.

"Oh no. Oh no no no," Rose muttered, gripping her wand in both hands and fiddling with it. "No. No this wasn't supposed to happen."

Worry looked at her sharply. "What—what do you mean? What *was* supposed to happen?" Had the fairy somehow planned this?

Rose's eyes widened, her tiny, pointed face flushed. Her wings fluttered, and she disappeared with a small pop.

Discussion Question:

Do you have any guesses about why Hope and Worry felt so much lighter at the top of the tower? Are there times that you've felt light like that? What were you doing? Next time you're on a swing set or riding in a car as it goes over a hill, or in an elevator just as it starts to go down, pay attention to what that feels like. Those are all moments where you feel a little bit weightless.

Chapter Five:
Sea Riddles and
Syllogisms

WORRY stared up at the moon, hoping to catch one last glimpse of her sister, trying to see where she went. *I'm coming, Hope. I'll fix this.*

She glared around the empty tower, still breathing heavily. "Rose!"

But no fairy appeared. An empty stillness descended, leaving the night feeling eerily calm. Only the faint smell of dragon smoke hung in the air.

Shaking, Worry swept up her belt and the few coins that were within easy reach, stuffed them into her pockets, and flew down the stairs.

Her mind was whirling. Where was the dragon taking Hope? What did Rose know? What had she meant, this wasn't supposed to happen? Fort was going to be furious, but she would fix this. She would know what to do, Worry was sure of it.

Worry collided with Fort halfway down the stairs, but the woman was a stable as a tree and Worry only bounced off her legs.

Fort knelt, picking Worry up and gripping her by the shoulders. "What are you doing here? I told you to— Where's Hope?"

Fort's green eyes bored into Worry's, and she felt herself shaking.

"A . . . a dragon," she gasped out.

Fort's grip tightened and her eyes went wide.

"Are you sure?"

"We have to do something! It took—it took . . ." She couldn't finish the sentence.

"No. No this can't be," Fort said.

"We have to get her back!"

Fort released Worry and stood, shaking her head, her hand going to her sword hilt.

"This is bad. This is very bad." She paused.

Worry had never seen Fort speechless before, but it looked like she really needed a moment to think. Worry's chest felt like an empty void. If Fort didn't know what to do . . .

Her ankles tingled and she looked down to see Kepler sitting on one of her feet.

Fort noticed him, too.

"This was your doing, wasn't it?"

Kepler gave an innocent meow and flicked his tail.

"I know you can talk," Fort said.

Kepler hissed, his hackles rising.

What was going on here? Worry didn't have time to try to figure it out. With every second that passed, Hope was farther away.

"Fort?" she said. "I'm so sorry. We broke into the tower. But . . . the top of the tower was so strange, and then a dragon came, and it took Hope. It was heading for the red moon. What do we do? How can we get her back?"

Fort ran a hand across her brow, looking deeply exhausted.

She knelt again, and Worry noticed her hands were shaking.

"Worry, I am so sorry. But there's no getting her back. She's gone."

Worry shook her head. No. No that couldn't be.

"She's not gone! I saw where she went! She went to the red moon!"

Fort stood in one swift movement. "Worry, I'm sorry, but . . . the fact that you saw a . . . a dragon . . . well this is very, very bad." One hand went to her throat, and the other rubbed her sternum, her eyes glazing over. Worry had never seen Fort so undecided. She looked . . . afraid.

Her expression was grim. "More are coming. This is only the beginning."

"What do you mean?"

"This is what happened before. It's what nearly ended the Scholar Knights. It's why I'm the only one left."

"What can I do?"

Fort's gaze was far away. "There's nothing you can do. I wish you had hidden like I asked." Worry wished she could shrink to the floor. At last, Fort looked straight at her. "Please,

267

Worry. Your sister is lost, but if I don't act quickly, the rest of the world might be lost, too."

Fort's words twisted like sharp splinters in her heart. There was nothing Worry could do. She couldn't do magic; she couldn't help her sister. She'd already made things worse. She looked down at her feet and nodded.

Fort clapped her on the shoulder. Her gloved hand was heavy.

"I'm sorry," Worry said.

Without another word, Fort sprinted up the tower, drawing her sword.

Worry sank down, sitting on the steps, wrapping her arms around her knees, and bowing her head. Kepler nuzzled her hand. All Worry could think about was Hope disappearing into the night sky.

She couldn't do nothing. She couldn't hide while her sister was in danger. "I'm coming for you, Hope," she whispered, looking upwards. She said it more for herself than for her sister.

But what was she supposed to do now?

"Rose?" she whispered to the empty air. "Please talk to me."

No one answered. Only Kepler stared back up at her.

Worry heard a crash from high above and leapt to her feet. She started up the stairs again, then paused. Fort didn't want her help. She'd only tell her to go back to her room.

There was no way Worry was just going to go back to her room now, even though she'd already made things worse. She turned and sprinted down the rest of the stairs, Kepler close on her heels.

When they were out of the tower, Worry darted down a narrow passage into an unused classroom, slamming the door behind her. Kepler hopped through the closed door and stared up at her, licking a ghostly paw.

"Kepler, what is going on?" she demanded. "Did you know that would happen?"

Kepler rubbed his paws over his nose, flattening his pointed moustache. "No, of course not. I didn't know that would happen."

"What else do you know? Tell me everything."

"Sea turtles travel thousands of miles and lay their eggs on the same beach they were born."

She groaned, but really, she walked right into that one. "Why do you do that?" she demanded.

"Pufferfish expand into a ball to evade predators."

Worry grimaced. "Is there anything you can tell me that isn't sea facts?"

"Yes, of course. I don't really care for sea facts much myself."

"Then why— No, never mind, don't answer that." She pursed her lips, pacing back and forth. She had to get Hope back. To do that, she had to figure out what was going on. Because there was clearly a lot more happening here than people were telling her. Rose wouldn't talk to her, but that wasn't surprising. Fairies were very shy and often only spoke with their chosen knight.

Fort wouldn't talk to her either and that stung her more. She clearly only saw Worry as a burden.

"What is going on?" she muttered to herself, trying to hold back the panic that kept threatening to overwhelm her when she thought about Hope imprisoned by a dragon on that far-away moon.

And Kepler wasn't telling her anything useful. Although. She tapped her chin. Maybe she could figure out something from when he told her sea facts and when he didn't.

She sat cross-legged on the floor and took a deep breath. It was hard to think when everything felt so urgent. But running around panicking—which was what she'd really like to do most—wasn't going to get Hope back. Maybe she'd allow herself some running around panicking time later.

"Okay, Kepler. What are some things you can tell me that don't have to do with the sea?"

Kepler sat up straight, his eyes wide and excited, his moustache perked. "Oh, thank you, what a fantastic question." His tiny tongue licked out and back in. "Well. I could speak about the castle. About the Scholar Knights. About the sea, and the earth and the sky, but no higher. I can speak about people who look at the sea, or the earth, or the sky, but no higher."

Worry's eyebrows lifted. "Hmm . . . so, you can't talk about . . . the stars. Or the people who look at stars?"

"A giant squid eye can be up to ten inches in diameter," Kepler said, looking deeply pained.

"Wow, that's big," Worry said. She briefly wondered what it would feel like to hold one. "We have to focus," she said.

"I will focus like a giant squid eyeball focuses on a fish!" Kepler assured her.

She nodded absently. "Okay, is there anything else useful you can tell me?" It occurred to her that Kepler was the one who'd led them to the tower in the first place, so following his advice might not be a very good plan. But she'd known Kepler her whole life, and of everyone in this castle he was the only one at least trying to give her information.

"There are some books missing from the library," he commented.

This was intriguing, although she wasn't sure how she was supposed to go looking for books that weren't there.

"Can you show me?" she asked.

Kepler opened his mouth, raising a paw, but with what was clearly a lot of effort, shut his mouth again. She was slightly curious to hear what sea fact he'd managed to avoid saying.

"All right, I'll take that as a no," she said.

"Thank you. I greatly appreciate your line of questioning."

She wished she'd thought to ask him about his strange interest in the sea long before. "Have you known many Scholar Knights?" she asked.

"Oh yes, a great many," said Kepler, suddenly serious. "I was very good friends with several of them, in my youth."

She wondered what had happened but knew better than to ask by now.

A strange question occurred to her. "Were you always a cat?"

"Dolphins have unique whistle-names for each other."

Whoa. If Kepler hadn't always been a cat, what had he been?

Luckily, Worry already had an idea of where those missing books might be. The benefits of years of exploring. She wove her way through a maze of staircases, down into the enormous library. One whole wall of the library was floor-to-ceiling windows that looked out over the ocean. Right now, the ocean was dark, illuminated only by moonlight. The syzygy had passed for that night, and flecks of red, blue, and green glinted off the ocean, bathing the library with a dim, watery glow of shifting colors.

She hurried through the long rows of empty reading tables, her feet silent on the thick, dusty carpet, then wove a familiar path through the endless shelves. Back and back and back she went, arriving at last at a small, locked door.

The iron key she'd found last year fitted perfectly, and she ducked inside, coughing as she inhaled dust, and batting away the spider webs.

Inside, the room was lit by glowing magic orbs. One large, white orb hovered in the center, with three smaller orbs rotating around it. One red, one blue, one green.

"Kepler is that—" but she cut herself off, seeing that Kepler was looking determinedly away from the object. The last time she'd been here she hadn't paid much attention, had assumed it was simply a fancy magic lamp. But now it was obvious what it represented.

She approached, seeing that the red moon had moved past the blue and green orbs, which rotated together as the great pearly planet moved beneath them.

It was a model of their planet and the three moons.

The last time she'd been there, she'd opened a few of the books, but they were mostly indecipherable symbols and diagrams, and she'd given up.

She reached out and plucked the little green moon from where it hung. It was surprisingly cool. Holding it up, she moved farther into the room, sending long shadows arcing away from the green glow of the orb.

At the very back of the room was an ornate shelf set into the far wall. On it were five gold pedestals. On the first rested an ancient, leather-bound book. The other four were empty.

Engraved on the front of each pedestal was a name. She read them off one-by-one, trailing her finger over the letters.

"Aristotle. Galileo. Newton. Einstein." She paused, her finger hovering over the final name. She looked at the ghost cat, who was staring out into the ocean, but watching her out of the corner of his eye. "Kepler."

Why was there a book with the name of her cat here? Or rather, a missing book. She ran her hands over the pedestal, looking for any other engravings or maybe a secret button, but there was nothing.

Leaving that for later, she approached the first book.

The front cover was embossed with a crown of laurel leaves and the spine read 'Aristotle' in gold letters. Gently, Worry opened it.

273

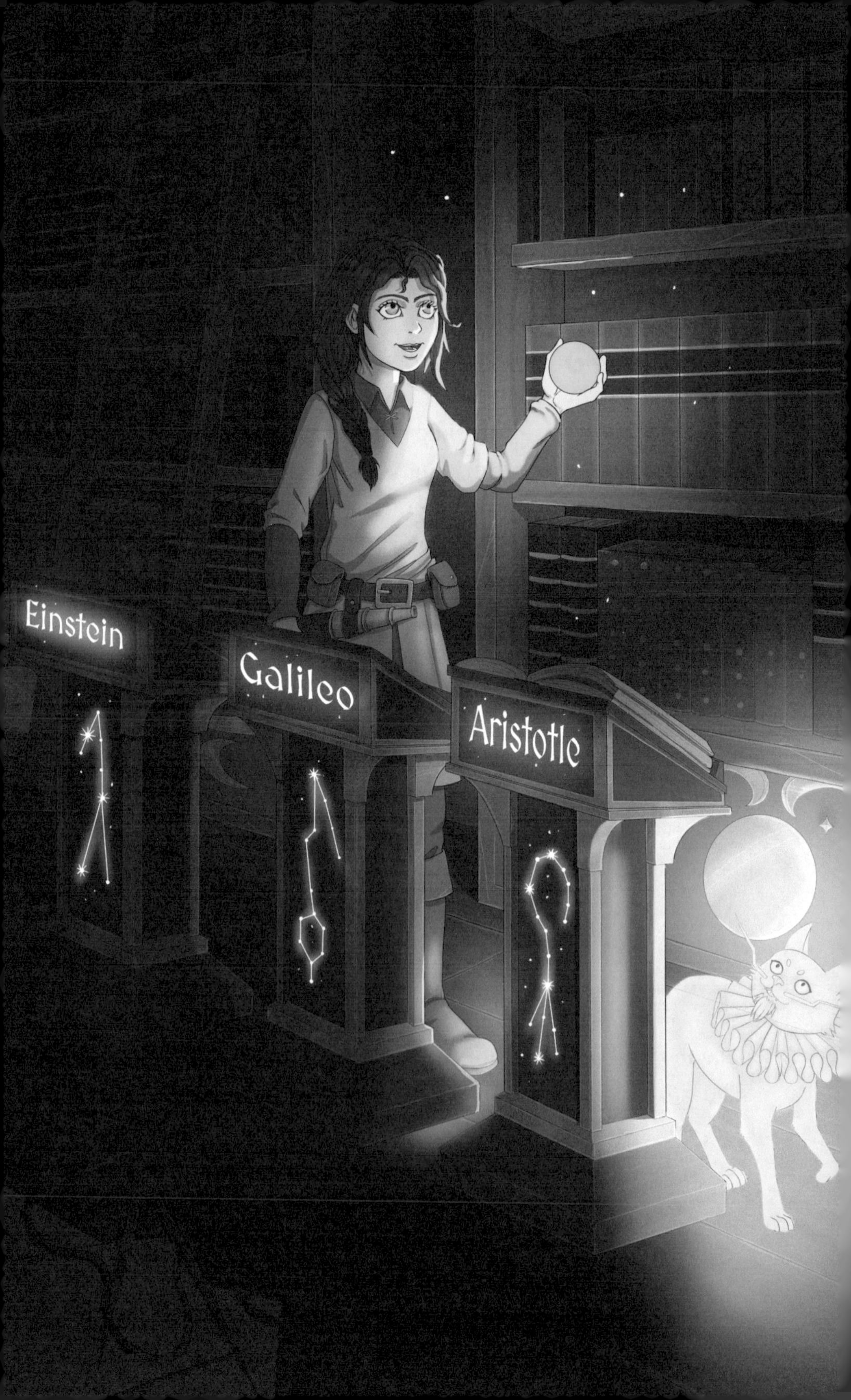
Einstein
Galileo
Aristotle

The inside was blank: crinkly, ancient parchment, weathered and water stained, but no writing.

She flipped through a few more pages. All empty.

She paused, staring at a blank page. A tiny scrawl of ink appeared.

To speak with the Father of Logic, you must master the tools of logic.

Worry already considered herself fairly logical, except when it came to her unrealistic anxieties. She waited, and more words appeared.

Complete the Syllogisms

"Kepler, do you know what a syllogism is?" she asked, bracing for information about clams or something.

"They're logical statements. Formal logic. Usually, you're given two pieces of information, and you have to put them together. See what logically follows."

"Hmm, okay. Thanks."

That didn't seem too hard.

The words disappeared, and more took their place.

All fairies have wings.
Bluebell is a fairy.

Worry considered this. Was there anything she could conclude? If Bluebell was a fairy, and all fairies had wings, then Bluebell must have wings.

She pulled her quill and ink from her bag and, feeling slightly terrible for writing in what was probably a priceless ancient artifact, carefully wrote out *Bluebell has wings.*

A sparkling sensation went through her fingers, almost like she'd dipped them in fairy dust, and the words disappeared. She let out a sigh, grateful that her writing wasn't going to forever mar the book.

Correct.
If the tide is high, the mermaids will come close to shore.
The tide is high.

Worry chewed the end of the quill, then stopped herself. Well, it seemed there was one thing that logically followed.

The mermaids will come close to shore.

Again, her words disappeared, replaced by a new riddle:

If you tickle a giant, he will laugh.
The giant is laughing.

"Hmmm . . ." Worry wondered aloud. Her first instinct was to say that someone had tickled the giant, but . . . what if someone had told the giant a particularly good joke? He could be laughing for many reasons. She frowned and wrote out her answer.

I don't think we can conclude anything.

Words replaced it almost immediately.

Well done.

276

A strong smell of ink filled the room, and the pages rustled, flipping back and forth as if in a gust of wind. They filled with writing.

Some Syllogisms to Solve:

1. If you give Fort a cupcake, she will be happy. You gave Fort a cupcake.

2. All dragons have scales. Hortense is a dragon.

3. If a dragon is angry, it will breathe fire. A dragon is breathing fire.

Answers: 1. Fort is happy. 2. Hortense has scales. 3. We can't conclude the dragon is angry. Something else might be making it breathe fire. Maybe it has indigestion or is trying to reheat leftovers.

Chapter Six:
The First Teacher

WORRY flipped through the ancient book. "Is there something in particular I'm supposed to be looking for?" she asked Kepler, but the cat only gave her a pained look and went to stare out the window into the darkness.

The pages filled with complex notes and diagrams. Arrows pointed everywhere. She paused at a detailed sketch of an octopus. There was a whole page of notes on fish skeletons, and then a long essay on virtue and how balance made one a good person. Then intricate sketches of ferns and the structures inside flowers.

Worry scratched her head. *Did one person write all of this?* The handwriting all looked the same.

One page went into detail about how to persuade others, which Worry thought she might come back to next time she tried to convince Fort to teach her to be a knight.

Fort. Her stomach flipped over as she remembered why she was here. She'd been so caught up in the logic puzzles that

278

she'd almost forgotten Fort was off trying to prevent some secret impending disaster. And Hope had been carried away by a dragon.

She flipped faster through the pages, looking for anything that might give her a clue as to what was happening and what she should do.

At the very end, there was a nearly blank page that had only one word on it.

Hello?

Worry frowned, then she picked up her quill and scratched out a response.

Hi?

Ah, hello, the parchment answered. Worry read the words aloud, so Kepler could follow along, even though he didn't seem to be paying attention.

Who are you? she asked. The words disappeared, and more began to take their place.

My name is Aristotle. In my world I am often called The First Teacher. Some call me The Founder of Logic or The Father of Biology. I am also famous for my philosophy, my ethics, and my principles of drama.

One person could do all that?

Wow, that's a lot, Worry wrote. *How did you learn all that?*

My father was a physician. He sparked my interest in biology. From there, I became interested in a great many subjects.

Nice to meet you, she replied. *Um, how am I speaking with you?*

Many years ago, the fairies created this book and others like it to allow scholars from your world to ask me questions.

Is it uncomfortable, being a book?

Only when people ask me illogical questions. There was a pause. *But it is kind of you to ask. What are you hoping to understand?*

Worry considered whether it was safe to be writing to a talking book. But she didn't see how else she was going to rescue her sister, so she continued.

My sister was kidnapped by a dragon from the top of a tower here. The dragon took her to one of the moons. I need to figure out a way to rescue her.

I see. That sounds difficult. Tell me, what did you observe?

Observe?

Yes, what did you see? The first step in understanding anything is to carefully observe.

Worry described everything she could remember, from the lightness at the top of the tower to the fairy's exclamation at the end.

Hmmm . . . I see. Most fascinating. In my world, we have only one moon. And no dragons.

Worry chewed the end of her quill again.

What do you know about my world? she asked.

Very little, I confess. I mostly answered the astronomers' questions.

Worry frowned. *What do you mean, the astronomers? Don't you mean the Scholar Knights?*

No; the Scholar Knights weren't interested in speaking with me.

There were astronomers here?

Assuming you are in the Castle of the Scholar Knights, then yes. There was a small group of astronomers doing research there as well.

Worry's heartbeat quickened. Fort had never mentioned this group. *What did they ask you?*

They asked me about the celestial spheres and how to reach them.

Worry gripped her quill hard. The astronomers had wanted to reach the moons? Had they achieved it? If so, maybe she could do the same!

Aristotle continued, *I told them that it was impossible. Everything in nature has its place.*

Worry's heart sank. *What do you mean?*

I mean everything is composed of five elements. At first people thought there was just earth, water, air, and fire, but I added a fifth: aether, which is what the heavens are made of. Earth and water naturally move downwards. Air and fire naturally move upwards. Aether belongs in the heavens.

When Aristotle said this, Kepler growled and flattened his ears.

Aristotle went on. *Everything has its natural state. Things prefer to be stationary and will naturally come to rest without some force to keep them moving. I am quite curious about these dragons. If they truly can reach the celestial sphere, perhaps they are made of aether. It would be quite wonderous to see a creature made of aether. Perhaps your sister's natural place is also in the outer, heavenly sphere . . .*

Something about this struck an uncomfortable chord for Worry. She'd often felt like she and Hope were just fundamentally different from one another. Hope belonged someplace better than Worry. It was a horrible thought. That maybe Worry was simply like earth and water. Heavy.

She paused, her quill hovering over the page. Her throat suddenly felt thick.

Kepler batted her gently on the side of the head. She hadn't even noticed him climbing onto her shoulder. She glanced at him, and he rolled his eyes, leaping away for one of the bookshelves.

She shook her head. That was silly. Obviously, Hope hadn't wanted to be carried away by a dragon. She took a deep breath and continued.

What else did they ask about?

They asked about the tendency of objects to fall. I told them that objects that are heavier fall faster, and that they fall more slowly through thicker substances.

Kepler hissed and lashed his tail.

They also asked me about the possibility of a vacuum, of a completely empty space. I told them that was impossible, because objects would move infinitely quickly in such a space. And that would be impossible.

Worry could sort of see how Aristotle might have concluded this. It was like reasoning with the syllogisms. Objects move slower through mud than through water. The thinner the substance, the faster the object. If a substance is infinitely thin, the object will move infinitely fast. It seemed logical, on its surface. She wondered if there might be more going on, though.

Did they ask you anything else?

There was a longer delay than usual before Aristotle replied. The handwriting became messier, with little flicks and scratches and dots of splattered ink.

They did ask me quite a lot about tides. Such a complex topic. Such a regular, repeating phenomenon, but so different in different places. I . . . I think it must be the wind. Winds move waves, and . . . and they must also cause the tides.

But winds are so chaotic, Worry wrote. *Why would they blow in such a uniform way?*

Perhaps . . . perhaps from heat from the sun.

Worry considered this. It didn't seem very likely. Why had the astronomers been interested in them?

Did they ever say why they wanted to reach the moons?

Not to me. But I know they had other books. They spoke with me quite a lot early on, and then, when they had their other books, they stopped. It's been nice talking with you. I haven't had a student in a long time.

I'm sorry. There haven't been astronomers here in a long time, either. Otherwise, I'm sure they would want to speak with you.

That is very kind of you to say.

I have to go now but thank you for the information.

Of course. Best of luck to you in your quest. I sincerely hope that you are able to rescue your sister. Should she not be made of aether and destined for the stars.

Worry snapped the book shut and stared at the other golden pedestals. Aristotle had a lot of interesting ideas, but many of them seemed not quite right. Maybe the astronomers had felt the same way. Her pulse quickened, and she twirled her quill through her fingers, thinking. The silence of the room closed in on her, all sound muffled by the books and the layers of dust. Kepler crouched, darting a paw under one of the shelves, his tail flicking back and forth.

So there had been another group of people here, besides the Scholar Knights. Astronomers. Maybe these astronomers had found a way to reach the red moon. Maybe the information in the other books was more useful. Maybe someone had stolen or hidden them because of this.

The idea of travelling to the red moon, knowing there was at least one dragon waiting for her was more than a little worrying, but if there was a way to do it, Worry was going to try.

Test Aristotle's Ideas:

Aristotle was a brilliant person who contributed so much to our understanding of the world, but there was a lot he got wrong. Still, those ideas were a valuable first step in our understanding of the world, and it's easy to see why he would have concluded some of the things he did, based on what he saw in the world. The world is complicated, and we can't always perceive the factors that cause things.

In this activity, let's try to see if we can disprove Aristotle's ideas, and maybe understand what he got wrong. Firstly, let's look at the idea that heavier objects fall faster. 1. Take a piece of paper and a rock. 2. Drop them both from the same height. Which one hits the ground first? 3. Now, do the same experiment again, but this time crumple the paper up so that it is the same size and shape as the rock. 4. Drop them both from the same height. What do you notice? Do they land at the same time? Closer? You see, what Aristotle didn't consider was that objects are falling through air, which slows them down. Flatter, lighter objects are more affected by air than are the more compact, aerodynamic objects.

Aristotle believed that it was impossible to have empty space, but nowadays we are able to pump all the air out of a container using a vacuum pump. What would it really look like to drop objects in a container without air? Watch this YouTube video to see. It's pretty mind-blowing. "Brian Cox visits the world's biggest vacuum | Human Universe - BBC"

Chapter Seven:
Circles and Secrets

WORRY knew better than to ask Kepler where she might find the book with his name on it.

The cat leapt onto her shoulder again, cooling and weightless, and together they climbed the steps out of the library, bursting out into a stone hall. A gargoyle snorted awake, peering at her through bleary eyes.

"Sorry to wake you," Worry whispered, and the gargoyle hmphed, tucked its head under a wing, and went back to sleep.

Worry put one hand on her hip and rubbed her chin with the other.

Where could the book possibly be?

Another library? In a secret passageway?

Moving down the hall away from the gargoyle, Worry pulled out her maps and spread them over the stone floor. She had several of the various sprawling wings of the castle and a few more of the surrounding countryside.

The castle of the Scholar Knights was a day's ride from the nearest villages. She hadn't left the castle since she'd been brought there as a baby. Not for the first time, she wondered where she'd come from. A nearby village? Farther?

Was there some secret underground bunker filled with treasures nearby? The parchment crinkled as she ran her hands over it, peering closely at names and labels.

If there was a repository of secret knowledge, the safest place for it would probably be the castle.

She'd explored every inch of it, though. A hundred times at least. She'd found a few secret closets, yes, mostly by looking at blank spaces on the map, but she'd thought she'd found the last of them years ago.

She waved Kepler a little closer so she could use his light to read by.

Time passed, and Worry's eyes began to get heavy. She yawned widely. Her mind felt foggy, but somewhere in this castle was a book, and she was determined to find it.

"I need a break," she said finally, her vision blurry. Kepler hopped onto her shoulder and together they wandered the halls of the castle, past snoring enchanted statues.

What am I even looking for? Worry wondered as she passed under an arch of glowing purple flowers from which soft jazz music emanated.

She tapped a stone frog, then twisted it, and a passageway opened. Passing into the darkness, she was glad of Kepler's light. He'd been mostly silent, occasionally starting to mutter something, but cutting himself off.

Maybe it was time to ask Fort again. Maybe now that the first night of the syzygy was past, and the moons would be out of alignment for a few hours, she'd be more open.

The passage sloped down, and Worry walked slowly, running her hands along the walls and looking for anything out of the ordinary. Anything that might hint at another secret door. Although, she knew that on the other side of the left wall was the library and on the other side of the right wall were a series of cobwebby classrooms full of empty glass jars. But this was the tunnel she had explored the least. Mostly because it was so long and boring.

She squinted, struggling to see, and realized Kepler's light was growing dimmer.

"Kepler, wake up," she whispered.

"I am awake."

The light didn't change.

She lifted an eyebrow. "Does your light usually get dimmer?"

"I haven't noticed, to be honest."

She turned around and walked back up the hall. Gradually, Kepler's light increased. She tried it a few more times to confirm. Yes, he was definitely brighter at one end of the tunnel than the other.

Intrigued, she retraced her steps, this time watching as Kepler's light dimmed and flared. It was hard to pinpoint, though, with the twisty passages, some higher and some lower. She'd think she was onto something, with the light getting brighter and brighter, only to find herself stuck at a dead end.

She needed to be more systematic.

She retrieved the little green ball representing the moon from the library, and wandered the castle until Kepler was exactly as bright as the moon, then she marked the spot on the map.

Then she set off for a different part of the castle, wandering around there until again she found a spot where Kepler was again exactly the same brightness as the moon. Again, she marked the spot on the map.

"What are you doing?" Kepler asked.

"I have an idea," she said, heading off for a new part of the castle.

"What?"

"Let me see if it works first, then I'll explain."

Technically, she only needed three dots, but the castle was so complicated and consisted of floors and half floors and balconies and angled ramps—and who knew how accurate this map was anyway—so she added more and more, until she was certain.

Flushed and grinning, she spread the map on an oak desk below a window. The sky outside was dark, the red moon neared the horizon, about to set.

"Look!" she whispered to Kepler. "Look at the shape!"

"A circle?"

"Exactly!"

"Well done. Geometry is a worthwhile pursuit, to be sure. And, um . . . How is that helpful?"

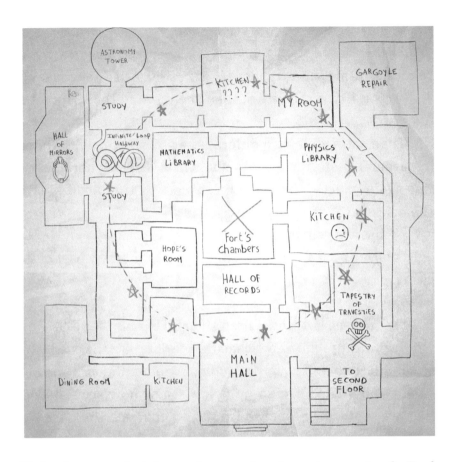

"I think you get brighter when you're closer to your book. Each of these dots is a place where you were exactly as bright as the little moon, which means you were exactly the same distance from your book."

Kepler went very still. Not even his tail moved.

"Every point on a circle is the same distance from exactly one place," she said, pausing for dramatic effect. "The center."

With a flourish, she connected the dots into a smooth circle. She peered closer, her quill hovering over the map. She

290

poked her quill right in the middle, making a single dot on the center, and her chest tightened, her stomach turning over.

It was Fort's chambers.

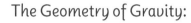

The Geometry of Gravity:

There are two shapes that are particularly important to our understanding of gravity. One is the circle, and the other is the ellipse. They're both super useful for a lot of things, actually, and understanding what they are fundamentally is not only interesting but helpful later on. So let's learn to draw them!

For this activity, grab a piece of string, two thumbtacks, a piece of cardboard, and a pen. First, let's draw a circle. Place the cardboard flat on the ground. Tie the string to the pen, then thumbtack the other end to the middle of the piece of cardboard. Hold the pen upright, like you're going to draw on the cardboard, and move it to where the string is taut (not sagging). Now, keeping the string taut, use the pen to draw on the cardboard. If you go all the way around the thumbtack, you'll have a circle! By using the string, we're keeping the distance from the center to the pen constant. This way, every point on the circle is exactly the same distance from the thumbtack.

Now, let's draw an ellipse! This time, cut a length of string and thumbtack each end of it to the cardboard, making sure the string is loose in between. (The string should probably be about half again as long as the distance between the two thumbtacks.) Now, pull the middle of the string away from the thumbtacks until the string is taut. Place your pen there, holding the string in a kind of triangle shape. Now you can start to draw. Try to move your pen in such a way that the string is always taut. You should end up with an elongated circle- an ellipse! This also works well with nails. For a video of this, search on YouTube for "draw a PERFECT ellipse with a string and two nails".

So, what's the difference between a circle and an ellipse? Well, a circle is a shape where every part of it is exactly the same distance from the center. An ellipse is like a circle, but it kind of has two centers. We call each of these points a "focus." In our activity, each of the thumbtacks is a focus of the ellipse. Because we tied a string between the two of them, we kept the total distance from the pen to each of the two foci (foci is the plural of focus—like octopi and octopus,) the same. So, wherever you are on the edge of an ellipse, if you measure the distance from that point to each of the foci and then add those distances together, you'll always get the same amount. Kind of complicated, but interesting!

Chapter Eight:
Books both Judgmental
and Hidden

THE door to Fort's chambers was shiny red madrona. Its frame was a single, curved branch lifting up and back down. "Fortitude Knightward" had been artfully burned into the door's surface, surrounded by sprays of maidenhair ferns.

Worry gulped. Fort could be back any moment. What would she do if she found Worry breaking into her rooms?

She pulled a key from her bag.

"You have a key to Fort's chambers, too?" Kepler hissed.

Worry blushed and hunched her shoulders. "I know I shouldn't. I just . . . She lost it one time and we all searched for hours and hours and finally I found it and . . . I just . . . made a teeny tiny copy before returning it."

"How did you copy the key? Are you learning smelting in your spare time?"

She giggled. "No. I found this cabinet that duplicates things you put in it. Or sometimes it turns them into cupcakes."

"Seems like a risky thing to do with Fort's keys."

"True. It worked, though!" She inserted the key and, with a quick glance over her shoulder, turned it. The door clicked open. "And it's helpful to Fort, too, really. Like when she loses them again. Which she has. What if she'd left a candle burning in there?"

"I should hope Fort wouldn't leave an open flame in her chambers," Kepler said dryly.

"She might, though. She's lost her keys twice since then. I think she's starting to be suspicious of why I keep "finding" them."

"You do skulk about often."

"I'm not skulking," Worry huffed. "If I can't study magic, the least I can do is study . . . everything else. And anyway, Fort made me the castle's caretaker. I take that seriously."

"A fair point," Kepler said, nodding his silvery head.

Gingerly, Worry stepped into the room, Kepler slipping in around her feet.

She stood in a dim office. Shelves of books filled one wall from floor to ceiling. A slight shudder, like a wave, went through their spines and a few floated off the shelves towards her.

"Legacy and Tradition: Respecting the Authority of One's Elders," was the title of the first.

"Er, no thank you," Worry said, gently nudging the book away. It floated back to its shelf with a slight air of misgiving.

Where would Fort have hidden an ancient, enchanted book? She bent down and reached her hands around Kepler.

"Can I pick you up?" she asked. The hair stood up on her arms as a chill went through her.

"I will float along, pretending you are carrying me," Kepler said.

With both hands, Worry held the weightless ghost cat up, pointing him towards various parts of the room, but the shifts in light were so subtle they were hard to interpret.

She turned to see that two of the books had been sneaking up on her.

"Openness and Transparency: The Case for Always Being Honest with Those Around Us," read the closest one.

"No, thank you," Worry said, hurrying through a doorway into the next room.

She passed a cozy sitting room with a large river rock fireplace and a mullioned window looking out over the dark, star-flecked ocean.

Beyond that was a small bathroom tiled with polished seashells, and after that a spartan bedroom.

Kepler's light illuminated a narrow bed in one corner, with a heavy trunk sitting at its feet. A threadbare wool rug muffled her steps. At a single narrow window was a slim gold telescope pointing horizontally out across the bay.

She thought she heard something and froze, tilting her head.

"Kepler," she whispered. "Did you hear that?"

He darted away through a wall and her chest clenched.

Seconds later, he returned. "No one's here. The hall is empty."

Her chest loosened a fraction.

She did a quick search of the room. There was nothing under the bed or under the rug. None of the stones were loose.

She approached the telescope. What had Fort been looking at? Bending slightly, careful not to bump the device, she peered through the eyepiece.

It took a few moments to get close enough that the image resolved into sharp focus. She sucked in a gasp. There was that many-spired castle she'd seen in the Tapestry of Travesties.

"Kepler, do you know what that place is?" she breathed. A shock of cold went through her face as Kepler joined her at the telescope, and she jerked back.

"Ow, jeez, I would have moved."

Kepler shrugged, his ruffle jiggling. "Efficiency. I figured we could both look just as easily."

She rubbed her face. "What is that place?"

"Some sharks have to keep swimming to breathe," he said heavily.

Her eyebrows lifted.

A bump from somewhere high above jolted her back to focus. Fort might return at any moment, and there was one place left to look.

She knelt in front of the trunk.

"Don't tell me you have that key, too," Kepler said.

"Of course not."

That didn't mean she didn't have options, though. Worry pulled out her lockpicks.

"You sure make a habit of learning disreputable things," Kepler said.

Worry frowned and her stomach churned. She didn't want to break into things. "This castle is full of ancient locks that Fort's lost the keys to. I wouldn't have been able to get into half the rooms without this."

Maybe Fort hadn't actually lost those keys, though. Maybe those were more secrets. Although, she didn't know why the room with all the chamber pots would have been some giant dark secret. Or the room full of canned asparagus.

And Fort did have a habit of losing things. Sometimes when people were so focused on giant, lofty challenges, they lost sight of the little everyday things, Worry reasoned.

The trunk clicked open with a burst of green fairy dust.

Inside were two tiny, very old blankets. Faded and worn. Each one had a name embroidered on it. The pink one read Hope, and the blue one read Worry. The lettering on Hope's was done in elegant gold loops. The 'W' on Worry's was also, but the tailor seemed to have run out of energy on the rest of the letters. They were done in a straightforward, businesslike script. Worry sighed.

Gently, Worry put them aside. Beneath that was a sketchbook. Worry flipped through it, recognizing Fort's handwriting on the labels. There were sketches of Worry and Hope, just doing everyday things. Farther back were rougher sketches of other people. A kind looking woman with a thick braid over one shoulder and a fluffy shawl read "Mistress Serenity". A tall, muscular man with a thick curly beard, many colorful tattoos, and a corduroy vest was labelled "Unity". Worry let out a long, sad breath. These must have been Fort's teachers. The last of the knights before her.

There were no other students.

With a pang of guilt for invading Fort's personal sketch-book, she put it aside.

Something clanked.

Frowning, she pushed aside another book, and a glint of metal caught her eye. A golden disk on a velvet chain. "For Bravery and Service to the Realm," Worry read aloud. Her eyes widened and she ran her fingers over the cool indentations. Fort had never mentioned winning a medal.

She flipped it over, but only a date was written on the back. Twenty years ago . . . Worry briefly counted on her fingers. Fort would have been around thirteen.

Gently, she set the medal aside. Below that was a sword. Its blade was dull and chipped, and its hilt was wrapped in worn, cracked leather.

She slid her fingers around it reverently, but then something below the sword caught her eye.

Her heart stopped.

Underneath was an ancient, leatherbound book. A glowing ribbon like woven seaweed made of light, was wrapped tightly around it, binding it closed, secured with a tiny shell clasp.

Forgetting the sword, she reached in and extracted it, running her fingers over the ancient cover. The golden letters reflected in the ghostly light. "Kepler."

"We found it, Kepler," she breathed.

Kepler started to say something about Narwhals, when a loud bang sounded from the entryway.

"Who's there?!" Fort shouted.

Worry hastily dumped everything but the book back into the trunk, shut it as quietly as she could, and dove under the bed. Kepler disappeared through a wall.

Fern zipped into the room, leaving a trail of sparkles as she shot to and fro.

Worry shrank back into the far corner as Fort's boots appeared.

She stopped in the middle of the rug. Green light tilted this way and that.

"I heard something," Fort said.

"I've checked everything. I didn't see anyone," Fern said, her voice high and sparkling.

Fort's boots moved away, towards the window, and Worry relaxed a fraction. Then Fort's hands appeared, bracing against the floor. She knelt down. There was only one thing to peer under in this room.

Worry grimaced, tensing, ready to explain, to be shouted at.

With a tiny pop, Fern appeared next to her. Without saying a word, or even looking at her, she tapped her wand. A thin, wavery veil surrounded her.

Worry's mouth dropped open, her whole body taut with tension, staring at Fern. *What is she doing?*

Fort's head appeared, and Fern lifted her wand higher, as if she'd come under the bed simply to illuminate the space.

Frowning, Fort moved this way and that, peering into all the corners, but her gaze slipped across Worry as if she wasn't there.

Worry's mind reeled. Fern was tricking her chosen knight. That wasn't supposed to be possible. Fairies chose their knights and then aided them, advised them. It was an ancient order that had always been this way.

Worry's stomach went cold, and she wanted to crawl out from under the bed, through that strange transparent veil, confess everything to Fort, and try to figure out what was going on together.

Fern still wasn't looking at her. *What are you doing?* Worry thought. *Why are you helping me?* Was she working with Kepler? *Am I doing something wrong?*

But Fort had told her there was no way to rescue Hope. And she'd been keeping things from her for years. Worry wanted to know the truth, and she wouldn't give her sister up for anything.

Even if it destroys the last of the Scholar Knights?

Worry pushed the thought aside. She had no reason to believe that would happen. Information couldn't hurt anyone, could it?

At last, Fort pushed up off the floor and collapsed onto the bed. It creaked and sagged under her weight.

"Guess I'm pretty jumpy tonight," Fort mumbled.

"Here, let me warm up your tea, and I'll get a fire going," Fern said gently. A moment later the room was warming and the smell of blueberry tea wafted in.

"Have you seen my notes? I can't find them anywhere."

"Oh yes, you left them in the hallway when you stopped to look at that painting."

"Ah, thank you," Fort stretched, stifling a yawn. "I'm so tired. But I should be doing more. I sent word out again though, sent out the call for every able-bodied fighter for thirty miles to get here as soon as possible. I tried to make it sound more urgent this time, but I still don't know if anyone will come." Her voice was tight, heavy and thick. The next words caught in her throat. "I lost her, Fern. I lost the last one. She was such a sweet girl. I hate to think—" Fort's voice cracked.

There was a long, heavy silence.

"There's one left," Fern said.

"Are you sure you haven't heard anything from Bluebell?"

Worry bit back a gasp. Who was Bluebell? The name felt like a warm bath, like perfect love and safety, like a cozy room on a stormy day.

"No, nothing," Fern said. "She's truly gone, it seems."

She's lying again, Worry thought immediately. She had no reason to think this, no evidence, but she felt in her gut it was true. *But why?*

"Well, you of anyone would know."

Fort slurped her tea and yawned heavily again.

"We've got . . . eighteen hours until the next one starts. I need to ready the rest of the defenses. Hopefully the others will be here by then. I'm just . . ." she yawned again. "I'm just going to take a quick . . . a quick . . ."

Fern caught the teacup neatly just before it hit the floor.

For the briefest moment, her eyes locked with Worry's.
She looked conflicted. Guilty?
She vanished in a cloud of green sparkles.

Using Gravity to Find the Invisible

How can we discover something we can't see? Gravity! That's how astronomers found the planet Neptune. Neptune is a gigantic planet for our solar system. It's 17 times the mass of the Earth! It's also extremely far away. (It's the farthest planet from the Sun, except for poor Pluto, who despite what scientists say will always be a planet in my heart.)

Astronomers and mathematicians were observing nearby Uranus, when they noticed a slight wobble in Uranus' movement. They realized that there must be some giant object passing nearby, like a giant magnet passing near a metal ball, pulling it towards it just slightly.

They used math to calculate where this secret massive planet might be hiding. They pointed their telescopes in that direction, and they found it! That must have been an amazing moment. I bet they felt like geniuses.

Let's practice finding invisible objects! Gravity is a lot like magnetism in many ways, except that magnetism is much, much stronger. So, we'll use magnets in this activity to represent gravity.

Get some magnets (4 or 5) and a piece of stiff paper or thin cardboard. Place the magnets on the ground, spaced apart, and balance the paper over them. Try to keep the paper flat.

(So, you're using the magnets kind of like table legs.)

Now take a metal ball or marble and roll it across the paper. Try to roll it so that it passes near a magnet by not quite directly over it. Notice how the magnets affect the motion of the metal ball. This is just like how strong gravitational forces would affect a mass travelling nearby.

For one other cool solar-system activity, check out "If the Moon Were Only One Pixel: A Tediously Accurate Scale Model of the Solar System." https://joshworth.com/dev/pixel space/pixelspace_solarsystem.html

Chapter Nine:
Tides

WORRY winced as Fort gave a loud snort and rolled over. The bed creaked and groaned.

It had better not break.

Worry weighed her choices. If she snuck out, and Fort woke up and saw her . . . She shook her head. She couldn't afford to wait until Fort left.

Tucking the book into her bag, Worry squirmed her way out from under the bed. Keeping flat to the floor, she crept across the spare wool rug.

Fort grunted and mumbled something.

Worry froze, staring at her. Fort had bundled up her blankets and was clutching them to her chest, curling her body around them. Her eyes twitched under her lids. "No," she said. "Eggs."

That sure was a stressful-sounding dream to be having about breakfast. A pang of sympathy hit her. Fort tried so hard at everything. And her own fairy godmother was lying to her!

What must it be like for Fort, being the only Scholar Knight? Hope felt so much pressure, being the only student here. And she had Worry for company and sympathy. Fort was the only Scholar and had been the only student in her day, too. Was it nice to have had all those teachers, or did that make the pressure even worse? And then, to have the teachers pass on one at a time, leaving Fort completely alone in this castle for years. Well, except for Fern, of course. No wonder Fort refused to tell Worry anything. She must feel like she had to do it all on her own.

Don't worry, she thought. *You're not the only one trying. I'll fix this.*

Even as she thought it, it felt a bit silly to think that she could do what Fort—smart, powerful, unstoppably hard-working Fort—couldn't.

Worry slipped out of Fort's chambers with a massive sigh of relief and broke into a run. She sprinted for the nearest exit and pushed her way out into the salty night air. Kepler reappeared at her side as she descended the steps two or three at a time.

"What happened?" Kepler asked.

"Fern hid me!"

"Fern? No. But . . . was it a trick?"

"Only on Fort," Worry said, out of breath. She sure was doing a lot more running than usual. *I should have thought of practicing this.* Having keys was good but running up and down staircases all night was a type of practice that hadn't occurred to her.

She spilled out onto the beach and skidded to a stop in the rocky sand.

Pulling out her own tiny telescope, she scanned the island on the other side of the bay. A tiny bit of reflected moonlight caught her eye.

There. The outline of a spire.

There must be a reason Fort had been watching that castle, and a reason the Tapestry of Travesties had shown it to her. She'd just better be careful not to fall in that bottomless chasm.

A vast expanse of water stretched between her and the island, but the tide was receding.

"What's the plan?" Kepler asked.

"Well, I could look for a boat, or try to make one, but . . . I think the tide's on its way out, and I have a feeling that we might be able to reach the other castle at low tide. If it's low enough. Do you know how long it takes for the tide to go out?"

Kepler only stared at her; his lips clamped tight.

"Fair enough," she said. "I wouldn't have thought tides had anything to do with astronomy, though." She interlaced her fingers behind her head and stared at the lapping waves. "Maybe I'll give it a minute, see if the tide looks like it's going out far enough. I'll read your book in meantime." Kepler's ears perked up and he ran three quick circles around her.

"Will you keep watch for Fort?" she asked.

Kepler spun around, his tail flying out. "Yes! I'll let you know if she's coming. Don't leave without me!"

"Of course not!"

He sprinted back up the stairs, and Worry sat on the bottom step, pulling out Kepler's book. A cloud of fireflies drifted over, hovering around her shoulders and illuminating the pages.

"Thank you," she whispered, running a hand across the leather cover, putting a fingertip on the cool seaweed that bound it. Would opening it break the enchantment on Kepler?

Gently, she tried the shell clasp, and it clicked open. Unwinding the seaweed, its glow fading, she waited for Kepler to return, excited, but nothing happened. She shrugged and opened the first page. Enchantments could be tough to break.

Words and diagrams and lengthy equations appeared on the pages as she turned them. Unlike in Aristotle's book, the last page had no disembodied writer to talk to, only a sketch of a cat with a pointed moustache.

She returned to the first page and began to read.

There were long lists of numbers, observations that Aristotle would have approved of, and tables of data. Sketches of the sky with unfamiliar planets labelled in their positions.

To her excitement, there was a whole section on tides.

"There are two tides per day," Worry read aloud. "I believe they are caused by the moon, but I don't know how, only that that seems to be the case. It is some harmony I don't understand."

"Caused by the moon!" Worry exclaimed. How did that work? "In a twenty-four-hour day—oh, that's the same as here, I wonder if the tides work the same, too—that would mean twelve hours per tide, or around six hours in and six hours out."

She lifted her gaze to the moonlit sand. A crab scuttled across the silvery surface and disappeared into a hole. The bay was a long expanse of exposed sand, littered with clumps of seaweed. The island poked up out of the water about a mile away, its base rocky and exposed, its top spiky with evergreens.

"Okay, it was high tide right before the syzygy, so I probably have an hour or two until the tide's at its lowest point. Does the tide always go out the same distance, though?" She tried to remember how far the water usually went out, wishing she'd paid more attention.

She flipped another page. Kepler's world had only one moon, it seemed. How strange! If they only had one moon, then why were there two tides per day? And would the tides in her world work the same as in his? She stared up at the moons. Only the red moon moved around the planet. The other two were fixed. So maybe only the moving moon caused the pattern of tides? But how could that be? Did the shape of the beach matter?

She struggled to keep it all in her mind. Three moons, one moving. A high tide around every twelve hours. A regular rhythm, but with varying depths.

She understood now why Kepler had been so annoyed when Aristotle said the tides were caused by the wind. But she also understood why it had been so hard for people to figure out.

She looked again across the bay at the tiny island that was her goal. Only a small amount of water remained between it and her.

Science Activity:

Sometimes in science, we know why something happens, but other times we only know that it does. This was the case for Kepler. He had a large amount of data from Tycho Brahe about how the moon and planets moved, and he used it to figure out that the planets moved in elliptical orbits, and he was sure the moon caused the tides, but he didn't know how that was happening. Still, having good data and noticing some patterns are a good first step on the road to understanding.

In this activity, let's take some data of our own, and we'll see why it was so tough to understand the tides.

Choose a location that is near the ocean. It can be near where you live, if you have tides, but you could also pick a place you'd like to go to, or a place you saw in a movie. I'll use Langley, on Whidbey Island.

Next, get yourself a notepad to take some data! Each day for a full week, record the times of the high tides at your location and the times when the moon is highest in the sky. You can also draw a picture of the moon to depict whether it's full, half, quarter, etc. For your notes on the moon, you can either observe directly, or you can use the SkyView app to follow its path, or the *Sky and Telescope Interactive Sky Chart*. Just input the day, time, and zip code of your chosen location.

For the tides, you can observe them directly or you can use the *US Harbors Tide Charts*.

After you've taken all your data, what do you notice? Do the tides correspond to the position of the moon in a regular way? What might be affecting this?

You might notice a pattern, but you might not. It turns out that even though the moon causes the tides, they vary a lot because they're also affected by the shape of the coastline, the gravity of the sun, and the rotation of the Earth! This is part of why figuring out how the world works can be so tough. There are so many things that all have an effect. We'll learn more about this in later chapters.

Chapter Ten:
Pendulums

A YOWLING like a siren reached her ears. Kepler shot around the base of the castle, pelting towards her.

"Time to go!" he shouted.

She slammed the book closed and hastily stuffed it into her bag.

"What's—"

"No time, no time, let's go!" he shouted, whizzing past her in a blur of light.

She leapt to her feet and took off after him, her bag banging against her side and her boots splashing through puddles.

"What's going on, Kepler?" she yelled, gaining on the ghost.

"Fort figured out you took—you were in her quarters."

Worry craned her head to look behind her, stumbling over the uneven ground, to see if Fort was running after them. "Is she—"

"Nope, nope. She's got reinforcements now."

"Soldiers?"

"Volunteers. From the neighboring villages."

"Ah, well, great."

"Yes, except they're after you now. I told them I'd seen you down in the library, but that won't slow them down for long." He gave a frustrated growl. "I really wish I could do things sometimes. Like close doors. And turn locks, for instance."

Worry pumped her arms, her pounding feet splattering mud. It soaked her pant legs but sailed right through Kepler.

"Anything else I should know?" Worry asked.

"An octopus can change color and texture to blend in with its surroundings!" he shouted.

"That sure would be handy!"

"Yes," Kepler said.

They were about halfway across the muddy bay, and Worry's boots were sinking inches deep with every step in the thick mud, when a distant shout reached her ears.

Against her better judgement, she turned briefly to see a group of adults emerging from the castle, shouting and pointing at her.

They took off at a run towards her. They looked like they might have practiced running a time or two more than she had.

She yelped and picked up the pace, slipped on a clump of seaweed, and splashed into a puddle. Flailing, with the incorporeal Kepler trying to help her up and succeeding only in sending chills through her, she pushed herself back up. *Okay, Worry,* she thought, *just run as fast as you can without falling.*

She fell a few more times before she reached a narrow channel of black water flowing between her and the island. She barely paused at the edge before wading in, holding her satchel over her head. "Please don't be deep," she muttered.

The icy water rose to her chest, and she felt like she'd been fully submerged in a giant Kepler. Kepler floated across the surface, urging her to hurry.

The frozen current tugged at her, and she pushed her legs forward, nearly losing her footing on the sand that gave way beneath her feet.

Finally, the far bank appeared, the water became gradually shallower, and at last she emerged, dripping and shivering, on the far side.

She didn't stop, just struggled in her wet clothes to the rocky base of the island.

A narrow set of stone steps wound up through smooth, red-barked madrona trees, their wide yellow leaves littering the ground.

Worry was grateful for the climb, even though her leg muscles burned in protest and her wet pants chafed, because it warmed her slightly.

The air around her lightened and the sky overhead became a paler shade of gray as the sun began to rise. Far below, their pursuers were gaining. She was only halfway up the dizzying steps when they crossed the channel and started up after her.

She swallowed hard and pushed herself to climb faster, grabbing tree branches to haul herself up the steep steps.

At last, she stumbled onto the top: a bare promontory of black volcanic rock and sparse yellow grass. There, only feet away, was the chasm she'd seen in the Tapestry of Travesties.

The chasm was a sudden gash in the black rock, as if the island had split in half. On the other side of the chasm rose the many-spired castle. Its lean was even more pronounced up close. The central tower tilted at almost a forty-five-degree angle to one side. The other spires were straighter but leaned at their own crazy angles in all directions.

She could also now see that it was covered in silver symbols. Planets, moons, comets, mathematical equations. Large balconies extended on all sides, each with its own large telescope, pointed at the heavens.

A thick metal cable overhead ran from one side of the chasm to the other, and from this cable three pendulums hung, each a different size and shape, and each its own length. They swung towards her and away, each with its own rhythm and speed. Her stomach gave a swoop as she watched, imagining trying to jump from one to the next.

She approached hesitantly, knowing the villagers would be there any minute, and peered down into it. A cold wind, like damp breath hit her face. The sun wasn't high enough to send light far down into it, so she could only see a few feet.

"Hurry," Kepler said. "We've got to get across."

He skittered over to the edge and peered back down the steps. "They're a lot better at stair climbing," he said, sounding both panicked and impressed. "You've got maybe a minute."

315

Her heart thundered, remembering the little image of herself from the tapestry, falling into the chasm.

She gulped, picked up a rock and dropped it in, just to see. Maybe it wasn't that deep.

She listened, and for a long while she heard it falling. Slowly, the sound faded, but she never heard it hit the bottom. She dropped a few more in, just in case she'd missed the sound of the impact.

Nothing.

A horrified groan escaped her lips.

"Come on, come on," Kepler said.

"Hang on," Worry said, noticing a plaque and a set of gears at the edge.

"Thirty seconds," Kepler said.

"If I don't take my time to figure this out, there's no point anyway," she said.

The plaque had an image of her planet, with a little "you are here" arrow indicating that she stood at the edge of a pit that ran the full diameter of the planet. She frowned. It looked like the chasm went all the way through the center of the planet and out the other side. That wasn't possible, was it?

She thought of Aristotle and his idea that earth and water wanted to be as far down as possible. What would happen in a pit like this? Would they fall to the center of the planet and then stop, stuck there?

That didn't make sense, because she knew that when she dropped something it fell faster and faster. So, when it got to the center, it must be going really fast.

But when you crossed the center of the planet, you'd be going upwards again. That didn't make sense at all. She picked up another stone and tossed it into the air. It rose a few feet, slowed down, paused, then fell back down. Would that happen in the tunnel? Would she fall through to the other side of the planet?

She didn't have time to think about this, she had to get across, so she turned to the panel. Three levers and three cranks were lined up in two rows.

Randomly, she pulled the first lever. A brake was applied, and the first pendulum ground to a stop, hanging straight down. She pulled the second and third, and those pendulums stopped as well. Well, it was nice that at least they weren't moving anymore. But the first was too far away. She knew she couldn't jump that far, and even if she could, she couldn't get to the second, let alone the third.

She started them swinging again. The first pendulum came close enough to the edge that she could have jumped to it, but it was out of sync with the next pendulum.

I see. I have to adjust them so that the second pendulum is closest to me when the first pendulum is farthest away, so that they're close enough to jump between them.

"Back away from the machine, Worry," a deep voice rang out.

She spun around and saw the last of the five adults climb over the edge. They were a motley group, with patched clothing and battered swords, but they were each several feet taller than she was and looked barely winded from their long climb. Worry didn't understand how that could be possible.

Faint early morning light shone in their eyes. She raised her palms in a placating gesture. "Please, I'm just trying to help," she said.

"Fort said as much, but you're to come with us," the leader said. He took a step closer.

"Please," she said again. "Please, I need to get Hope back."

"We know you want her back, but that's impossible. The best thing you can do now is not make any more trouble for Fort. She sent us to get you, when we should be back defending the castle for . . . what might be coming."

The others were nodding. "You're wasting valuable resources, kid."

Worry swallowed. There might be truth to what they were saying. Yes, she was trying to help, but she didn't know what was going on. Because Fort refused to tell her.

"Look," Worry said. "That totally makes sense, and I want to go back and help, but I can't do that unless Fort will be honest with me."

"You're just a kid," he said.

Her throat tightened and tears rose in her eyes. "Maybe, but I still have to do something. I can't sit around hiding, not knowing what's happening."

"That's a mistake," he said. "You're making things worse."

"You've already made things worse, by opening the tower," another added.

Worry scanned their faces and saw only earnestness. She swallowed hard and shook her head, looking down. Who was she to be trying to fix things? She was just making a mess of everything.

Out of the corner of her eye, she saw something strange. There, in the chasm, a rock appeared, floating, for a second, before falling back down. She blinked, her vision swimming with tears.

Another rock appeared, rising from the depths, pausing, and then falling back down. *What?* They were familiar rocks. They were the ones she'd dropped. She thought of Aristotle, of her own ideas about what would happen with a tunnel that went all the way through the planet.

A very, very risky idea occurred to her.

A thousand objections immediately suggested themselves.

The villagers were edging closer, raising their hands. One carried a length of rope looped across her chest. If they caught her, they'd bring her back to the castle and lock her up.

"Please, I just need to get my sister back. I just need to help."

"We can't promise that, kid."

Desperately, she scanned the narrow promontory on which she stood. All sides were steep cliffs. There were only the stairs in front of her—with the grownups in her way—and the chasm at her back. No other ways off this ledge.

She took half a step back, and the leader lunged for her.

A yowling, white blur shot in between them, colliding straight with his face.

"Ah!" he shrieked, pawing at his face, waving his arms and shaking his head as if trying to wave off a mosquito. "Cold!" he shrieked. The others dove in to help. Kepler leapt between them, like a surprise internal ice bath. She had only a second to make up her mind.

Clenching her fists, she stepped backwards off the edge of the chasm.

Safety Notes:

Don't try this at home! Worry's planet is special. It's smaller than Earth, so it has less gravity, and it has a tunnel going perfectly through its center. Will she be okay? What will happen as she falls through the chasm? To understand that, we'll need to understand some things about gravity!

In the last activity, we saw how hard it can be to understand the world, because there are so many complex factors that go into each phenomenon. How can we fix this? One way is to ask ourselves a simpler question. Simplify or slow down the thing we're looking at, to try to understand it better, and to try to rule out some of the many complicated factors. Many scientists and mathematicians use this trick to solve complex problems. I love using this trick when I'm solving puzzles!

So, what's a simpler gravity situation? Pendulums! Legend has it that Galileo Galilei was staring at a chandelier swinging back and forth in Pisa Cathedral when he realized he could use its motion to understand something about gravity. What causes a pendulum to swing? Gravity!

Pendulums Activity:

In this activity, let's figure out what affects the speed of a pendulum. All you need is a stopwatch, and a weight tied to a string. A necklace with a pendant works great. To start, hold the necklace by one end with the weight dangling down. Grab the weight and lift it up and to the side a bit, keeping the string taut. Have someone start the stopwatch at the same time as you let go of the pendulum. Watch the pendulum swing down and back. Keep your hand holding it as still as possible. Stop the stopwatch right as soon as it comes back to its starting point. The amount of time this takes is called the period of the pendulum. (You could also let the pendulum swing 3 times and then divide the time you get by 3, sometimes this helps with accuracy.)

What do you think might affect the time this takes?
Would the weight affect it?

Try adding more weight to your pendulum (maybe add another pendant to your necklace.) Make sure you keep the starting point of the pendulum and the length of the string the exact same! (When we're experimenting, it's important to only change one thing at a time so we know what causes what.) You might want to make a little table in your notebook to record the weight of your pendulum and the period of the swing so you can see if there are any patterns.

Next, let's see if length of the string affects it! This time, keep the weight exactly the same, but repeat your measurement of the period with different lengths of the string. Does the period change?

You could also try playing around with the *Phet Pendulum Lab*. Try changing the string lengths and the weights and see what changes the time it takes to swing back and forth.

Bonus challenge question: Does the starting height of the pendulum change its period?

Results: Making precises measurements is tough, but what you should notice is that the mass doesn't affect the time the pendulum takes to swing back and forth. This directly contradicts Aristotle! Why? Because it means that different weights are falling at exactly the same speed. Aristotle thought that heavier objects would fall faster, but Galileo showed with his pendulums that they don't! The surprising fact about pendulums is that it doesn't matter how heavy the weight is, or how high you start the swing from (as long as it's not a super big angle). There are only two things that affect the speed and period of the pendulum: 1. The length of the string and 2. The strength of gravity.

One super cool fact: you can use pendulums to measure how strong gravity is. If you were suddenly teleported to a random planet, and you didn't know which one, you could use a pendulum to precisely measure the strength of gravity, which you could use to figure out which planet you were on! (Assuming you were somewhere in the solar system and had a table of the gravitational strengths of the different planets...)

Chapter Eleven:
The Bottomless Pit

WORRY screamed as she plunged into darkness, the dank air whistling in her ears as she fell, as if into the throat of some enormous, subterranean dragon.

She screamed until she ran out of breath, then sucked in more of the dank air and screamed some more, all the while falling faster and faster.

Eventually, when nothing horrible had happened, she stopped screaming.

The wind rose and rose, plastering her hair straight up; her braid was like a lifted tail. She squinted against the blackness, but there was nothing.

At any moment, she expected to career into something. The side of the chasm, some ill-placed ledge. Maybe a giant tongue would lick out and scoop her into the mouth of some invisible monster.

She screamed again, thinking of the monster and what it might feel like to be chewed up. But, when that didn't happen, and she continued to plummet without incident, she stopped.

It was surprising how quickly one got used to speeding through the center of a planet at speeds faster than one thought possible.

By waving her arms, she could change her position. It was like swimming, and she realized she could change her speed. Feet first was fastest. Belly first, with her arms and legs spread wide, was the slowest. She'd never noticed before how powerful air could be! It was so light, barely noticeable usually, but at high speeds, it really made a difference! What if there were no air here? Had Aristotle missed the effects of air, too?

Eventually, she realized she was slowing down.

I think I've passed through the center of the planet. Was she now blasting up towards the other side?

This seemed to be the case. Slower and slower she went. She whizzed past colorful, flickering lights, too quickly to make out their shapes.

Light dawned up ahead. She sped towards the brightness, the spot growing larger and larger. The closer she got, the slower she fell. Could it even really be called falling anymore? Or was she now flying?

Through the hole above, she began to see trees, fireflies, more flickers of colorful lights. Slower and slower she went, at last just barely popping through the hole, rising like a whale lifting out of the ocean in a graceful leap.

She had a quick glimpse of evening light. Orange rays slanting through campfires. Great trailing moss hanging like shawls from ancient trees. Everywhere, around the campfires, lounging in trees, fluttering over the hole, were delicate gossamer fairies.

Lilting music cut out as she rose into their midst. They stared openmouthed at her. She gave the tiniest of waves as she paused, then, with a swoop of her stomach, began to fall back into the hole.

A few of the fairies whizzed after her, but she was quickly gaining speed, and they couldn't catch her. For a while she went back to screaming.

She felt it this time, that moment she passed through the center of the planet. That moment when she was no longer speeding up but just for the briefest of moments there was that same weightless sensation she'd had at the top of the Astronomy Tower. And then she was gradually slowing again.

As she approached the opening she'd originally started at, she scanned the bright spot for something to grab onto. She definitely didn't want to risk another fall through the center of the planet.

She reached her arms up and prepared to grab whatever appeared.

She lifted gently above the hole, to almost the height she'd started at, extended her foot, and stepped back onto the ledge she'd leapt off several minutes earlier.

She grinned, full of exhilaration and triumph. The others were gone.

Her stomach went ice-cold as a ball of light collided with her. It roiled through her shoulders, neck, out one arm, then back to her stomach again.

"Ow, Kepler, eesh!" She dodged out of his way.

Silvery tears were dripping from his pointed moustache. He wiped them away with his tiny paws and stared mournfully up at her.

"I watched you disappear," he said quietly.

She knelt and ran her hands over his back. "I'm so sorry to worry you, Kepler. I'm fine. I dropped some rocks in earlier and they came back. I thought I could trick them into leaving."

His eyes widened. "That was incredibly . . ."

She expected him to say something like 'brilliant' or 'brave.'

". . . dangerous."

"Oh. Yes." That, too. "I had to, though."

He let out a long sigh and crouched lower. "Well, it sure worked. They watched the hole for a while, then your screaming cut out and . . . they felt awful. They're on their way to let Fort know."

Worry's stomach twisted. Fort was going to feel horrible, too. Worry didn't want to add to Fort's burdens. *I have to keep going, though.*

"Are you okay?" Worry asked Kepler.

He sat daintily. "Oh, yes. I'm all right, thank you."

She let out a long sigh. There was a ringing in her ears from the wind, and her stomach was still adjusting to being stationary.

She turned and stared up at the castle, silhouetted with early morning sunlight.

It was time to cross the chasm.

Who hasn't tried to dig a tunnel to the other side of the Earth? Could you actually make a tunnel through the center of a planet? This is such a fun thought experiment! The first answer is probably not on Earth, but possibly on Worry's planet, which is much smaller. The centers of planets get incredibly hot because of the weight of all the rock and dirt and oceans pressing down on them. The temperature at the center of the Earth can get up to around 10,000 degrees Fahrenheit. Iron melts at only 2,800 degrees, steel melts at 2,500 degrees. Wood burns at only 400 degrees. So, all our tools that we might use to dig or reinforce the tunnel would be destroyed. Not only that, but the pressure at the center of the Earth is 3.6 million atmospheres, which means it's 3.6 million times the pressure that we feel. (Have you heard that diamonds are made by squishing carbon? Well, that only takes about 60,000 atmospheres of pressure.) But Worry's planet is much smaller, and it doesn't have a liquid core, like our Earth does. (Side note, did you know that the Earth used to be solid rock? It didn't use to have a liquid core, but eventually over time, as the weight of the planet compressed itself inward, its core melted. This is called the "Iron Catastrophe"! You can read more about all this fascinating stuff in the *National Geographic Education article entitled "Core"*. But back to Worry's planet. Her planet is still solid rock, so it might be more doable. If you could dig this tunnel, then what Worry experiences in the story is exactly what would happen. As you fell down the tunnel, you'd go faster and faster. The air would get hotter, too, from the increased pressure. Your ears might pop just like when you swim deeper underwater (the atmosphere is like a liquid, too, it's thinner and lighter than water, but still very heavy! We just don't notice it because we're used to it.) One of the weirdest things about going through the tunnel is that the force of gravity gets less and less as you go down. The math of this is a little complex, but basically, only the mass that's below you affects you. The stuff that's above you gets balanced out. So, as you fall, it's like you're standing on a tinier and tinier planet. You're still speeding up, but not speeding up as much as you were initially. (You would also probably hit what we call "terminal velocity" which is where you're not speeding up anymore because the force of the air pushing on you is balancing out the gravity pulling on you. So, you end up going at a constant speed.) In the very center of the planet, if you could stop yourself there, you would find yourself in a cavern where you were completely weightless. Just floating around as if you were in a spaceship! But it would be hard to stop there, because you'd be going incredibly fast at that point! In fact, you'd shoot right through the center of the planet as if you were fired from a rocket. As long as you didn't hit the walls of the tunnel, you'd head straight up to the surface on the far side! If there were no air resistance at all, and if the planet were perfectly circular, you'd rise just above the planet's surface on the other side, just like a ball thrown into the air pauses for a moment at its peak, and then you'd fall straight back through. You'd arrive at exactly the spot you left! As long as you never hit the walls or slowed yourself down in any way, you could bounce back and forth like this forever! It would take you exactly the same amount of time every time you bounced back and forth. In fact, you could even set your watch by it or build a clock that used this to measure the time, just like grandfather clocks use pendulums to measure the time.

Story Prompt: Could you imagine a planet with a tunnel like this, or maybe many tunnels? What would people use them for? Brainstorm, outline, or write a short story about someone living on a planet like this. Are they human, or some other kind of creature? Is there air on their planet?

Chapter Twelve:
The Leaning Castle

WORRY cracked her knuckles and approached the chasm again. What if she jumped in again? Could she fall through and pop back up on the other edge of the chasm? Too risky. It was such a long distance through the center of the planet that the tiniest amount of speed to the side might cause her to hit the edge of the tunnel.

She examined the panel with its three levers and three cranks. Flipping each lever to the 'off' position, she stopped the pendulums from swinging. Then she spun the cranks. These cranks changed the lengths of the pendulums.

If I make them as different as possible, their differences will be more extreme, and I can see what happens. She made one as short as possible, one as long as possible, and left the third where it was.

When the pendulums were swinging, she immediately saw that the shorter string made the pendulum swing back and forth faster. The longest string took the longest amount of time.

All those pendulums look different. Doesn't it matter that one is heavier?

She reset them all to the same length and started them moving. They all swung at exactly the same speed now.

How strange. The weight doesn't seem to matter. That's not what Aristotle would have expected.

An idea hit her. Keeping them all the same length, she started the pendulums swinging one at a time, so that when the first was as far away as possible, the second was as close as possible, so that they nearly touched. Then, when the second was as far as possible, the third was as close as possible, and those two touched. Because they were all going at exactly the same speed, they kept up this regular pattern.

"Impressive," Kepler said.

"Well, I had a lot of time to think. While I was in the bottomless pit of despair."

"I suppose bottomless pits of despair are good for that," Kepler said.

Clenching her fists, she hopped onto the first pendulum, moving with it as it swung. Landing on it changed its swing a tiny amount, but it was a lot heavier than she was, and it didn't change much. She easily leapt to the second pendulum, and then the third.

With a triumphant yell, she landed on the other side.

Spinning around to see if Kepler had made it, she watched him hop up to the cable that crossed the chasm and trot calmly across it.

He leapt gracefully down to join her and sat licking his paw with a slightly smug expression.

She pouted. "Had you thought of that the whole time?"

"Yes."

"Why didn't you say anything?"

"You looked like you were having fun."

She opened her mouth to protest, then laughed. "Okay, yeah, that was pretty fun."

Together they climbed the marble steps to the foot of the leaning castle. Above an enormous door were engraved the words "Philosophy is written in this grand book, the universe, which stands continually open to our gaze."

How beautiful, she thought. There was so much to see and understand in the world. So much that we took for granted every day.

Below that, a second line read "It is written in the language of mathematics, and its characters are triangles, circles, and other geometric figures . . ."

She thought of how she'd used her knowledge of circles to find Kepler's book, and how within that book she'd learned that the moons travelled in ellipses around her planet. Math was sometimes hard, but, like learning another language might let her speak to people from other kingdoms, in a way, math let her speak to the universe. The hair on her arms stood on end, and she shivered.

As she stood transfixed on the threshold, marveling at the beauty of the world, the door was thrown open. A boy about her age stood staring at her.

He wasn't quite solid, but he wasn't fully transparent like Kepler. He looked mostly like a boy, but with the occasional shimmer, and she could just make out the far wall through him. He wore elegant purple robes and a jaunty purple hat.

He glanced down at her cat. "Hello, Kepler," he said. "It's been a while!"

"Narwhals have a tusk that is actually an elongated tooth," Kepler said.

"Ah, right. Still enchanted, my friend? Sorry, buddy."

"You know Kepler?" Worry blurted out.

The boy smiled widely at her. "Hello, my name is Galileo." He placed a hand flat on his chest and gave an elegant bow. His hat fell off.

"Oh. Hi. My name's Worry."

He snatched his hat back up and thrust it onto his head, looking at her curiously. "Really?"

"Oh. Yeah."

"It's not a nickname?"

"Unfortunately, not."

"That must be rough."

"It's not my favorite, no."

Galileo nodded sympathetically.

"Sorry, are you an astronomer, too?" she asked.

"Oh, yes, I am!"

"And you're not enchanted?"

He glanced around at his tilted castle. "I mean, I'm sort of under house arrest here. Like I was towards the end of my actual life on Earth." He sighed. "But no. Not enchanted."

333

"You look too young to have been arrested," Worry said.

"Oh, I just prefer this. Just like Kepler prefers being a cat. Reminds me to stay curious. Would you like to come in?"

"Yes, thank you," Worry said. "I'm wondering if you can help me with something, actually."

He led her into the castle, which was lit by chandeliers swinging to and fro in a way that was slightly dizzying. She quickly told him the story of the tower and Hope, and Kepler's enchantment.

"You reopened the tower?" Galileo said, his voice rising with excitement. "That's wonderful!"

Her stomach churned. "I'm not so sure. Do you know what happened to it? Why they sealed it off? Why the astronomers are all gone and almost all the Scholar Knights are, too?"

"No. All I know is that they built it to reach the red moon. Telescopes work better when you bring them up high. There's less air between you and the stars, so things are clearer."

"Did they ever actually reach the red moon?" Worry asked breathlessly.

"I don't know. They mostly asked me about my telescopes, and what I knew about gravity."

Worry's heart caught in her throat. "Do you have a telescope I could use to see the red moon?"

"Yes, I have several."

Her heart flipped over. "Can we go look?"

"Well, the red moon is below the horizon now. It will rise later tonight. We can look then, if you'd like."

"Yes! Please. Thank you!"

"My pleasure! I make all my telescopes myself. I even grind the lenses myself. Or I did. When I could touch things." He waved a transparent hand through a nearby lamp sadly. "The astronomers and I were actually working on turning this whole castle into a giant telescope. Maybe you could help me polish the lenses?"

"Of course," Worry said. "I'd be happy to."

He grinned and ran up a spiraling staircase, motioning for her to follow. She pounded after him, thinking ruefully that yet again she found herself sprinting headlong up a staircase. Kepler silently followed.

At the top of the tower was a giant circular window. It was made of glass around two feet thick at the edges and four feet thick in the middle. Through it, Worry could see the blue sky, distorted by the lens's shape. Galileo pointed to a pile of cloths.

"The astronomers were here working on it a while ago. I guess it's been decades now. I kept hoping they'd come back. It's incredibly frustrating to be a ghost and not be able to make anything anymore."

"I can imagine," Worry said, picking up a cloth and gently polishing the enormous lens. She felt like she was standing inside a giant eyeball, looking out. "You don't happen to know how to break Kepler's enchantment, do you?" she asked.

"I don't, sorry," he said.

"But you knew him? Here?" she asked.

"On Earth. We were scientists at the same time. He had very good ideas. We both disagreed with Aristotle, which was a very unpopular opinion at the time."

Worry scrubbed a little harder at a speck of dirt on the lens. "He seemed very wise," she said.

"Brilliant, absolutely brilliant," Galileo said, fiddling with his brooch. "But he missed some things."

"Like what?"

"Well, he thought heavier things fall faster."

"They don't?"

Galileo grinned and motioned for her to follow him to an open window. They were at the top of the leaning tower. Looking out, she could see the ground far below. She really hoped this tower would stay up.

Two ornate vases, one large and green and one tiny and yellow, were perched on the windowsill.

"Push them over the edge," Galileo said.

Worry did a double take. "Are you sure?"

He nodded.

Checking to make sure nothing was below, she pushed the two of them off. They plummeted to the ground, shattering at exactly the same moment.

Almost as soon as they had shattered, they reappeared, whole, on the windowsill. Her eyebrows lifted.

Kepler hopped up, his tail twitching in anticipation, and batted a paw at the vases. His paw went right through, and he meowed plaintively at Worry. She obediently pushed the vases off again. Seeing them hit the ground at exactly the same time again, despite their sizes, she frowned at them.

"But Aristotle said—"

"He didn't realize that air was messing up his results," Galileo said. "Lighter things like feathers are more affected by the air, so they fall slower. But if there was no air, everything would fall at precisely the same speed."

"That's so weird," Worry said. "How did you figure that out?"

He pointed to one of the swinging chandeliers. "Pendulums! I noticed that the mass of a pendulum doesn't affect how fast it goes. Understanding gravity is hard, because things fall so quickly. It's hard to figure out what's going on. Pendulums, and rolling things down gradual inclines, slowed things down enough for me to figure things out."

"That's so clever," she said, and he smiled. "So . . . what about . . ." she hesitated. This was the question she was most afraid to ask. Was Hope just destined to be somewhere else? "Aristotle said that earth and water both moved down, and air and fire naturally move up. That . . . things all have their own natural places?"

"A pretty idea, but wrong," Galileo said with confidence. A great weight lifted off her heart. As if its natural state was not in fact to weigh her down. "No, Aristotle thought the Earth was the center of the universe and surrounded by crystalline spheres. And that everything had its own natural place. And that the stars and planets moved in spheres. Which is all incorrect. He really loved spheres. I see why. They're very nice shapes."

"True, yes," Worry said, moving back to the great lens and resuming her polishing.

Galileo's voice rose in excitement. "But you have to go with the evidence! And from all my observations, all the evidence was pointing towards Copernicus's idea that the sun was in fact the center, and the Earth and other planets moved around the sun."

"Fascinating," Worry said, trying to picture this.

Kepler gave a mournful yowl and put his head in his paws.

"They move in ellipses, as my friend here discovered."

Kepler looked slightly more cheerful.

"And faster when they get closer to the sun, and slower when they get farther away."

"So even planets speed up and slow down?" Worry asked, amazed.

"Yes!"

"Why don't we feel that?"

Galileo opened his mouth and closed it again. "Huh. You know, that's an interesting question."

Her stomach warmed. Fort's response to Worry's questions was usually to tell her not to ask them. Or that her questions would bring destruction to the world. This was definitely nicer.

"Anyway," Galileo said. "People did NOT like me saying Aristotle was wrong. No, they did not. The Roman Inquisition put me under house arrest for the last years of my life."

"I'm sorry. What's the—"

"But I kept learning! And writing! I found that the distance travelled by a falling object is proportional to the square of the time it has fallen! Hah! Take that, Aristotle!" He punched the air.

338

"Er, yes. Bet that made him feel pretty silly," Worry said, having no idea what any of that meant.

Galileo looked at her. "Oh. Sorry. What I mean is, let's say an object falls one foot in a certain amount of time. It's speeding up that whole time, so it's falling faster and faster. When it's fallen for twice as long, it will have fallen four feet. When it's fallen for three times as long, it will have fallen nine feet. Four times as long, sixteen feet, and so on."

"I see. By 'square' you mean you're multiplying a number by itself. Two squared is four, three squared is nine. So, when you've fallen 3 times the time, you've fallen 9 times the distance. Very strange."

"Exactly!" Galileo said. His eyes were lit with excitement.

"Do you know why that is?" she said curiously.

He waved a hand. "I simply make observations and see patterns. I don't know what makes things fall. Newton might, though."

"Newton?" Her pulse quickened. That was the name of another of the missing books.

"Yes, but you probably already talked to him. He's in the Astronomer's Tower."

She shook her head, frowning. "I didn't see—wait, there was a locked door. Maybe he was in there?"

Galileo snapped his fingers. "You know, the last time I saw the astronomers, they left a key here." He pointed to one of the stones in the wall. "See if you can pry that stone out."

She just managed to get her fingers around the edge of the stone and pry it out. In a tiny space beyond, was a large iron key. Amazed, she pulled it out, examining it. It was iron, heavy, cold in her hands. She secured it in her bag of keys.

"Thank you!" she said.

He nodded. "Newton. I'm sure he'll have the answers you're looking for."

Science Activity:

The Exploratorium has a musical experiment you can do to get a feel for what Galileo discovered. It's called *Falling Rhythm*. (Search 'Exploratorium Falling Rhythm' to find it.) To do this activity, get a measuring tape, a cookie sheet, a long piece of rope or string, and some washers to act as weights. First, tie a weight on the string every foot. Stand on a stool and hold one end of the string, so that it dangles down, with the first weight just touching the ground. Put a cookie sheet below, to make the sound louder. Drop the string onto the cookie sheet. Listen to the pattern the falling weights make as they hit the sheet. You should notice that they hit closer and closer together, since they're speeding up. Now, untie the weights or get a new piece of string. Now tie one at the 1-inch mark, the 4-inch mark, the 9- inch mark, 16 inches (1 ft, 4 inches), 25 inches (2 ft 1 inch), 36 inches (3 ft), and 49 inches (4 ft 1 inch). Again, stand on the stool, with the string dangling. The closer-together weights should be closest to the ground. Now, drop the string and listen to the rhythm they make! It should sound like a regular drumbeat. This is because the longer things fall, the farther they go with every second.

Chapter Thirteen:
A Hopeful View

WORRY and Galileo spent the afternoon polishing lenses and tidying Galileo's workshop. He seemed very happy to have company and chattered on about math and telescopes.

"What about tides?" Worry asked. "How do those work?"

He frowned and scratched the back of his neck, dislodging his ghostly hat. "Er, well. I'm pretty sure it's because of our motion around the sun. You know how if you're carrying a bowl of soup, it sloshes around? I think that's what causes it. Maybe. It's just a guess."

Kepler put both paws over his face, but Galileo pointedly ignored him.

As evening closed in, Worry's anxiety rose. The second night of the syzygy was beginning. On the other side of the bay, Fort and her soldiers would be preparing to defend the kingdom from attacks. From more dragons. *I'm okay, Fort.* She tried to imagine Fort hearing the words. Hoped it would comfort her.

Galileo and Worry sat in the depths of the central tower, where a second great lens pointed up at the first lens. Together, the two lenses made a powerful telescope.

As they made the final adjustments, the red moon appeared, again creeping high into the sky to join the other two moons.

They sat in silence, staring up through the lenses at the magnified sky overhead. Waiting as the light in the observatory became redder.

Galileo sighed in contentment. "It's been so long since I looked through a telescope," he said softly. "For the last several years of my life, I was nearly completely blind."

Worry looked at him sympathetically.

He shrugged. "I saw more than most in my life, though. I saw farther into the solar system than any human before me. I was the first to see the moons of Jupiter." He went silent, lost again in remembering.

The red moon appeared at the edge of the lens. Worry gasped, moving closer, squinting her eyes and straining.

Bit by bit, it edged into view, until it covered the whole lens.

The details! The red surface was pockmarked with craters, and she could see every rock and ridge. "It's not smooth at all," Worry said softly.

"That surprised me, too," Galileo said. "And another of the things that disproved Aristotle. The moon and the sun weren't perfectly smooth, celestial objects like everyone thought they were."

She scanned the surface for any sign of her sister. Red canyons, pillars of rock. To her surprise, a great ocean came into view. In the center of this ocean, she saw a tiny red stone island. In the center of this was a tiny, silver speck.

Worry wasn't breathing. She didn't move. But the silver speck did.

It shifted, moving slowly right, to the edge of the island. It hit the edge and moved back, left as far as it could go. Like someone pacing.

Worry gasped and bit back a sob of relief.

She dropped to her knees, her hands on the floor, joy flooding through her. Her sister was alive.

"Are you sure you don't want to stay a little longer?" Galileo asked as Worry gathered her things.

"I'm sorry, I'd love to, but I need to go. There's only one more night of the syzygy. I need to get back."

Galileo looked down at his hat, which he was holding in his hands.

"Of course, I understand."

There was a long pause.

"I'll come back, though, and visit," Worry said. "I mean, we've got a lot more lenses to polish!"

Galileo brightened considerably, but then his face tensed up again. "I'm sure you'll be very busy, though. You're training to be a Scholar Knight, aren't you?"

Worry flinched. "Oh, um, no actually. I don't have a fairy godmother."

344

"You don't? But your name? It was given to you by one, was it not?"

She sighed. "Yes. But she disappeared."

Galileo gasped and lifted a finger, as if he were pointing at the ceiling. "She did? I—I can't believe I didn't think of this earlier. But I believe I've heard of you."

Worry froze, her gaze lifting to his. "What do you mean you've heard of me?"

"A traveler came to visit one rainy night. She came in to get out of the storm. I—" he blushed. "I pretended to be a scary ghost for a while. Sometimes it's fun to think I'm haunting this place . . ." He scratched the side of his head. "Anyway, she was not amused. And she already knew who I was. She said she was on her way to the castle of the Scholar Knights. Where her nieces were studying."

Worry's heart stopped. She wasn't completely confident in Galileo's sense of time, but . . . did she and Hope have an aunt somewhere?

"What did she say?" Worry prodded.

"She said she'd gone to correct a mistake. You see, one of the fairy godmothers had been in an incredible rush. She'd appeared at the birth, had been about to pronounce the name, had just said the first letter, when she stopped and looked up into the sky. She'd looked suddenly terrified. She disappeared before she finished the name."

A strange sense of unreality washed over Worry. It was as if someone had slipped a giant lens in between her and the memories of her entire life. Everything looked different.

Her mouth went dry, and it took her a few tries before she was able to speak. "What was the letter?"

"W," Galileo said. "I wish I'd thought of it when you first arrived. Especially because your name is so . . . unusual."

"Depressing, you mean?" Worry said faintly, but her mind was spinning.

"Er . . . not the usual tone of the Scholar Knights. They can be a tad . . . grandiose I feel."

The fairy godmother only said the first letter. That had been her fairy godmother, Worry felt sure of it. *My name might not be Worry at all.*

"But . . . why . . . why am I . . . How did I get my name?" she wondered aloud.

"That I do not know."

What did she mean for my name to be? Worry stood, motionless, her eyes unfocused, staring straight through Galileo. *Wonder? Warmth? Warrior?* She thought back to every time she'd ever questioned herself. How often in her life had she dismissed her own thoughts as worries?

Worth? Tears sprang into her eyes.

"Thank you," she said, her throat thick with emotion. "Thank you for telling me this."

He looked at her sympathetically. "Names can be heavy burdens sometimes."

She nodded, her mind still whirling, remembering every time she'd been annoyed at herself for worrying.

"Do I . . . do I seem like . . ." she trailed off, finding herself too afraid to ask the question.

"You seem very level-headed," Galileo said, guessing at her question. "You ask interesting questions. I saw you leap into the bottomless pit of despair, you know. Not many people go in there. At least on purpose. You seem . . . thoughtful. But just because one can see possible bad outcomes doesn't mean one is overly worried, or that one should dismiss those thoughts out of hand. There might be . . . useful information in those thoughts."

Worry nodded. *What is my name? If it's not Worry, what do I think of myself as? Who am I?*

It was something she'd have to . . . consider. Maybe something would occur to her. Until then, what was most important was getting back to the castle and figuring out how to rescue Hope.

"It was lovely to meet you," she said. "Thank you again. I'm sure I'll be back soon."

His eyes lit up. "That would be wonderful! I wish you all the best in your quest, Miss W."

She smiled and, Kepler at her heels, hurried back down the steps.

Chapter Fourteen:
Newton

THE castle was buzzing with activity. Groups of heavily armed men and women jogged through the halls, lighting their way with blazing torches. Worry dodged through secret passageways and crept through halls, narrowly avoiding being noticed several times.

When she reached the main level, she emerged from a stairwell and bumped right into a guard. He looked just as shocked as she felt. He reached for her, but she stumbled back, slipping out of his grasp and scrambling away.

Her feet pounded the floor, and she dodged into the Hall of Mirrors, only a few feet in front of him. She dove behind a mirror just before he rounded the corner after her.

She could hear his heavy breathing, only a few feet away. His footsteps clicked across the stone floor towards her, pausing to peer behind each mirror he passed. He stopped right in front of the mirror behind which Worry crouched.

It was a mirror that showed your ideal hair style, and she heard a slight intake of breath, and a ruffle as he ran his fingers through his hair.

She closed her eyes, expecting at any second to feel his hand descend on her shoulder.

A tiny skittering noise reached her ears, and she opened her eyes to see the spoon she'd given the olive to.

It shot out of its labyrinth, jumping excitedly at the man's feet and pointing out the other door frantically.

"You sure?" the guard asked.

The spoon gestured frantically.

"Thanks, little guy," the guard said and ran off in the direction the spoon had pointed. Straight into the infinite loop hallway.

Worry exhaled slowly. He'd find his way out, but it would likely take hours.

"Thank you," Worry whispered. The spoon bowed its head, and she continued on her way.

At last, she made it to the Astronomy Tower.

The door was open.

Had it really only been a day and a half since she and Hope had last stood here?

Deftly, she slipped inside and approached the second, locked door.

Galileo's key fit perfectly.

She crept inside, shutting the door quietly. Kepler arrived at her side, looking uncharacteristically reverent and solemn.

349

He straightened his fluffy collar and looked up at her, eyes wide and excited.

They moved farther into the dark expanse. Kepler's light expanded, filling the dark corners and illuminating a large circular room.

Tapestries on every wall depicted dragons. Dragons of every shape and size and color, glittering, soaring through the skies across a background of stars and planets. Worry stared in wonder. These were not terrifying monsters. There was something joyful about the way they were depicted. Wonderous and exciting.

"Newton?" she whispered, her voice echoing through the dark, still space.

There was only silence.

Worry approached a wooden contraption in the center of the room. A wooden scaffolding surrounded a large rickety cage flanked by gears and levers. Thick chains extended into the darkness overhead.

Finally.

An elevator.

Stepping onto the central platform, Worry glanced at Kepler, who nodded. She flipped the switch.

With a groan and a great clanking of chains, the elevator lurched upwards.

Relishing the effortless upwards motion, Worry examined the walls as they went. More mathematical drawings, more paintings of dragons, some with people standing next to them. Smiling, happy people holding telescopes.

350

What had happened? Had the dragons and the astronomers been working together? They didn't look like evil people conspiring to commit terrible atrocities. But then, Worry didn't know anyone who had committed any atrocities, so she didn't know what they looked like.

The ride lasted a very long time. Again, as she rose higher and higher, she felt lighter and lighter. She vastly preferred this calm speed to her fall through the pit of despair. She sat cross-legged, watching the paintings go by and talking with Kepler.

"What do you think my name is?" she asked him at last.

"I don't know," he said. She was surprised not to hear a sea fact.

"Do I seem like a Warmth to you? Or maybe a Warrior?"

"Hmm . . ." he twisted his moustache. "I suppose you could be Worldly now."

"Mmm . . ." That didn't feel right. "Wit?"

"Fort would probably call you Wily."

"Or Wild," Worry added. "Am I Wacky?"

"No. You're Watchful, though."

That was too close to Worry for her liking.

The elevator gave a shudder and began to slow. Worry's heart sped up and she climbed to her feet, staring up into the darkness. A flickering light glowed up ahead. She stared at it, holding her breath and willing it to resolve into a glowing figure. Someone who would tell her how to rescue her sister.

The elevator platform lifted into an ancient workshop. Windows ringed the room, and a staircase at the far end led to a small trap door in the ceiling. Next to this, an enormous canon crouched, pointing through a hole in the ceiling. Tools lay scattered around it, like someone had been working on it recently. In between the windows were floor-to-ceiling chalkboards covered in smudged writings.

Hesitantly, Worry took a step inside, which accidentally became a short leap in the low gravity.

A roaring fire burned in a grate at one end, filling the room with flickering light and shadows. A figure stood hunched over the fire, their back turned to Worry.

"Newton?" she said hesitantly, although this was no ghost.

The figure jerked and wheeled around, her mouth dropping open.

It was Fort.

She was holding a thick, leatherbound book.

Her expression softened, a look of joy and relief crossed her face, then swiftly turned to rage.

"What—what are you doing here? I thought—"

"I'm okay. I'm sorry I tricked those people. I just had to . . . I had to know." Her eyes flicked to the book in Fort's hand. "Is that the book of Newton?"

Fort's expression hardened. "So, it really was you who stole Kepler's book. You're working with them, aren't you? How long? This whole time? I wondered why a girl without a fairy godmother was brought here. It was all lies, wasn't it?"

352

"What? No, of course not. I— What are you talking about?" Worry asked.

Fort moved closer to the fire; her eyes locked on Worry. "Who are you really?"

"I . . . I was going to ask you that. What is my name, really?"

"You tell me."

"I don't know!" Worry cried in frustration. "I was just talking to Galileo, who said that—"

Fort blanched, and her cheeks flushed a hectic, angry red. "So, you are conspiring with them! It's true. And you must have found a way to break the protection spell I put around Kepler, didn't you? You've been lying to me this whole time."

Worry gaped, infuriated at the unfair accusations. "Of course not! And no, but . . . but *you* were the one who put this spell on Kepler? Why?"

"To protect the world! To hold together the last vestiges of this society!" Fort's voice rose to a desperate pitch. She sounded like she might cry. "And all this time you've . . . you're the one who opened the tower. You sent your sister there on purpose, didn't you?" Fort took a step towards her.

Now Worry felt like crying. "Of course not! I'm trying to get her back! Why won't you tell me anything? I just want to know what's going on!"

Kepler was inching away from her, moving around the edge of the room, trying to get behind Fort.

Fort saw him and spun around. "You!"

Kepler took another step towards her, but Fort held up a hand and he froze, unable to take another step.

"Please, Fort," Worry said. "I swear I don't know anything. Hope wanted to break into the tower—"

"Right. Blame your sister. Convenient."

"No—I . . . I didn't mean to. I just have to get her back! I . . . Will you please tell me my real name, at least?"

"Your name is Worry," Fort said. "You came here with your sister, with only a W sewn onto your baby blanket. I paid attention, watched what you said and did, and I picked your name."

"You named me this? But . . . but what if you were wrong?"

"Clearly, I was wrong. Maybe your name was Wreckage or Woe."

Worry drew herself up taller. "Fort, that's just mean. I swear I knew nothing about the astronomers. I've been trying and trying to figure out how to get to the moon so I can get Hope back. And I'm sorry I'm messing up your plans. I completely believe that you're trying to do the right thing, but you've kept me in the dark and I have no idea what's going on!" Her fists were clenched, and she realized she was shouting.

Fort's eyes narrowed. "At the last syzygy, a horde of dragons came from the red moon. They'd been planning this with the astronomers, unbeknownst to the Scholar Knights. The astronomers wanted power. They never liked that they were always second place to the knights. They lured the scholars out of the castle, just like you lured Hope, and then they brought the dragons in for their attack." Fort was breathing heavily. "There were almost no survivors."

Worry's eyes widened. "That's horrible. Were you there?"

"My teachers were there. They would barely speak of it."
She shook her head.

"But . . . where did the astronomers go?"

"The last of the knights were still very powerful. Those
who survived, after the dragons disappeared, they attacked
the astronomers, driving them into exile. They locked up the
books and sealed the tower. Which you apparently figured out
how to open. But even after that, no one wanted their children
to join the knights anymore. They started putting wards up
when their children were born, so the fairies couldn't give
them names. And so, the order of the Scholar Knights began
to die."

Worry struggled to make sense of all this. It felt like there
were pieces missing from the story. Was it really power the
astronomers had wanted? Her eyes went to the book in Fort's
hand. The answers would be in there, she was sure of it. She
couldn't just take Fort's word for it. Not anymore. Not after the
years and years of lies.

"I want to help," Worry said. "I want to trust you." She
swallowed. "Can I please just read the book?"

"These are secrets I am sworn to protect," Fort shot back.
"I won't let you call the dragons back."

She lifted the book. Kepler's eyes went wide. "No, please,"
Worry said.

Fort tossed the book into the fire.

The ancient cover caught immediately, flames licking
around its edges. Sparks of magic hissed and exploded like
fireworks.

Worry felt like she was falling into the pit of despair again.

Fort turned to her. "Where's the Kepler book, Worry?"

Worry blanched and Kepler began to struggle against the invisible wall Fort had put up. His tiny paws flailed in empty space, like he was digging a hole in the air.

Instinctively, Worry clutched her bag and took a step back.

"It won't hurt him," Fort said. "The book is only a gate. It's a doorway, not a person."

She reached out a hand and stepped towards Worry.

"No," Worry said. "You can't."

But there was nowhere to run. She took another step back and found herself lifting into the air, as if she'd taken a bounding leap. The syzygy must be nearby.

Fort lunged for her as Worry drifted back down. Worry's feet hit the ground just in time for her to push off to the side, careening towards the fire. Fort sailed past, her arms swiping the empty air where Worry had been a second earlier.

She narrowly avoided crashing into the flames. She reached into the inferno and yanked the book out, immediately dropping it as the heat seared her hands.

Without thinking, she dropped, belly first, onto the ancient, flaming book, wrapping her arms around it. The flames went out. Tears pricked the corners of her eyes, seeing the charred and smoking book.

Fort approached, moving between her and the elevator.

I'm trapped.

"Kepler!" she yelled. "What do I do?"

Fort lunged for her again, sailing straight for her.

She can't change direction, Worry realized. Without the floor to push off from, Fort had no way to turn. Worry scooped up the book and dodged out of her way, leaping again to the far side of the room. She found herself next to the staircase below the trap door.

"Don't despair!" Kepler shrieked. His voice was strangled, as if his collar were choking him, trying to prevent him from speaking. "Whatever you do, absolutely do not despair! Like before. When you were in despair. Don't do that!"

"What?!" Worry yelled. *What is he talking about?* "Like the pit of despair?"

"Right! Definitely not that!"

"But there's not a—" she looked up at the trap door. "Oh. Oh no."

Fort's expression went livid as Worry hurled herself up the steps. She narrowly missed Worry's ankles as she yanked open the trapdoor and hurled herself out into empty space.

It was an utterly still night. The sky overhead was clear and cloudless, a vast expanse of stars and nothingness.

I wish I had time to consider this, Worry thought as she crouched and then leapt upwards with all her strength.

Chapter Fifteen:
The Leap and the
Truth about Gravity

IT WAS slower than falling in the pit of despair had been. Gentler. She was already slowing down, but very gradually. Drifting upward in the vast emptiness.

Slower and slower, with the world opening below her. She saw the vast, dark ocean, its surface flecked with moonlight. And Galileo's leaning tower on the island across the bay. And in the distance the hulking dark shapes of mountains.

Craning her neck, she looked up to see the red moon expanding, appearing larger and larger as she drew closer.

Minutes passed, and Worry marveled at the stars, at the castle growing smaller below.

Again, Worry was surprised at how quickly one could get bored. Gently, she opened the book of Newton, terrified that all she would see were crumbling, charred pages.

As she cracked open the cover, smoke began to pour out, billowing into the shape of a man in long robes. His hair was on fire, and he coughed, but he was scribbling something on smoky paper.

"Just a second, just a second," he said, writing furiously.

Worry waited patiently, still rising slowly into the air.

He paused to chew on the end of his quill, staring out into empty space. After a few seconds of this, he blinked, then yelped and whirled around. He looked from Worry to the ground far below, and then to the moon overhead.

"Hello," Worry said. "Are you Newton?"

He cleared his throat. "This . . . this is a dream. Or I'm dead?" He looked down at his smoking, translucent body. "Ah. Dead." He glanced back at his work in frustration. "I don't suppose you'd let me finish what I was working on?" He peered more closely at her. "You're not at all what I expected."

"You're not dead," Worry said. "The fairies made a book that lets us ask you questions."

Newton frowned. "That . . . that doesn't sound . . . like something that is scientifically possible."

"I'm not sure how it works," Worry said.

Newton looked around him again. "But . . . fairies. And . . . okay, so I'm a . . . I'm a spirit?" He poked at his ghostly stomach with a transparent finger. It went straight through. "Oh. Oh no. I am going to have to rethink so many things now . . ." He looked both overwhelmed and fascinated. "But fourth rule of reasoning! New phenomena mean we rethink the ideas!"

"If it helps, my world is different than your world."

Newton scratched his chin. "Well, third rule of reasoning: if something is a physical law in one place it's a physical law everywhere. So . . . but, what do you mean a different world? Oh, the New World? Virginia? New Spain?"

"Ummm . . . maybe? To be honest I don't know."

"Huh." Newton put his hands on his hips and surveyed the empty void around them. "Well, this truly is most fascinating." He looked down at the planet they were slowly drifting away from, and then up at the moon they were approaching. "Are we . . . in the heavens?"

"I think so, yes."

"And you're sure I'm not dead?"

"I'm not sure of anything at the moment."

"Fair enough. Been there myself plenty of times. What did you say your name was?"

Worry opened her mouth, but something made her pause. She didn't want to give the name that Fort had given her. It was a name that had made her doubt her own thoughts her whole life. She couldn't guess what the fairy had wanted to name her, but part of her didn't want that name anyway. It was another name to try to live up to, or to fight against. A name with pressure and assumptions and roles. "I'm Abigail," she said, feeling a warm glow in her stomach that might have just been nausea caused by currently being a human projectile.

"Lovely to meet you, Abigail," Newton said. He looked again at the moon. "Fascinating. Absolutely fascinating. What is happening?"

"I jumped, and now I seem to be floating towards the moon. I'm hoping to make it there, but I don't know if I will. Do you know?"

"Oh, certainly. I do not know but I can easily calculate it. What speed did you jump with? What are the masses of your planet and moons? What is the distance between their centers?"

"Umm..."

Newton frowned. "We can't answer any questions without data! An understanding of the world requires an understanding of numbers."

Abigail nodded. "Galileo said something like that, too."

Newton's face lit up. "Galileo?!"

"Oh, yes, I just spoke with him. Do you know him?"

Newton sat down cross-legged, propped his elbows on his knees and his chin in his hands. His hair still burned merrily. "I wish. I love Galileo. He died the year before I was born, unfortunately. So close! But I've read all his works." He sighed dreamily. "He was so smart. Lots of evidence for the ideas of Copernicus, which I love. The sun being the center of the universe and the Earth travelling around it. In elliptical orbits, as Kepler discovered."

"Oh, you know Kepler, too?"

"No, he also passed before I was born. How do you know him?"

"He's my cat."

Newton considered this.

"I...I think I will have to treat this as a very strange dream. I'm not sure I'm quite ready to throw out my whole Principia Mathematica. Despite the Fourth Rule of Reasoning."

"That's understandable," Abigail said. She glanced up at the moon again. "Can you tell me what's happening? I really need to make it to that moon. My sister's there. She was kidnapped. Aristotle said that maybe she just belongs there."

Newton rolled his eyes. "My apologies for the eye roll. That was very impolite of me. Aristotle was extremely brilliant. It's amazing, really. Did you study Aristotle in school? I did. His ideas were still incredibly popular in my time, the late 1600's, even though he was writing in the 4th century BCE. Isn't that wild? Two thousand years later! But he used too much philosophy in his attempts to understand the natural world, in my opinion. True understanding requires experimentation. That's where it's at."

"I wasn't allowed to go to school."

"Oh, because you're a girl?"

"What? No. Why would that matter? Because I don't have a fairy godmother."

"Huh. An equally illogical reason, I suppose." He paused. "Is my hair on fire?"

His hair sent off a cheerful shower of sparks.

"Yes, it is. So . . . if the moon isn't celestial and, in the heavens, because it's made of aether and destined to be there . . . why is it there?"

Newton grinned. "Well! Let me tell you! It's pretty incredible, really. I was surprised when I figured it out."

Abigail lifted her eyebrows.

Newton continued. "One of my greatest accomplishments, and I have many, many accomplishments, was my Law of Universal Gravitation."

"What's that?" Also, why did everyone have laws? She supposed it was the need for certainty. As someone currently floating farther and farther away from everything she'd ever known, out into an infinite void, towards a strange new world inhabited by dragons, she could understand the desire for certainty.

"Well, it turns out that everything is attracted to everything else."

"What? What do you mean?"

Newton rummaged in his pockets and pulled out two more quills. He held them up at arm's length. "If I let go of these two quills, they would ever so slowly start to move towards one another."

"But . . . I've never seen anything like that."

"Well, no, you wouldn't have. And excellent question! Well done! Using your observations to discern the truth! Lovely. But be careful, because things are complicated. Sometimes things are so gradual that we can't perceive them, or there are other phenomena getting in the way."

"Like air resistance?"

Newton looked even more impressed. "Yes, exactly like that."

"That's why Aristotle thought bigger things fell faster."

Newton pointed at her. "Well done! Wow! Yes!"

Abigail felt like she must be glowing as much as Kepler did when he was near his book.

"Anyway, this attraction that all mass has for all other mass, it's very weak. So tiny that we can't notice it in our everyday life. But it's there." He pointed down at the planet. "See how enormous it is? That's why we can feel the effects of gravity. The more mass there is, the greater the force." He cleared his throat. "Apologies. Force is simply a push or a pull. People really were upset at my idea of gravity, though. Because usually a force is an obvious push or a pull. You have to be touching something. But gravity doesn't work that way. It's called "action at a distance" and it's a fairly strange idea."

"I can see why. How do things pull on each other without touching?"

"I have no idea! But that's fine. These things are complicated. It took two thousand years, and many brilliant scientists—Kepler, Galileo, Copernicus," he cleared his throat again, "me . . . to refine and change his ideas based on our experiments. I'm sure people will figure it out in the future."

"Wow . . . so all of this . . . every time anything falls . . . it's because mass is attracted to mass . . ."

"Yes, which is why things all go the same speed, if you ignore air resistance. The more massive something is, the harder it is to get it to speed up—that's my second law, you know—but also, the more massive something is the more gravitational force it experiences. Those two things balance out exactly and they speed up—accelerate—in exactly the same way."

"Amazing! But . . . why don't the moons crash into our planet?"

"Moons? You have several? Fascinating. We only have one. But that's something pretty incredible. The answer is that the moon is always falling."

"But . . . if it's always falling, then why doesn't it . . ."

"Why doesn't it hit your planet? Well, because it's falling *around* your planet. Imagine standing on the surface of your planet. You throw a ball as far as you can. Maybe from the top of that giant tower you have."

"Okay, I can imagine that."

"Your planet is curved, like all planets. So, as the ball travels in a straight line, the ground is curving down away from it. If you threw it fast enough, then the speed at which it fell would be exactly equal to the speed at which the ground was curving away from it."

"That's . . . that's so strange!"

"Indeed. So, your moons are all constantly falling towards you, but because they're going around your planet, the ground is always falling away. Like a dog trying to chase its tail."

"But . . . one of our moons moves and the other two are in the same place all the time."

"Ah, no, they only look that way. You have daytime and nighttime on your world, do you not?"

"Yes."

"Well, that's because your planet is spinning."

"Ohhh . . . So, our planet is spinning, but the moons are going around at exactly the right speed that they look like they're staying in the same place. That's so strange."

"Yes, the world is a strange, amazing, magical place. Even without fairy godmothers!"

"But why did I feel so light when I was at the top of the tower during the syzygy?"

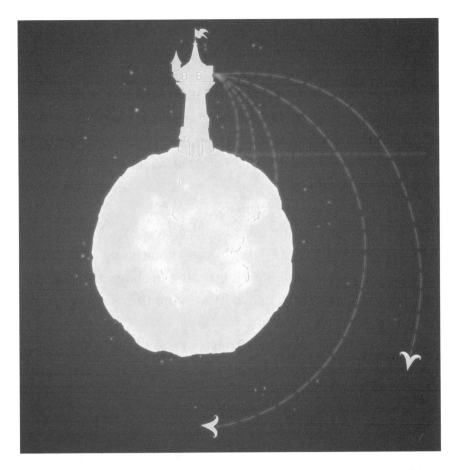

"I'm going to make some assumptions here, but that was likely because the gravity of the moons was pulling you upwards. That's what's happening now. The gravity of your planet is pulling you down, and the gravity of your moons—which is weaker because they are smaller and farther away—is pulling you up."

"So, am I going to make it? I mean, I know you don't have numbers, but . . . any guesses?"

"Well, it all depends on what the speed of your jump was. One thing working in your favor is that gravity gets weaker as you get farther away. It's what we call an Inverse Square Law. If you get twice as far away, gravity gets one fourth as strong."

"Oh, kind of the like the squaring thing with the distance something falls?"

"Yes, that's a square law as well, but the distance is increasing rather than decreasing, in that case. Here, gravity decreases as we get farther away. It all depends on whether you jumped fast enough. If you did, then at some point we'll reach a place where the force of gravity from your moons is greater than the force of gravity from your planet. If you can get to that tipping point, you'll start to fall towards the moon."

Abigail blanched. "How fast will I fall?"

"Well, generally when we throw things upwards, they end up back where they started, going exactly the same speed. But in your case, you jumped from a tower, which means you've got farther to fall on the other side. But also, the moons are smaller, so their gravity is weaker." He shrugged and lifted his hands, palms upwards. "It's complicated! I really can't say how fast you'll be going."

His smoky form shifted, as if an invisible breeze were blowing him away. He dissolved into eddies and then reformed.

"Whew, this book of yours doesn't seem to work all that well."

"Fort burned it."

"Ah. Well, that explains my hair." He scratched his head and stared up at the slowly approaching moon. "I wonder what having three moons does to your tides . . ."

Abigail perked up. "So, the moons do cause the tides?"

"Oh yes indeed. As I said, gravity pulls on all matter. Oceans are matter, and they move much more easily than rock and soil do. In my world, we have a single moon. The pull of the moon and the sun combine to make the tides. Yours must be complicated! Although, the fact that two of your moons are geosynchronous—they stay in the same spot in the sky—might make it simpler. Hard to say!"

Abigail was beginning to get a sense of just how complicated the world could be. Just how much tiny variables could change our perceptions and make understanding anything so difficult. It was much easier to jump to conclusions about things. To assume things were as simple as they looked. That tides were blown by winds and the planet was the center of the universe because everything looked like it spun around them. It had taken two thousand years of very smart people taking very careful measurements to figure out that that wasn't the case. And even the great Galileo was wrong about tides.

I wonder what I'm wrong about, Abigail thought. And this time she didn't dismiss the thought as pointless worrying, but something worth considering.

"But you know," Newton said casually, "I'm not sure it's gravity you need to worry about in this situation."

"No? Why's that?"

"Well—and I don't know how things work in your world—but in mine, air gets thinner as you get higher. At some point you should reach a place with very little or no air."

"That sounds bad." She took an experimental breath. The air did feel thinner. Was she lightheaded? She thought she might be, she just hadn't noticed.

"Quite, yes. But . . . well, perhaps you will discover otherwise!"

He cleared his throat. "The other—small—problem is that the moon is moving quite rapidly. As I said, it is orbiting. Moving horizontally at a very high speed to keep from falling into your planet . . . That might pose a problem for you as well . . ."

"Ummm . . ."

"Imagine jumping onto a galloping horse. If that horse were galloping at two thousand miles per hour."

"That doesn't seem like it would work well."

"No, not at all. But you weren't entirely stopped. You were spinning along with the surface of your planet . . . anyway, like I said, I really wish I knew the masses and distances involved here . . . I feel like I'm alarming you."

"Oh, no. I'm fine," Abigail said, breathing a bit more rapidly than was necessary, trying to tell whether the air was disappearing. "Just . . . wishing I'd taken a few more measurements before jumping . . ."

Newton nodded. "Yes . . . on the other hand, sometimes we do have to just try things."

Abigail looked down at her fingers. Were the tips blue?

"Any ideas?" she asked Newton. "What should I do now?"

The fire on the side of his head gave a little pop and a shower of sparks rained down.

"Hmm . . ." he said. "Well, maybe if you . . ."

The smoke shuddered, and his form dissolved like a whisp of cloud on a windy day.

"Newton?" Abigail closed the book and opened it again. "Newton, are you there?"

Nothing.

A wave of dizziness washed over her, and she took a few panicked breaths. The air felt thinner, colder, she struggled to breathe.

I really should have thought this through. She panicked, struggling with all her might to draw the thin air into her lungs. *Hope made it. I can make it.*

The red moon swirled in front of her, like an apparition taunting her.

Hope, she thought muzzily. Her eyelids began to close.

Two faint pops jolted her awake. Something warm and sparkling surrounded her, and suddenly there was air again. Thick and breathable and lifegiving.

The spots and flashes faded from her vision and, shaking her head, she looked around to see Rose, pink and gold and sparkling with gossamer dragonfly wings, and Fern, green and clothed in tendrils of delicate moss and surrounded by glittering dewdrops and rainbows.

They didn't look at her, but they waved their wands, gently tending to the sphere that surrounded her.

Aristotle would have liked this, she thought dizzily.

370

The moon was getting larger, but she was moving so slowly she was nearly stopped.

I'm not going to make it. I'm going to stop and fall back.

But, like a ball rolling over a hill, she seemed to reach some invisible peak over which she gently toppled.

Then, just as gradually, she was picking up speed again.

Suddenly, up was down and down was up.

She'd been flying upwards, up from the surface of her planet, into the sky, but now, everything had reversed. Down was the direction of the red moon, and she was falling towards it, gaining speed.

How strange, she thought. *I thought down was . . . down. But it's actually . . . towards the . . . the biggest thing nearby?* She wasn't sure.

But she was picking up speed.

At first it wasn't too much. When she'd gone about as far down as she'd originally gone up, she was going slower than when she'd first jumped. But after that she gradually picked up speed. The ocean she'd seen from Galileo's telescope sped towards her.

Gravity Simulation:

Play around with gravity! Follow the link below or search for "Phet Gravitational Force" to try out a little simulation of what gravity is like. You'll see two spheres, like planets. There are black arrows at the top, pointing towards each other. These arrows show you how strong the gravitational force is between the objects. You can also tell because the stick figure people are holding the masses apart. If gravity gets stronger, they'll have to pull harder.

Try dragging one of the masses back and forth. Does that affect the strength of gravity?

Now play around with the mass sliders. If you make one bigger or smaller, does that change both the arrows or only one?

Is there a way to make the two arrows have different amounts of force or are they always the same? Try making it as hard as possible for the two stick people. What do you need to change about the mass and the distance to make the force of gravity as big as possible? What about as easy as possible? https://phet.colorado.edu/sims/html/gravity-force-lab/latest/gravity-force-lab_all.html

Chapter Sixteen:
Finding Hope

THE fairy bubble protected her.

She splashed into the water, the force of her impact taking her several feet underwater. A luminous jellyfish stared at her wiggling its tentacles, and then the bubble shot back up, popping above the waves and settling down to float.

A swift current pulled it along until it bumped up against some shallow rocks and popped.

Abigail splashed down into the water, quickly getting her feet under her and standing.

The water was about knee deep, extending as far as she could see in all directions.

It was also daylight.

A pleasant, salty breeze was blowing, and silver and orange fish leapt from the waves, snapping bugs out of the air.

Looking back up the way she had come, Abigail saw an incredible sight. Her own planet, bright and silver and green with life, mostly in shadow, but glowing at the edges.

Behind it was the sun, glowing brightly, but looking like a crescent moon, partially eclipsed by her own planet. Her jaw dropped and she quickly looked away, the brightness hurting her eyes.

This was what the syzygy looked like from the red moon. Not the ominous nighttime alignment of colorful spheres, but a shadowy silver planet eclipsing the sun.

Where was Hope?

Shading her eyes with her hand, she scanned the horizon.

She didn't have time to search the whole moon. At least the water was smooth and shallow, and she could see for miles in every direction. Picking a direction at random, she splashed through the clear water, sending ripples out in every direction.

The gravity was so light here that every step sent her sailing through the air. It was almost like flying. She leapt, gliding several feet before slowly splashing down. It almost felt like she could keep floating forever.

Newton had said that if you threw something fast enough, it would orbit. Even jumping as hard as she could, she still splashed back down. Curious, though, she pulled a coin from her bag and threw it as hard as she could. To her astonishment, it sailed over the horizon. She stood, hands on hips, watching the place where it had disappeared, until, moments later, something whacked into her back.

She groaned, spinning around, panicked and expecting to see the dragon. But there was no one behind her.

Glinting in the water below her was the coin. It hadn't travelled all the way around the moon, had it?

She threw it again in another direction, with exactly the same speed.

This time, she spun around, scanning the smooth horizon.

Not long after, it came gliding up around towards her. She caught it deftly, her eyebrows lifting. Then she grinned.

Making a very slight turn, she threw the coin again. Again, she caught it when it came around the other side.

"This moon really is smooth," she muttered to herself.

She repeated the process for a few minutes, throwing it all the way around the moon again and again until one time, it didn't return.

Maybe I didn't throw it fast enough, she thought. Her arm was getting tired. She tried again with another coin. It still didn't return. That meant it had hit something. Like an island.

Hoping she was going the right way, Abigail sprinted off in the direction she'd thrown the coin that hadn't returned. She took great leaping strides, soaring over the surface of the water.

A thin column of dark smoke appeared in the distance. She splashed towards it, a rising current now dragging at her knees, and an island materialized. She stared at it, open-mouthed. It was the island she'd seen through Galileo's telescope. She'd made it.

The water now rose to her mid thighs, and she struggled along, slipping in the sand and waving her arms as she went. The red island grew, getting taller as she approached.

She arrived at the base of a sheer red cliff, extending straight upwards. Turning right, she began to make her way around the island, looking for a way inside.

Seabirds nested in the cliffs, diving and calling to one another.

Something gold glinted, catching Abigail's attention.

There, at the foot of the great red cliff, half-submerged in the water, was a solid gold cage with thick bars. Sitting on a large stone in the center of the cage, her knees drawn up to her chest, her clothes and hair soaked, was Hope.

"Hope!" Abigail called, overjoyed, splashing towards her sister.

"Worry?" Hope shivered and stood, leaning against the bars. "What are you doing here? How did you get here?"

Abigail reached through the bars, wrapping her arms around her sister and holding her tight. "I jumped. Are you okay?"

"You . . . you jumped?" Hope leaned back, her blue eyes wide, taking in her sister. "I'm okay, but . . . I tried to escape. The dragon was keeping me up on the top of the island, but at the last syzygy, I ran. It caught me and locked me in here."

Abigail leaned back, too, scanning the area for any sign of the dragon. She noticed horizontal lines on the sheer red cliff, and her stomach went cold. Those were water lines. Showing how high the tide usually rose. And they were even with the top of the cage. Would the tide be higher or lower than usual during a syzygy?

"Hope, how long have you been in here? How high does the water get?"

Her sister swallowed hard. "Umm . . . only a few hours. The water was lower before." Her voice quavered. "All this was bare rock a while ago. I guess I hadn't . . . hadn't noticed."

Abigail pulled back and frantically began searching for a way to open the cage.

"The door's over there," Hope said, pointing. "But she melted it shut. There's no key."

Hope wrapped her arms around her soaked and tattered pink dress.

"Don't worry," Abigail said. "I'll get you out."

Again, her sister gave her that look: surprised, like she was meeting a stranger.

Abigail ran her hands quickly over every bar, testing and tugging on it, but the cage was solid. She didn't have anything to pry it open with, either. She tried shaking the cage, thinking she could move the whole thing, but it wouldn't budge.

Clenching her fists, which were cold and clammy from the saltwater, she looked up at the cliff. "Where's the dragon?"

Hope's eyebrows climbed higher into her disheveled silver hair. "You'd better get out of here. It'll only lock you up, too, Worry."

Abigail pulled her sister into another quicky hug, the gold bars cold and hard between them.

"Hold on for just a little longer, okay?" she said. "I promise I'm going to figure out a way to get you out of there."

Science Note

How high will the tide go? You might have noticed in the tide charts that they change from day to day and month to month. What affects how deep the tides will be? Will the tide be higher or lower than usual during the syzygy?

It turns out that the gravity from the sun and the moon together create our tides. Interestingly, the moon creates two high tides, one where it is, and one on the other side of the Earth. This is because gravity gets weaker as you get farther away. The moon pulls on the water nearest to it, lifting it up, but it also pulls on the Earth, pulling it slightly towards it. It pulls less on the water on the far side, which gets left behind, creating another high tide. The sun does the same thing, although it has less of an effect because it's farther away. Check out the Exploratorium video *Dance of the Tides* to see a visual of how this works.

On Earth, we have a similar situation to the syzygy, which is when the sun, moon, and earth are in alignment. We call this a 'spring tide'. There is also what's called a "neap tide" which is when the moon is not in alignment with the sun but is instead at a right angle. There's a cool simulation of how this works here: *https://beltoforion.de/ en/tides/simulation.php.* In the simulation, try clicking "neap tide" and "spring tide" one at a time. What do you notice about the tidal bulge? (The blue oval shape represents the ocean. The more stretched it gets, the higher the tide will be.)

During the syzygy on Abigail's planet, the tide will probably be similar to the spring tide, because all the planets and the sun are in alignment, meaning they all work together to make the tide bigger.

But many more factors influence the tides. Some places on Earth only have one high tide, because of the way the Earth's axis of rotation is tilted. The shape of the coastline affects the tides, too, as does the rotation of the Earth and the positions of the sun and moon. Because of this, high tides can be before or after the moon is at its highest point and can vary a lot from day to day and month to month! Complicated! No wonder it took so long for us to figure it out.

You can also watch Neil deGrasse Tyson talk about the tides on YouTube: "*Neil deGrasse Tyson Explains the Tides.*"

Chapter Seventeen:
The Dragon's Lair

FOLLOWING Hope's directions, Abigail jogged around the base of the island until she came to a gaping maw of a cave. The opening extended forty feet overhead. The tide made a roaring, sucking noise as it swept in and out of the cave. Stalactites stabbed down like fangs.

Abigail took a deep breath, straining her ears for any sound, and made her way inside.

It was an echoing, hollow place. A warren of tunnels leading up through the center of the island. A cool wind brushed ghostly whispers into her mind.

The crash of the ocean receded as she moved deeper into the lair. The walls were crystal, like dark corroded mirrors encrusted with salt. Here and there one gave a flicker or burst of light. One cracked in half right as she passed, and she flinched. For a moment, she stood there, shaking, her breath coming in short gasps. But she thought of her sister, trapped outside. She took a deep breath and stood up straighter.

I don't know what's in here, but whatever it is, I will figure it out.

The cave smelled like burned seaweed and the dripping of water sounded like footsteps.

She passed ancient empty halls and a place where enormous talons had scraped deep gouges into the walls. She avoided looking at them too closely.

On tiptoe, Abigail climbed higher, following the largest branch of the tunnel as it wound up and down and around.

A great groan echoed through the space, and Abigail clapped her hands over her ears as two more lifeless crystals shattered.

Pressing close to the wall and crouching, she crept forwards.

The tunnel opened out into a massive cavern. Columns thicker than tree trunks stretched a hundred feet into the air, supporting an arched ceiling. Into this ceiling were stone carvings of dragons in flight. Their eyes and talons and tails encrusted with jewels.

It was like a massive library with stories and stories of shelves, all with arched balconies and nooks and statues of fairies. But there was not a single book. The whole place was empty. Nothing rested on the shelves. No jewels, no books, no treasures of any kind.

A great hole in the ceiling was open to the sky above, and a column of sunlight angled nearly straight down, expanding like a spotlight and illuminating a small section of floor below.

In this tiny column of sunlight lay the dragon.

Here it is.

Its long, scaled tail with six silver spikes was curled around its body. Its eyes were closed, and its muscular arms were wrapped tightly around something Abigail couldn't quite make out.

Strangely, it reminded her of Fort, clutching her blankets to her chest as she slept.

The dragon gave another earsplitting groan, and a thick tear leaked out of the corner of one scaly eye.

The dragon was crying.

Ever so quietly, barely breathing, Abigail descended a set of steps.

Her boot dislodged a pebble, which rolled and then tumbled down, the noise of its fall echoing painfully loudly. Abigail froze.

The scaly eyelid shot open, the amethyst eye with its red pupil fixed directly on her.

The legs uncoiled, the talons flexed, the leathery wings lifted, their spikes extending. Terror shot through her as the creature sent a burst of fire over her head, narrowly missing her.

Abigail raised her hands high, fixing the dragon with a pleading stare. "Um, hello? I'm sorry to bother you. Please, could I speak with you?"

The dragon's talons scored deep grooves in the stone, and it opened its jaws. Flames licked out of its mouth, curling through its spikes of charred teeth.

Fear locked Abigail in place.

Between its feet were two oblong chunks of stone, each giving off a faint glow. One pink, one blue.

The bright purple eye followed her gaze to the stones. The pupil contracted to a tiny slit, and the dragon dug its talons further into the stone, giving an earsplitting roar. Dust and chunks of stone rained down from the ceiling.

Abigail threw her arms over her head but stood her ground.

"I'm sorry to barge in like this," she yelled at the top of her voice. "Could I please speak with you for a moment?"

Another burst of fire shot overhead, and the dragon stalked towards her, opening its massive jaws.

Abigail winced and dodged behind one of the enormous columns. She peeked around the column and saw the dragon stamping on the floor, moving a few feet towards her, and then back to the rocks again. As if unwilling to leave them. As if it were protecting them. Like a bird might protect its eggs.

The dragon's eyes were wide, and it scanned the upper reaches of the cavern, looking from the opening in the ceiling to the various tunnel entrances. It shot another quick blast of fire at Abigail, but then did a quick spin, whirling around and looking this way and that, ready for an attack from all sides.

"I'm the only one here!" Abigail shouted, then wondered whether that had been the best thing to reveal. Luckily the dragon clearly didn't believe her.

Were its forelegs trembling? She'd seen a dog's legs shake like that once, after it had been attacked by a large eagle.

"Sorry to frighten you!" Abigail tried.

This seemed to have an effect, but not the one she'd hoped for. The dragon faced her and charged. The ground quaked with every pounding step, its muscular tail slashed behind it, and flames exploded from its mouth.

It closed the distance between them with blinding speed. Abigail didn't even have time to flinch. Her mouth was open, her eyes wide as the monster sped towards her.

At the last second, a tiny, sparkling blue light zipped in between them.

"Endure, wait!"

Abigail's stomach and arms felt like they were suddenly filled with champagne. Bubbly and sparkling.

The dragon skidded to a stop, only feet from the column Abigail crouched behind.

In between them was a tiny blue fairy.

She had shoes made of hermit crab shells, curling at the points, a tiny crown of starfish, and a dusting of blue sparkles on her skin. Earrings made of polished sea glass adorned her tiny, pointed ears, and her gossamer wings were edged with sea foam.

"It's happening again, Bluebell," the dragon said, its voice a low growl. "They've come to destroy the last of the eggs."

"No, it's okay. I promise. This is her; this is Wisdom."

Bluebell turned and smiled, her blue eyes locking with Abigail's. Abigail felt like there had been a piece of herself missing all these years, she just hadn't realized what it was. This was her fairy godmother. She was sure of it.

Slowly, she registered what the fairy had called her.

"Wisdom?" she asked. "You named me Wisdom?"

The dragon shifted its massive bulk and darted a terrified glance back at its eggs.

Bluebell frowned, giving her a polite smile. "Yes, of course. You . . . you didn't know your name? I announced it." She pulled her wand anxiously to her chest, gripping it with both hands.

Abigail explained what she'd thought her name was, and why. Bluebell's polite smile faltered. "Oh my. Oh . . . oh I am so sorry. I . . . I was in a rush to . . . well, to get here . . ." Her pointed ears drooped.

"Whoa," Abigail said, her head spinning, imagining what her life might have been like if she'd thought of herself as Wisdom. At first, it felt powerful, but then, an equal amount of pressure set in. Like every thought she had must be perfect, well-considered. Like she needed to learn as much as possible about everything and then analyze all that information until she found the absolute best solution. It was paralyzing.

I'd rather just be Abigail, she thought.

Did Hope feel this way? It must be a lot of pressure to feel like you needed to be optimistic all the time. Especially optimistic for the sake of others.

Hope. Her stomach dropped.

"Bluebell, Hope's trapped in a cage outside." But the fairy must know that already.

Bluebell's hands twisted more tightly on her wand. "Yes, I know," she said grimly. She turned to the dragon. "Endure, please, I've told you. Hope and Wisdom are here to help. To end all this. To make things safe for your eggs."

She glanced pleadingly at Abigail.

Abigail locked eyes with the dragon, who was watching her distrustfully. "Your name is Endure?"

The dragon blinked; two sets of eyelids flicking across its corneas. She shuffled back a few steps, closer to the eggs. "It is."

"Why are you called Endure?"

She lowered her head a fraction of an inch. "I was a hatchling when the knights turned on us. I did not have a name yet." Her gaze made another piercing survey of the room, looking for threats.

"What do you mean, when the knights turned on you?" Abigail asked.

"First, only a single egg was missing. Stolen. A terrible betrayal. But then the rest came. They attacked us here, destroying all our eggs except these two, which I managed to hide. Many dragons were lost, then." She hung her head, and her voice quaked. "Only a few, very old dragons remained. They named me, a tiny hatchling, Endure. It would be up to me to continue the line of the dragons, to watch over the eggs. To endure. They warned me that, when the planet covered the sun again and our world went dark, the knights would be back to destroy the last of us. Slowly, one by one, the old dragons died, and only I was left."

"That sounds so lonely," Abigail said. "And terrible. I'm so sorry."

Endure lifted her chin, her face tightening. "It is simply how things are. And I have watched over the eggs all these years, waiting until they are ready to hatch. But then the sky darkened, and the great sphere in the sky covered the sun. The ancient pathway between the worlds opened, making flight between very easy. I couldn't just cower in fear. I went to go see. And there I saw you and your sister. I thought you must be preparing an attack." She ran a large talon along a crack in the floor. "I wasn't thinking. I . . . I thought that maybe if I had one of yours, I could bargain . . . But then I didn't know what to do with her. I learned you'd all but forgotten about us. Then I realized that others might come looking for her, or she might go back and divulge what she'd found." She closed her eyes, grimacing. "I might have invited exactly what I'd feared."

"The knights attacked you first?" Abigail couldn't quite believe that. There had to be more going on. Why was everything so complicated?

"Yes." Endure's voice was firm.

Abigail took a few—very slow—steps towards Endure. She gently extended a hand and laid it on the dragon's shoulder.

Endure's eyes shot open, and she leaped backwards. After a few panicked breaths, she relaxed.

"Wow. That is . . . that is so awful. I'm so sorry we scared you by going up into the tower."

Endure eyed her warily.

Abigail turned to Bluebell. "But why are you here?"

"Dragon eggs can't survive without fairies," she said simply. "We have an ancient pact with the dragons. We care for their eggs, and in turn they assist our knights."

"Is that why Fern lied to Fort about me being under the bed?" Abigail asked.

"You were under my bed?"

Fort's voice rang out through the empty cavern as she stepped out of the shadows, swinging her sword. Fern fluttered anxiously at her shoulder, trailing green sparks.

"Fort! How did you—"

"I jumped, just like you did."

Endure froze in a crouch, her eyes wide and terrified as she watched Fort approach. It was strange to see something so huge and powerful look so scared.

"When were you under my bed?"

Abigail swallowed hard. "Yesterday. Right after I stole Kepler's book."

Fort's face was hard as stone.

"I'm sorry," Fern said in a high, pinched voice. "I promise I've never done anything like that before."

"Except that you knew there was another fairy up here, protecting the dragon that attacked the knights, that destroyed our order?"

Abigail felt desperately sorry for Fort. Now that Abigail knew what it felt like to have a fairy godmother, she couldn't imagine what it would feel like to learn that her fairy had been lying to her. And she definitely knew what it felt like to not understand what was happening.

"Fort, I think there's more going on here than you and I know," Abigail said loudly.

Fort was about to speak, but she took a step closer to the eggs, and Endure suddenly lunged for her, fire blossoming from her jaws.

"Endure, no!" the fairies shrieked.

She swung her great, spiked tail at Fort, but Fort lifted her hands, and a ball of bright green energy surrounded the dragon.

Endure slowed, as if she were encased in glowing green honey. She thrashed and struggled, and Fort grimaced, sweat pouring down her cheeks. Her jaw clenched and she took another labored step towards the eggs.

Abigail's mind spun. *I have to stop this. I don't know what's right, I don't know who started this, I don't know if the dragons really are a threat to the knights or if it's the other way around, or what the astronomers had to do with all this.* No one was listening to her, and in one more second Fort would reach the eggs.

Someone had to stop this, but the fairies weren't doing anything, and both Fort and Endure were too terrified to listen to one another let alone Abigail. She had to make them stop, had to make them pause and listen and try to figure out what had really happened. She swallowed hard and glanced at Bluebell. Her fairy godmother. *I have a fairy godmother,* she thought. *I'm a Scholar Knight now. And I am going to stop this.*

Fort took another shaking step towards the eggs. Endure thrashed against the green glowing sphere, which flickered in and out.

Abigail sprinted between them, scooped up the eggs, and jumped.

With gravity so weak, she shot upwards, straight for the opening in the ceiling.

Fort yelled, Endure roared, but Abigail didn't look down.

She was losing speed as she went, but only gradually, and she shot through the hole in the ceiling easily, then drifted back down to land next to the opening.

She stood on the top of the island, a space of bare, red rock about fifty feet across.

Clutching the eggs, she ran to the edge. She needed more time. An idea hit her, and she grabbed a couple of small rocks, throwing them horizontally off the cliff.

Seconds later, both Fort and Endure—no longer trapped— flew through the opening. Fort stumbled, but got her feet under her quickly and, raising her sword, sprinted towards Abigail.

Endure lunged for them in a blast of fire. Fort sent a blast of glowing green energy at her again, but this time it only encased the dragon's wings. She couldn't fly, but she could still attack.

"Wait!!" Abigail shouted, holding the eggs over the edge, threatening to drop them. Endure skidded to a stop, her face a mask of rage.

The fairies fluttered about anxiously.

"Wisdom, please, don't do that," Bluebell said. "The dragons didn't start this conflict. I really don't think they did."

"The knights absolutely didn't start this, either!" Fort shouted. "If we let the dragons continue, they'll destroy what's left of us. They can't be trusted. They'll betray us again, Worry."

Abigail cleared her throat. "My name," she said, "is Abigail. And we are going to talk about this and figure things out."

Fort lifted her sword and advanced. "No. They could hatch any minute. I can barely hold off one dragon. I can't fight three. You, me, Hope. We'll all be gone."

On the far side of the island, Abigail saw what she'd been hoping to see. Three rocks appearing on the horizon. Thanks to Newton, she knew why.

"Okay, just hang on one second," she insisted.

"No," Fort said, raising her sword high, preparing to swing for the eggs.

Abigail threw the eggs horizontally off the top of the island, at exactly the same speed she'd thrown the rocks. Thanks to Galileo, she knew it wouldn't matter that their masses were different.

The dragon gave a panicked roar, but it couldn't fly.

"Don't worry!" Abigail shouted, "They'll be back! They're perfectly fine. They're orbiting. We just need a little more time to figure this out."

Endure glanced from her to the eggs, looking deeply skeptical, but the eggs did seem to be peacefully floating along in the low gravity.

Fort's sword clanged against the ground, and she gave a groan of frustration.

"I never, ever, ever should have taken you in."

Abigail gave a quick glance over the side. She could just make out Hope's cage from here. The water was several feet deeper, nearly up to Hope's neck.

Better hurry.

From her bag, she whipped out Kepler's book.

"Bluebell, I need your help," she said, and the fairy was at her side instantly. "A Scholar Knight made this enchantment. Help me break it."

"No!" Fort said, but Kepler jumped through her stomach, up in front of her eyes. Fort yelped and tried to bat him away. But her hands passed straight through him.

Abigail instinctively placed her palm flat on the book. With Bluebell at her side, she could suddenly sense the enchantment that wove around and through it. That sparkling, joyful feeling again filled her arms and stomach, and Abigail wanted to laugh. This was what magic felt like?

Guided by Bluebell, Abigail felt her own source of magic. It did have a sense of wisdom about it, but there was also something Abigail-like there, too, she was sure. It poured up like water dancing off a waterfall, sending up sprays and rainbows. The enchantment dissolved.

Grinning, feeling like she'd just tasted the best cookie ever, Abigail looked at Kepler. He'd dropped to the ground and was standing, feet splayed, a look of surprise and delight on his face.

"Kepler?" she asked. "Are you free?"

He straightened his back, adjusted his moustache, and fixed her with a serious look.

"Electric eels can produce a shock of six hundred volts," he commented.

Abigail's face fell.

He grinned slyly. "Just kidding. Couldn't resist, sorry. Tides are caused by the moon! Planets travel in elliptical orbits! The time it takes them to go around the sun depends on how far away they are!" He hopped into the air, doing a flip. "Ah I can't tell you how good it feels to say that! When Aristotle was talking about crystal spheres, I thought I was going to catch on fire."

Abigail laughed.

"Don't listen to him!" Fort said. "He's working with the astronomers!"

"Astronomers can never be trusted!" Endure growled.

They glanced at one another, surprised to be in agreement.

"Kepler?" Abigail asked.

He adjusted his fluffy collar and turned to Fort and the dragon. "It was the astronomers."

Fort kept her sword raised.

"For a long while, the castle was home to both the Scholar Knights and the League of Astronomers. There was a rivalry between the astronomers and the knights, though. The astronomers were jealous of the knights. Not only could the knights work magic, but every scholar had not only a fairy godmother, but a dragon as well."

Fort's jaw dropped and her sword tip lowered. She darted a glance at Endure who frowned suspiciously. Again, they looked surprisingly similar, Abigail thought.

Kepler went on. "The knights and the dragons worked together for centuries. Er, you might have noticed your names are slightly similar. In order to endure, one must have fortitude, you might say. You do have certain commonalities."

Fort now stared openmouthed at Endure, who pawed the ground uncertainly.

"It is the dragons who represent the core principles. The fairies are there to help their eggs hatch, and, when a dragon egg is laid, a fairy goes to the planet to pick a scholar knight for it. Together, the knights and the dragons defended the principles they stood for and tried to make the world a better place." Kepler's tail twitched. "Your world truly is an interesting place. I found it almost as interesting studying it as I did Earth. I don't think the other scientists took quite the same view as I did. But it certainly was fun. Unfortunately, the astronomers were jealous of the power and prestige brought to the knights by the dragons. And they wanted to study the dragons. How did they fly? How did they produce fire? Understandable questions, I might say, as a scientist."

The eggs appeared over the horizon and came drifting back towards them. Abigail gently plucked them out of the sky and set them on the ground. Everyone was so engrossed in Kepler's story that no one made a move towards them this time. With a thrill, she noticed again that one was pink, and one was blue. A lot like Rose and Bluebell. Did she have a dragon, too?

"The knights were extremely protective of the dragons and refused to let the astronomers even speak to them. The astronomers built their tower, saying it was only for observation, but they were able to figure out how to leap from the planet to the moon during a syzygy, and they stole an egg to study it."

Abigail's stomach dropped. How horrible. The dragons must have been devastated, finding their egg missing. They must have felt so betrayed. Endure gave an agonized growl. Fort glanced at her, her face an agonized mirror.

"The dragons, horrified and betrayed, thought the knights had taken one. The knights of course denied it. The dragons came and searched the castle, destroying parts of it in the process. They found the egg. The knights only saw the dragons attacking them."

Abigail thought of Aristotle and his syllogisms. How if you saw a dragon laugh, it might be because you'd tickled it, but it could also be because you'd told it a joke. It was so understandable, from both sides, how the misunderstanding had happened. The dragons thought only the knights could reach their home, and so they thought that the knights must have stolen their egg. The knights knew they hadn't, and only saw the dragons turning on them, attacking. None of them knew the astronomers could reach the red moon.

Abigail shook her head. It was so complicated. Was everything this complicated? It was so easy to misunderstand. Maybe there were still pieces of the story missing. She felt calm, though, hearing Kepler's explanation. This fit, this made perfect sense. And it was so tragic that both Fort and Endure had lived their whole lives alone and afraid, with the burden of the responsibilities they carried. She swallowed around a lump in her throat.

Kepler went on. "At first, the knights were confused, but then they fought back. It escalated into a horrible conflict between the dragons and the knights, which led to the near complete destruction of both. The knights didn't know that an astronomer had taken an egg, but they thought that the astronomers had somehow turned the dragons against them. They vowed to seal away all astronomical knowledge. The fairies and I were able to hide some of the books, but Fort found me and enchanted my book. Although the fairies managed to hide me in the castle. Eventually, all anyone knew was that astronomy was an ancient evil, and something bad had happened on the syzygy."

Fort gave a strangled nod. "That's what they told me. They would barely speak about it, though."

"I remember the knights attacking our stronghold," Endure said coldly.

Fort drew herself up. "I'm so sorry," she said formally.

"Wait, you believe me?" Kepler asked. "You've only ever thought I was an annoying, potentially dangerous astronomer demon cat."

Fort sighed. "That all makes sense. It fits. I . . . I always had questions. There was always so much secrecy. I guess I thought the secrecy was necessary somehow . . . because we were in a fight for survival." She glanced at Abigail.

"I'm sorry to you, too." She placed her sword gently on the ground. "I really did think I was protecting you."

"I know," Abigail said. "I can see why, too."

A scream followed by a gurgle echoed from far below. Abigail went cold.

"Endure, please, please will you release Hope from the cage? The water's still rising."

Endure looked from Abigail to Fort.

Fort waved her hands, and the green magic locking the dragon's wings in place disappeared.

Endure glanced at the eggs one more time. Panicked splashing came from below.

Endure spread her wings and darted over the side of the island.

Moments later, she reappeared, a golden cage clasped in her talons, water streaming off it, a bedraggled Hope collapsed on the floor.

Endure set the cage down, and gently, with precise bursts of flame, opened it.

Abigail darted in, her arms around her sister, pulling her up and pounding on her back.

Hope was still and silent.

No, Abigail thought. *I'm too late.*

Hope coughed, seawater gushing from her mouth onto the ground. Gasping, she opened her eyes and looked around at everyone. She gave a wan smile.

Abigail gripped her in a tight hug, her heart thundering.

Hope hugged her back.

*

Eventually, Hope pulled out of Abigail's vicelike grip and looked down at herself. She took a few experimental breaths and poked her stomach.

"You okay?" Abigail asked.

Hope shrugged her thin shoulders and picked a piece of seaweed out of her hair.

"I . . . I think so." She climbed to her feet but nearly fell right back over again, swaying. Fort caught her, holding her tightly by the elbow. "Okay . . . okay . . . yep, all good."

The pink egg groaned and rolled over. The air began to shimmer around it.

Endure gasped, then coughed, sending out a cloud of flame. She scooped the eggs into her talons, unfurled her wings, and took off. She swept upwards, then dove into the fortress below.

All three fairies zipped after her.

Hope pressed her palms together and lifted onto her toes. "Oh! Are the eggs hatching? I hope we didn't jostle them too much. I'm sure we didn't." She glanced at Abigail. "Baby dragons!" She sprinted after Endure, crouching at the edge of the hole and peering in.

Abigail and Fort stood alone now on the edge of the island. The wind whistled around them, and far below the waves lapped at the shore as the tide continued to rise.

Fort's hand was on her sword pommel, now sheathed, and she darted a glance at Abigail before looking down. She scuffed her boots in the dirt then straightened her shoulders and turned to face her.

"I really am sorry," she said, looking earnestly at Abigail. "I'm sorry for what I said earlier. About your intentions. I see you were trying to help."

Abigail thrust her hands into her pockets, but she smiled at Fort. "Thanks. It's okay. Things are so complicated sometimes. It's so easy to misunderstand. Especially when we're afraid."

Fort gave her an evaluating stare.

"Very true . . . You know, I'm sorry I gave you that name. I misjudged you. I think I named you based on myself rather than on you. I saw a Worry because I was worried."

Abigail shrugged, unsure of what to say. Not used to this open, apologetic Fort.

Fort suddenly stood, grabbing a handful of her hair. "Did I . . . no . . . I told them to wait to fire the weapon until I got there. Didn't I?" She looked around, but not seeing Fern, returned her gaze to Abigail. "Sorry, what was I saying?"

"Weapon?"

Fort waved a distracted hand. "I've been building canons. A lot of them. To attack the moon. We'd probably better head back in case . . . but I'm pretty sure I told them not to . . . but if I'm gone too long . . ."

That was troubling.

"But I wanted to say . . ." Fort went on. "Now that I know your name is Wisdom, I can see it. That's absolutely fitting."

"I guess worry and wisdom can look alike sometimes," Abigail said.

Fort nodded. "Very wise!"

Abigail's stomach clenched. "Thanks . . . but . . . honestly . . . can you just call me Abigail?"

"What? Why?"

"It's just . . . it's a lot of pressure. I'd rather be . . . somewhere in the middle . . . than feel like everything about me has to be a certain way."

Fort opened her mouth, then stopped herself, with a finger to her lips. She chuckled. "Fair enough. I was going to say that was wise, too. But . . . that's . . . very Abigail of you."

The tension went out of Abigail's stomach. She could just be Abigail. Not worried or wise, but a combination of both. And someone who could change every day.

"Thank you. And . . . I'm sorry I went through your stuff."

"You what?" Fort stood up straighter.

"When I got Kepler's book?"

Fort sagged. "Oh, right. Well, that's okay. All in all, I'm glad you did I guess."

Abigail twisted her fingers. "Um . . . can I ask . . . what was the medal for?"

"Medal?" Fort looked genuinely confused for a moment. "Oh. That." She waved a hand. "The capital was under attack. I figured out a way to fend off some . . . some . . . well I was going to say monsters but . . ." one hand went to her throat. "I hope I didn't misunderstand that, too." Her eyes glazed over, and she looked like she might be running through every memory she had looking for misunderstandings.

"I'm sure it was different," Abigail said hurriedly. Fort really didn't need anything else to worry about. "Umm . . . and . .

. there's still one book missing? Einstein? Do you know where it is?"

Fort unwillingly came back to the present. "Oh. No. That one was missing before my time, I think."

"Huh. I wonder where it is . . ."

"Well, you have my permission to search the whole castle!"

"Thanks!"

"All the keys, all the doors, everything I know!"

"Awesome!" Abigail smiled warmly, deciding not to mention she already had most of the keys, then glanced up at their planet. "Um, should we go check on your canons?"

"My what? Oh! Right! Oh no. Yes, let's go!"

Gravity Simulator

There's a really cool website (*www.GravitySimulator.org*) where you can play around with gravity in our solar system. What would happen if the Earth were orbiting around Saturn? Well, it would mess up Saturn's rings! You can see the effect simulated here! (Select the Saturn's Rings simulation and then click the play button in the lower left corner.) You can also see what would happen if gravity itself were stronger or weaker. Go to the full Solar System simulation, then click on the physics menu on the right-hand side. Lower down where it says 'Gravitational Constant' try increasing or decreasing that. Notice what stronger or weaker gravity does to the orbits of all the planets! "When Galaxies Collide" is also super cool!

Chapter Eighteen:
The Ideal Number
of Kitchens

ENDURE took some heavy convincing to leave the eggs, even for the short trip back to the planet. It was a harder journey than before, now that the syzygy had passed, but the fairies helped, and soon they stood again at the top of the astronomy tower, watching Endure flap away towards the red moon.

The townspeople were thanked and sent home, and over the next few weeks, while they waited for news of the eggs from Endure, Fort began Abigail's lessons on being a Scholar Knight.

Three weeks later, Abigail sat in what had once been a kitchen and was now her workshop. Rain pattered cozily on the glass domed roof. The walls were filled with shelves crammed with tools and all the magical objects she'd scavenged over the years.

Bluebell lounged against a glass bell jar, watching as Abigail bent her head over the set of brass scales she was tinkering with. A haze of sparkly blue fairy dust floated around them. Abigail gave a brass screw a final turn, then held her hand out over the scales, screwing up her face and closing one eye in concentration.

An explosion burst outward, crackling with bolts of blue energy. It enveloped both of them and then imploded in on itself.

Abigail ran a finger over her eyebrows. They were both still there. And not on fire.

"Nice," Bluebell said.

Abigail grinned.

The door behind her burst open.

"They're coming!!"

Hope collided with her, gripping her shoulders and spinning her around. "Come on come on come on! They'll be here any minute!"

She paused, suddenly noticing the crackling of energy in the room.

"Wow, what are you working on?"

Abigail's grin widened. "Oh man, so many things!" She gestured to the scales. "This will show you the worst possible outcome on one side and the best possible outcome on the other. The more likely thing will tip the scales."

She addressed the scales. "I'm considering going outside." A whirling sound emanated from the device. An image appeared on each side. On the left, Abigail walked outside, was immediately hit by a meteor, trampled by a herd of dear, and then kidnapped by pirates.

"You survived, though!" Hope said brightly.

On the other side of the balance, Abigail went on a pleasant walk through the woods, stumbling upon a magic flower. She picked the flower. Rubies, emeralds, and gold began to spill out of it. A few minstrels passing by began to serenade her, and a group of gnomes invited her to a magical feast.

"I could see that happening," Hope said.

The side with the minstrels tipped lower. It was apparently slightly more likely than the pirate scenario. Abigail frowned. "They're both too extreme, still. I need to adjust it. I want it to be useful for people."

"That's amazing," Hope said, grabbing her arm and tugging. "Come on . . . there's one more kitchen, and Fort needs our help."

Reluctantly, still thinking about how she would adjust the scales, she let Hope drag her away.

They sprinted past the library and down a corridor, a herd of kitchen implements at their heels. A kitchen doorway tried to hide unobtrusively behind a large potted plant, but Abigail saw it.

She waved a hand and with an explosion of blue fairy dust and the sound of harp strings, the kitchen turned back into a music room.

"You're getting good at that," Hope said.

"I mean, the castle's given us a lot of practice," Abigail said.

A large crash followed by several bangs and a shout drew them up a set of steps towards the old classrooms.

Fort lay frowning under a pile of stainless-steel pans. With a clatter, she pushed the pile off her. She waved a hand at it, and the pans turned into handkerchiefs, then ceramic mushrooms before merging with the floor tiles below. The stones now had a pretty mushroom design.

"Fern, did I remember to put the timer on for the cake?"

"Yes, you did."

"And the—is the turkey fully defrosted?"

"As of last night. Fully defrosted and in the oven!"

Her hands went to her head. "The crumpets! I think those were in the kitchen that we—"

"No, no, we moved those to the other kitchen before you vanished that one."

Fort let out a long sigh. "I'm glad you're keeping track of things." She caught sight of Abigail and Hope. "Ah, girls. Wonderful. I'm glad you're here." She stood, brushing herself off. Fern gave a cheerful wave. "This kitchen is particularly troublesome, and our guests will be here any moment. Could you give me a hand?"

They lined up facing the arched doorway. Abigail narrowed her eyes at the mint green rows of cabinets and innocent pastel pink table and stove. This was the strangest one yet.

It'd be no match for the three of them, she was sure.

They locked elbows.

There was a groan and a magical explosion. A cloud of pink, green, and blue fairy dust cleared.

The kitchen wavered slightly but was otherwise unchanged.

Something scuttled in one of the cabinets, followed by a muffled "Shh."

Abigail raised an eyebrow and darted inside. She threw open the cabinet door, Fort and Hope right behind her.

Silverware and cooking implements scuttled away, hiding behind a large, leather-bound book. A fork peeked out from behind it.

Another group of silverware held a tablecloth stretched flat between them. On this cloth rested several glowing balls, making indentations in the smooth surface of the cloth.

"Oh, they're reading!" Hope said.

"It's the last missing book!" Abigail said. "Einstein?"

A glowing head poked out from around a corner of the cabinets. "Oh, um, yes?"

Fort gasped and leapt backwards. Her sword rang out as she drew it in one quick movement. "Astronomers!"

Abigail held up her hands in what she hoped was a calming gesture. "It's okay, Fort!"

Fort took a few deep breaths, her hand pressed flat to her chest. She lowered her sword point a few inches but watched the ghost and the kitchen utensils warily. A few of them crawled out from behind the book.

Abigail addressed the ghost. "What are you doing here?"

The ghost ran a hand through his shock of poofy white hair. "Oh, well, these fellows had questions for me. I was just showing them about how matter bends the space around it." He pointed at the tablecloth. "Those glowing balls are like planets, you see? If you put a marble on there, it would roll into those little indentations the balls make. That's how gravity works."

Abigail had thought she'd fully understood gravity after talking to Newton about it, but apparently there were yet more and more layers. "Wow . . ." she said. "Umm . . . why?"

"That's the question!" Einstein said happily.

"Well, would you mind moving out of this kitchen for now? We want to turn it into something else."

"Oh, certainly, of course." Einstein said. Then he looked down at the book and at his own ghostly hands. "I don't suppose you could . . ."

"I've got it!" Hope gently scooped the book up, sending some spoons scurrying away.

Fort was taking long, slow, deep breaths behind them.

Kepler popped out of the ceiling and Fort flinched.

"They're here!" he said. "Oh, Einstein, good to see you."

"Johannes Kepler! Fantastic to see you as well." Einstein turned to Abigail and Hope. "What an absolute giant in the field, let me tell you. I'm a great admirer."

Kepler smoothed his moustache.

Fort cleared her throat, and they all turned to look. Her face was slightly pale, her jaw tense.

"Would you . . . care to join us? We are having a bit of a party."

Kepler's eyes widened and his tail twitched.

"I would be delighted, thank you," said Einstein.

"Galileo will be there!" Hope said.

"He will?" Abigail asked.

Hope waved a hand. "Oh yeah, you talked about how helpful he was. I thought we should invite him! I went over there and brought him back!"

"Oh! That's great! He'll be so happy to see you all," Abigail said.

A knock rang through the castle, accompanied by a series of chimes and gongs.

A thrill went through Abigail's stomach, and they all made their way to the great entrance.

There on the stone threshold stood Endure. Somehow looking even bigger and more powerful here on their small entryway courtyard. On either side of her were two tiny dragons: one pink, one blue.

"This is—" Endure began formally, but the tiny pink dragon was already a tiny pink blur making a beeline for Hope. It twirled around her feet a few times, crawled up to the top of her head, down one shoulder, then fell off doing somersaults. It sprinted back to Endure, then back to Hope, where it paused at her feet, staring up at her with large wide eyes, its head cocked to one side. "—Aspire. Aspire, this is Hope."

Aspire chirped and flapped up to perch on Hope's silver head. Hope laughed and patted it.

The blue dragon made its way sedately over to Abigail. Its name somehow found its way straight into Abigail's mind. "Hello, Discern," she said. It examined her cooly with its sapphire eyes. She suddenly had a vision of them flying together, years and years in the future. They were going to go so many places, do so many things. She couldn't wait.

But now, it was time for dinner. Everyone except Endure, who was too large to fit inside but would stay on a specially prepared balcony outside, went inside to the largest and best of the remaining kitchens.

Fort, Abigail, and Hope, with the help of the enchanted kitchen, had prepared a large feast with everything they or the baby dragons could want.

Discern spent most of the dinner calmly exploring every inch of the kitchen, poking into every cabinet and evaluating every cauldron and bundle of herbs. Aspire built herself a nest of Hope's hair and remained perched atop her head. Galileo set up a telescope at one window and spent most of the dinner deep in conversation with Einstein.

Abigail mostly sat quietly by herself, eating two warm, flaky pieces of bread with the thick stew Fort had made. Her stomach felt warm and full, and not just from the food. She watched her sister chatting happily, and Fort's shoulders slowly creeping down from her ears as she began to finally relax.

Kepler hopped up onto the bench next to her and she scratched him behind one ear.

"How's it feel?" he asked.

"Nice," she said.

"Nice to be able to finally do magic?"

"Yes, but you know, I think it's more that there was something not quite right in the whole castle. Fort was so scared; Hope was having to do it all herself . . ."

"I was constantly spouting sea facts . . ."

"Those were pretty interesting, honestly."

"Well, I'm glad to hear it, because do you know what's better than sea facts?"

She soaked up the last of the gravy in her bowl with a crust of bread and glanced at him. "What?"

"SPACE FACTS!" He lifted onto his hind legs and waved his front paws.

She laughed and took a bite of the bread. "Oh yeah? Like what?"

"If you connected the sun to our planet with a giant string, then as our planet moves, it would sweep out little wedged-shaped areas, right?"

Abigail frowned, chewing. "I think I could see that."

"Well, for any given amount of time, the area swept out would be exactly the same, no matter where the planet is in its orbit."

She tried to picture this. "Huh. That is pretty interesting."

"And did I ever tell you about the supernova I observed?"

"No, I don't think you did."

"Of course not! I was enchanted! Well, no time like the present. So . . . do you know what a supernova is?"

Abigail shook her head.

Kepler's eyes lit up. "Well! Let me tell you . . ."

Abigail listened as Kepler talked and talked, letting the warmth of the food and the cozy glow of the kitchen and the happy murmur voices all around lull her into a comfortable sleepiness.

She was happy to be here with the people she loved. Happy to have her own name without the pressure or expectation to be either anxious or wise. Happy to just be herself.

Gravity Writing Prompt:

Look back at your answers to the writing prompt at the end of chapter one. Spend 5 minutes journalling about what you've learned about gravity. Feel free to write whatever thoughts come to mind, or to use any of these questions to guide your thinking: Was there anything about gravity that's different than you thought? Were your thoughts similar to those of any of the scientists? (Aristotle, Kepler, Newton, Galileo, or Einstein?) What is your favorite fact about gravity?

The End

THANKS FOR READING!

✦

Thanks so much for reading, I hope you enjoyed the book!

If you have a moment, I would greatly appreciate an honest review on Amazon.

If you'd like more physics stories, worksheets, and games, you can check out my website: www.MathwithSarah.com.

One super fun free activity that's related to gravity is Starlight Starship: An Interstellar Voyage of 3-D Shapes and the Inverse Square Law. You'll find it on the books page!

Or you can try a free demo of The Sorceress of Circuits: A Steampunk Electricity Adventure on the games page!

You can also sign up for the Sometimes Science newsletter, where I sporadically send out updates about what I'm working on, free resources for learning physics in fun, hands-on ways (preferably in stories), and the occasional meteor shower heads-up.

Physics Fables Sneak Peek!

Physics Fables is an illustrated collection of short stories that teach physics concepts ranging from special relativity to magnetism for ages 8-10!

Sakura and the Many-Layered Sea:
A Tale of Density and Buoyancy

Once upon a time, on the oily shores of the Many-Layered Sea, there lived a girl named Sakura. You might think that an oily sea sounds worrisome, as if it were the result of a spill or disaster, but this was simply how the sea was. The top-most layer was a quarter-mile thick of oil and plentiful with swarms of oil eels. Which were delicious.

Sakura had short, straight black hair, wore little pink shell earrings, and was fascinated by the sea, as she was fascinated by many things. She had so many questions, but she could barely get them out because she was listening so hard, taking in all the information around her.

One night, she and her grandmother were up late repairing fishing nets. Winds moaned around the corners of their

little house, and the drumming of the rain on the roof drowned out all but the loudest cracks and pops from the fire.

"The sea dragon is angry with us today," her grandmother muttered to herself.

Sakura had never seen the dragon who protected the sea, but her grandmother often blamed him when the storms came up.

"Why is the dragon angry with us?" Sakura asked.

"Because we have taken too many of his eels," her grandmother said. "We try to limit how many we take, but this time of year there isn't anything else to eat."

"That doesn't seem fair," Sakura said.

"His duty is to protect the sea creatures," her grandmother said calmly, and for a while they sat in silence, listening to the rain pound like fists against their home.

"Tell me again," Sakura said, struggling with the unruly fibers of the netting. "Who lives below the oil?"

Her grandmother smiled, the firelight flickering off her glasses, but she didn't look up from her work. Sakura marveled as her grandmother's knobby fingers flew deftly across the fibers, untangling and repairing at a blinding pace.

"Below the oil is where the mermaids live, of course."

"And they will grant you wishes?"

"To a lucky few, yes," her grandmother said, twisting two strands of rope together. "Or that was how it used to be. They left in my own grandmother's day. They went to the center of the Many-Layered Sea, where the dragons go to dance, and no one has heard from them since."

420

"Why did they go?" Sakura asked.

Her grandmother shook her head. "No one knows."

"Then how do you know where they went?"

Her grandmother laughed. "I don't know. That's a good question. Maybe they told us why they left, and we didn't listen. Or maybe they didn't go there after all."

Sakura considered this, then jumped at a crack of thunder overhead.

The next morning, Sakura went out with her father to fish for the oil eels. Rain still poured from the sky in great sheets that sank into the oily waves, descending in great droplets to join the water layer far below. Sakura stared over the side of the boat, her nose close to the shiny surface as the thick waves slowly heaved and ebbed.

No shimmering shadows of eels today. She squinted, trying to make out the water below the oil, straining for a glimpse of a long-nosed mermaid looking back at her, or a flick of tail, but there was nothing. There were other, thicker layers below that, with unnamed armored creatures lumbering through it, she had heard, but she had never seen them either.

Science Note:

The Many-Layered Sea has a layer of oil on top and water below that. Why is the oil on top? Oil floats on water because it is less dense. What is density?

Well, if you had two buckets, one full of water and one full of oil, the bucket full of water would be heavier. Because the water is heavier, it ends up below the oil.

Density is the amount of stuff a given size object contains. Imagine taking a slice of cake and squishing it into as small of a ball as possible. You're packing it more tightly, which increases the density!

They caught only a single eel that day, and the next they caught nothing. For the next two months, barely anyone in the village caught anything.

The storms worsened. Great bruised clouds bubbled up, crackling with electricity and sending torrents of rain to be caught by the wind and blown into eyes and faces and open doorways. The whole village huddled together in the great meeting hall.

"We have to stop catching eels," her grandmother said, speaking in front of a crowd of elders. "We will only anger the sea dragon further."

"I haven't had anything to eat in three days," a young man said. "We have to catch something!"

Sakura raised her hand, but no one noticed her.

"We must be patient," an elderly man with a long beard said. "If the dragon sees we are obeying his laws, he will send more eels."

Sakura lifted her hand higher and waved it a bit. The eyes of the elders slid over her, like eels sliding over rocks.

"The sea dragon only cares about sea creatures. He won't take pity on us," the hungry young man said.

"Why don't we ask the mermaids for help?" Sakura cut in, unable to hold back, jumbling her words together until the room filled with a tiny beat of silence.

The silence stretched longer. A few eyebrows lifted. One or two of the elders glanced at Sakura's grandmother.

Sakura frowned. It was a better idea than doing nothing.

"Thank you, Sakura. Why don't you go home and tend the fire for me?" her grandmother said.

Sakura left the villagers arguing behind her, but instead of going home, she went to the rocky shore and stood, squinting against the rain, her hair tossed and tangled behind her by the gale. The waves swelled and crashed against the shore, filled with dark shadows of seaweed, but no eels.

There might not be mermaids out there.

The mermaids might already be gone.

She wrapped her arms around her empty belly, shivering.

If they did nothing, the sea dragon might take pity on them and send them enough eels to live. But maybe the sea dragon had decided he didn't want them eating his eels anymore.

Trying to catch more eels didn't seem like it would work, either.

Lightning stabbed down from the clouds like an angular trident.

She ground her feet into the smooth pebbles of the shore, listening to the crunch. Then she spun around in a whirl of pebbles, making for the docks.

She unlashed her small wooden boat, tossed the rope in, and jumped in after it. Her hands went through their familiar dance as she heaved up the mast and hoisted her coral-pink sail, webbed like the fingers of a gecko.

Thunder rumbled as she crashed through the swelling waves of oil. It splashed over the sides of her boat, and soon her fingers were slippery with it. The rain beaded up on her skin and trickled across it.

"I'm going to find the mermaids," she whispered to herself. But what if there weren't any mermaids, after all?

Science Activity:

To see density in action, grab a cup or bowl, a scale, some gravel, and some sand. Fill the cup with gravel and place it on the scale. How much does it weigh? Now, leaving the gravel, pour sand into the cup around it. What happens to the weight? By filling in the empty spaces of the cup, you've increased the density! The cup remains the same size, but it's more tightly packed, so it's heavier!

Sakura piloted her tiny craft up and down the waves for many hours until her stomach heaved along with the waves.

At first, she thought she might be imagining it, but a great rushing sound built and built, like a river heavy with snow-melt cascading over a cliff.

A spiraling whirlpool appeared a few hundred feet from her boat. It whirled faster and faster, and she could see the funnel extending deep into the oil, all the way to the water layer below. At last, in a great spray of water, a fearsome dragon with long whiskers appeared. He bared his golden teeth at her, his eyes flashing like the lightning behind him. Sakura cowered in her tiny boat, crouching behind the mast, and stared up at him wide-eyed. It was the sea dragon himself!

"Go back, Sakura," the sea dragon said, his voice washing over her like powerful waves that could crush her into the sea floor.

She clasped her hands and bowed, attempting to be as mannerly as she knew her grandmother would recommend. "Hello great sea dragon. It is an honor to meet you. I apologize for disturbing you, but my family is hungry, and I have to do something. I know you don't want us to eat your eels, so I am going to ask the mermaids for help in finding something else to eat."

"Your family disobeyed my wishes." The cold winds whirled around him, lifting his many long whiskers. His long scaly body whipped and curled in the wind like a ribbon.

From her respectful bow, Sakura noticed a tiny creature with large, luminous eyes hovering at the sea dragon's shoulder.

"I apologize for my ignorance, oh sea dragon, but . . . who is that?" She pointed.

"That is Clyde," he said in his booming voice.

Clyde waved tentatively.

She waved back, and the sea dragon frowned, his moustache drooping with displeasure.

"He is my assistant." The sea dragon cleared his throat and resumed his threatening expression. "Go back to your family." With a crack of thunder, he disappeared.

Sakura couldn't go back to her family. She already knew the dragon was angry at them. She readjusted her sail and continued on.

The waves rose higher and higher, and she thought she could hear the sea dragon's growl in the whistling wind.

Lightning struck her mast, and her beautiful sail disintegrated into flames. She quickly patted the flames out with a heavy cloth. She knew better than to toss fire into the Many-Layered Sea.

Her sail was destroyed, so she pulled out her oars and rowed.

The air grew colder and colder. Her breath rose in clouds, and the rain turned to swirls of snowflakes like the cherry blossoms that were her namesake.

The cold made the oil thicker and thicker, and rowing became very difficult, but Sakura pressed on.

"Interesting," she thought. "The water freezes before the oil does."

Science Note:

Different materials freeze at different temperatures. It's why we put salt on roads. Saltwater freezes at a colder temperature than water without salt.

At last, the oil froze solid. Sakura sat for a few minutes, straining against the oars, but finally she stood, stepped out onto the frozen surface, and pried her boat up out of the ice. There was a small, boat-shaped indentation in the oil.

"Interesting," she thought again, despite the cold and her exhaustion. "I wonder what makes the indentation exactly that size." She'd seen boats laden with goods that were lower in the water. She could imagine that the heavier boats would make a larger indentation.

She put her boat on her back like a turtle shell and trudged up the slippery, frozen surface, shivering. At the crest of a wave, she set her boat down and made a sled, sliding down into the next trough, where she picked it up and trudged up the next hill.

Night fell, and she slept in her boat, shaking with cold and listening to the soft flakes of snow collecting around her . . .

I hope you enjoyed this excerpt! You can find the rest of Physics Fables on Amazon!

About the Author

SARAH ALLEN was a math and physics tutor for twenty years before becoming a full-time fantasy writer. She earned her undergraduate degree in physics with both college and departmental honors from the University of Washington, and a master's degree in cognition and learning from Columbia University.

Her all-time favorite book is *The Phantom Tollbooth,* and her current goal in life—besides growing a few flowers that aren't eaten by deer—is to write the kinds of physics books she would have loved as a kid.

Made in United States
Troutdale, OR
05/31/2025

31752525R00246